Global Citizen
Action

◆

GLOBAL CITIZEN ACTION

EDITED BY
MICHAEL EDWARDS
JOHN GAVENTA

LYNNE
RIENNER
PUBLISHERS

BOULDER

Published in the United States of America and elsewhere in 2001 by
Lynne Rienner Publishers, Inc.
1800 30th Street, Boulder, Colorado 80301
www.rienner.com

Library of Congress Cataloging-in-Publication Data
Global citizen action / edited by Michael Edwards, John Gaventa.
    p.   cm.
   Includes bibliographical references and index.
   ISBN 1-55587-968-3 (alk. paper)—ISBN 1-55587-993-4 (pbk.   :   alk. paper)
   1. Political participation. 2. Direct action. 3. Globalization. I. Edwards, Michael,
1957– II. Gaventa, John, 1949–
JF799.G586   2001
323'.042—dc21

                                                                                        2001019070

Printed and bound in the United States of America

The paper used in this publication meets the requirements
∞ of the American National Standard for Permanence of
Paper for Printed Library Materials Z39.48-1984.

    5   4   3   2   1

Contents

I

Introduction

Michael Edwards

Ten years ago, there was little talk of civil society in the corridors of power, but now the walls reverberate with at least the rhetoric of partnership, participation, and the role of citizens' groups in promoting sustainable development. Though poorly understood and imperfectly applied in practice, concepts like the "new diplomacy," "soft power," and "complex multilateralism" place civil society at the center of international policy debates and global problemsolving (Edwards 1999). This radical change in international relations bodes well for our common future, but it is also a highly contested debate in which questions abound and answers are in short supply. In reality, civil society is an arena, not a thing, and although it is often seen as the key to future progressive politics, this arena contains different and conflicting interests and agendas (Scholte 1999). For their part, global institutions are still the prisoners of a state-based system of international negotiation and find it exceptionally difficult to open up to nonstate participation at any meaningful level. We may dream of a global community, but we don't yet live in one, and too often, global governance means a system in which only the strong are represented and only the weak are punished. Resolving these deficiencies is the essential task of the twenty-first century. This volume brings together a diverse group of scholars and practitioners to reflect on the lessons of recent social movements and the challenges that lie ahead. This introduction provides a short analysis of the changing global context as well as a conceptual framework for the case studies that follow and an overview of their contents and conclusions.

The Rise and Rise of Civil Society

Civil society is a contentious term with no common or consensus definition. The contributors to this book use it to refer, in very broad terms, to the arena in which people come together to advance the interests they hold in common, not for profit or political power, but because they care enough about something to take collective action. Civil society organizations are all those bodies that act in this arena, comprising a huge variety of networks and associations, political parties, community groups, and NGOs but excluding firms that are organized to make a profit for their shareholders and that generate no public benefits. NGOs (nongovernmental organizations) are formally constituted nonprofits that often dominate discussions about global civil society, but they are only one part of a much bigger picture. Although our contributors recognize that civil society organizations have different and sometimes conflicting normative agendas, they focus their case studies on those groups that share a broad commitment to democracy, human rights, and protection of the environment.

During the past few years, and especially since the much-publicized demonstrations against the World Trade Organization in Seattle in 1999, the term *global civil society* has been much in vogue. Although some of the case studies in this book do use this term, they refer more often to elements of *transnational civil society* or *international social movements* to describe a spreading web of networks of organizations based in different countries, usually but not always led by NGOs. Such transnational networks abound, but there are few global citizens to constitute a *global civil society* in the deepest meaning of that term. Citizens from different countries are certainly speaking out on global issues, but the rights and responsibilities of citizenship at the global level are ill defined, especially in the absence of a global state or culture. Nevertheless, the place of civil society in international affairs has risen dramatically since the end of the Cold War. Why is this? There are at least three reasons:

Changing Ideas About International Development

In recent years, there has been a significant move away from what was known as the *Washington consensus*—the belief that market liberalization and Western-style democracy offered a universal blueprint for growth and poverty reduction across the world. Central to the emerging *post-Washington consensus* are a number of ideas that place civil society at the heart of the development policy debate. First, a strong social and institutional infrastructure is crucial to growth and development: *Social capital*—a rich weave of social networks, norms, and civic institutions—is just as important as other forms of capital to these ends. Second, more pluralistic forms of governance and decisionmaking are seen to be more effective in developing a social consensus about structural changes in the economy and other key reforms. That is, shared ownership of the development agenda is seen as the key to its sustainability. Third, public, private, and civic roles are being reconceptualized and reshaped, in both economics and social policy; the best route to problemsolving lies through partnerships among these different actors. Fourth, international institutions require stronger public and political constituencies to support them; otherwise they will continue to lose legitimacy. Civil society is central to all these ideas, and to their successful application. Although the empirical evidence backing some of the underlying assumptions about these ideas is incomplete, there is already a consensus among the donor community that a strong civil society is crucial to successful development performance.

New Conceptions of Governance

Beyond the domestic arena, the second major shift highlighting civil society concerns a quiet revolution in the theory of international relations. When Kofi Annan talks of the "new diplomacy," he is echoing a common perception that the characteristics of global governance—the rules, norms, and institutions that govern public and private behavior across national boundaries—are changing in new and important ways (Annan 1998). As economic and cultural globalization proceed, the state's monopoly over governance is challenged by the increasing influence of private actors, both for-profit and not-for-profit (Rosenau and Cziempel 1992; Archibugi and Held 1995). Corporations and private capital flows react very quickly to the opportunities provided by an increasingly integrated global market. By contrast, the response of states and civil society is necessarily slow, fragmented, and messy because of the demands of democracy and the need to negotiate among so many different interests. In theory, civil society can be a counterweight to the expanding influence of markets and the declining power of states, but in practice there are few formal structures through which this countervailing authority might be expressed, especially at the global level. The result is a growing democratic deficit in the processes of global governance.

As Ann Florini puts it in Chapter 3, "the Westphalian system [of nation states] is neither divinely ordained nor easily swept away," but it is changing, and one of the most important of these changes concerns the expanding role of transnational civil society. In the twenty-first century, global governance is unlikely to mean a single framework of international law applied through a unified global authority. More likely is a multilayered process of interaction among different forms of authority and different forms of regulation, working together to pursue common goals, resolve disputes, and negotiate new tradeoffs among conflicting interests. The early stages of this model of governance, described as "global public policy" by some (Kaul 1999; Reinicke 1998) and "multi-track diplomacy" by others (Smith et al. 1998; Waterman 1998), can already be discerned in global environmental regimes such as the Montreal protocol and in the campaign case studies provided later in this volume. Over 20,000 transnational civic networks are already active on the global stage, 90 percent of which have been formed since 1970 (O'Brien et al. 2000; Runyan 1999). This form of governance is messy and unpredictable, but ultimately it will be more effective—by giving ordinary citizens a bigger say in the questions that dominate world politics and a greater stake in the solutions. For citizens of nondemocratic regimes, transnational civil society may provide the only meaningful avenue for voice and participation in decisionmaking.

Currently, civil society involvement in global regimes tends to operate through networks of interest groups, especially NGOs, rather than through formal representative structures (Keck and Sikkink 1998; Higgott and Bieler 1999). This raises important questions about the future role of global citizen action, especially issues of structure, governance, and accountability that may erode the legitimacy of civic groups as social actors in the emerging global order. These questions are taken up below and throughout the rest of this book. However, the role of civil society is certain to grow as global governance becomes more pluralistic and less confined to state-based systems defined according to territorial sovereignty.

It's Good for Business

In addition to the conceptual explanations, international agencies have become more interested in civil society, and more open to working with civic groups, for a simpler and more commercial reason—it is "good for business." They have found that operational partnerships and a broader policy dialogue contribute to more efficient project implementation and a lower rate of failure; a better public image and more political support, especially among key shareholder governments in North America and Western Europe; and research and policy development more informed and less constrained by internal orthodoxy. Given these tangible benefits, it would be difficult for any international agency to retreat from the trend toward greater civic engagement; the practical and political costs would be too high.

This positive assessment is a comparatively recent phenomenon. Prior to 1980, there was little structured contact between civic groups and multilateral institutions and almost no formal nonstate involvement in global regimes. Toward the middle of the 1980s such contacts became more frequent and more organized, including the consolidation of NGO advisory or consultative bodies for the specialized agencies of the UN system, the formation of the NGO Working Group on the World Bank in 1984, and some early global campaigning efforts around debt, structural adjustment, and popular participation (Willetts 1996; Weiss and Gordenker 1996; Fox and Brown 1998). Global civic organizing increased at a much faster rate after the end of the Cold War, with NGO networks increasingly sharing the stage with other civic actors such as international labor union federations and networks of professional associations. Successive UN conferences on gender, population, the environment, social development, and habitat provided a vehicle for these emerging civic alliances to test out their skills. Both the UN and the World Bank began to form strategic partnerships with key NGOs in ventures such as the Global Alliance for Forest Conservation and Sustainable Use and the World Commission on Dams (Florini, Chapter 3). The assumption underlying these partnerships is that "global civil society" can broaden democratic practice by creating additional channels for popular participation, accountability, consultation, and debate, thus improving the quality of governance and promoting agreements that will last. The World Bank, the United Nations Development Programme (UNDP), and many bilateral aid agencies have embarked on a systematic effort to increase their understanding of civil society and its role in these contexts and to enhance their capacity to engage effectively with civic groups at both the national level—through planning processes such as the World Bank's Comprehensive Development Framework—and the international level.

However, toward the end of the 1990s, critical questions about this phenomenon began to surface inside the international institutions, especially about the role of intermediary (advocacy) NGOs as a subset of civic actors. Because institutions such as the UN have in the past portrayed civil society as something of a magic bullet for state and market failure, it is not surprising that observers are now turning their attention to the failings (actual or perceived) of civil society itself. It is increasingly common to hear senior agency staff, academics, and journalists echo the complaints of some governments (especially in the South) that NGOs are self-selected, unaccountable, and poorly rooted in society, thereby questioning their legitimacy as participants in global debates. It is not that these commentators question the principle of civic engagement; they worry, rather, that the practice of civic engagement may be distorted in favor of organizations with greater resources and more access to decisionmakers in capital cities. At the start of a new century, there are forces acting both for and against the deepening of civil society involvement in global regimes.

From Rhetoric to Reality:
The Dilemmas of Civil Society Involvement

As a result of the political openings of the last decade, civic groups increasingly feel that they have the *right* to participate in global governance. Much less attention has been paid to their *obligations* to pursue this role responsibly or to concrete ways in which to express these rights. This is sensitive and difficult ground for all concerned. There are at least four areas of tension:

Legitimacy, Accountability, and Representation

The first set of issues—and by far the most contentious—concern legitimacy and accountability: Who speaks for whom in a global network, and how are differences resolved when participants vary in strength and resources? Who enjoys the benefits and suffers the costs of what the movement achieves, especially at the grassroots level? Whose voice is heard, and which interests are ignored, when differences are filtered out in order to communicate a simple message in a global campaign? In particular, how are grassroots voices mediated by institutions of different kinds—networks and their members, Northern NGOs and Southern NGOs, Southern NGOs and community groups, and so on down the line?

In the mid-1990s, North American NGOs generally claimed to represent a Southern consensus against the replenishment of the International Development Association (IDA, the soft loan arm of the World Bank), on the grounds that social and environmental safeguards were too weak. In contrast, Southern NGOs (mainly from Africa) tended to insist that IDA go ahead regardless of the weakness of these safeguards, because foreign aid was desperately needed even if its terms were imperfect (Cleary 1995, Nelson 1996, Edwards et al. 1999). On some issues (like debt or land mines), there is a solid South-North consensus in favor of a unified lobbying position. However, in other areas (especially trade and labor rights and the environment), there is no such consensus, since people and their civic representatives may have conflicting short-term interests in different parts of the world. As globalization proceeds, these areas will become the centerpiece of the international system's response, so it is vital that networks develop a more sophisticated way of addressing differences of opinion within civil society in different regions. However, very few networks have mechanisms in place to resolve such differences democratically (Covey 1995).

In cases like these, discussions often focus on the thorny issue of representation, though there are really two questions at hand: First, is representation the only route to civic legitimacy in global governance? Second, how representative must an organization be in order to qualify for a seat at the negotiating table? These questions are often conflated, with results that make sensible conversation about policy options impossible.

Legitimacy is generally understood as the right to be and do something in society—a sense that an organization is lawful, admissible, and justified in its chosen course of action. However, there are generally two ways to validate organizations: through representation (which usually confers the right to participate in decisionmaking) and through effectiveness (which only confers the right to be heard).

Legitimacy in membership bodies is claimed through the normal democratic processes of elections and formal sanctions that ensure that an agency is representative of, and accountable to, its constituents. Trade unions and some NGOs fall into this category, though whether these processes operate effectively and democratically is another matter. Agreement on some minimum standards in this regard remains an important part of the agenda for the future. By contrast, nonmembership NGOs define their legitimacy according to legal compliance, effective oversight by their trustees, and recognition by other legitimate bodies that they have valuable knowledge and skills to bring to the debate. No one expects Oxfam, for example, to represent third-world opinion perfectly, only that its proposals on debt and other issues should be solidly rooted in research and experience as well as sensitive to the views and aspirations of its third-world partners.

NGOs may have the right to a voice, but not necessarily to a vote in global fora. In this sense, the best representative of civil society is a democratically elected government, complemented by the checks and balances provided by nonstate membership bodies (such as labor unions) and pressure groups of different kinds. The resulting mix is very messy, but it mirrors standard practice in national politics and stands ready to shape the emergence of more democratic regimes at the global level too. As the case studies in this book make clear, transnational civil society is far from democratic, and few networks have democratic systems of governance and accountability. Nevertheless, the increasing voice of civil society groups on the world stage adds an essential layer of checks and balances into the international system, while helping to ensure that excluded views are heard. The challenge—which our authors take up—is how to structure global citizen voice in ways that combat, rather than accentuate, existing social, economic, and political inequalities.

It is no accident that questions about legitimacy are being raised at a time when NGOs have started to gain real influence on the international stage. In that sense they are victims of their own success. Neither is there any shortage of hypocrisy among the critics, especially when they appear to single out NGOs in contrast to businesses (and even many governments) that are even less accountable than they are. Nevertheless, the criticisms are real and must be addressed if NGOs are to exploit the political space that has opened up in the post–Cold War world. At the minimum, that means no more unsubstantiated claims to "represent the people" as well as an explicit recognition that voice and vote rest on different types of organizational legitimacy.

Global Citizen Action: Building from the Bottom Up

Globalization requires both governments and nonstate actors to link together different levels of their activity—local, national, regional, and global. For corporations (through the market) and governments (through intergovernmental structures like the United Nations), this is already possible, but civic groups have no parallel structure to facilitate supranational civic participation, nor do they have avenues for representation in intergovernmental bodies. All around the world, governments, civic groups, and businesses are already experimenting with dialogic politics at the local level, sharing in planning and decisionmaking to generate a better and more sustainable set of outcomes (Reilly 1996; Edwards 1999). These experiments are the local building blocks of future global governance. By laying a strong foundation for negotiations over labor standards, environmental pollution, and human rights, they offer the potential to connect ordinary citizens to global regimes. But this can only work if local structures are connected to more democratic structures at higher levels of the world system, which can ensure that sacrifices made in one location are not exploited by less scrupulous counterparts elsewhere. Recent tripartite agreements on child labor in Bangladeshi garment factories are a sign of the future in this respect, with factory owners, NGOs, and local government striking mutually advantageous local bargains within a framework of global minimum standards set out in the International Labour Organization (ILO) Convention (Harper, Chapter 18). Other regimes may follow this example by embedding local agreements in a nested system of authorities that balance necessary flexibility with a core of universal principles. Getting things right at the base of the system is crucial if global institutions are to grow from, and be accountable to, their ultimate constituents.

These problems are not helped by a tendency among some NGOs to focus on global advocacy to the exclusion of the national-level processes of state-society relations that underpin the ability of any country to pursue progressive goals in an integrated economy. There is always a temptation to "leap-frog" the national arena and go direct to Washington or Brussels, where it is often easier to gain access to senior officials and thus achieve a response. This is understandable, but in the long term it is a serious mistake. It increases the influence of multilateral institutions over national development and erodes the process of domestic coalition building that is essential to the development of pro-poor policy reform. In addition, the dominance of civic voices from the North reinforces the suspicion among Southern governments that these are not genuine global alliances but simply a new example of the rich world's monopoly over global debates. The NGOs concerned may see themselves as defending the interests of the poor, but it is still outsiders—not the government's own constituents—who are deciding the agenda. The asymmetry of global civic networks, a common theme in the chapters that follow, makes such criticisms inevitable. For example, only 251 of the 1,550 NGOs associated with the UN Department of Public Information come from the South, and the ratio of Southern NGOs in consultative status with the Economic and Social Council of the UN (ECOSOC) is even lower (Kendig 1999).

Addressing this problem requires a different way of building global alliances, with more emphasis on horizontal relationships among equals; stronger links between local, national, and global action; and a more democratic way of deciding on strategy and messages. The rising power of information technology and the Internet makes it much easier for networks to operate with less centralized structures, not to mention a flatter hierarchy. For example, the landmines campaign analyzed by Matthew Scott in Chapter 9 connected over one thousand NGOs together across forty countries, while Jubilee 2000 has successfully married local, national, and global efforts together around debt relief (Collins et al., Chapter 10). In Uganda, a network of local NGOs developed a dialogue with their own government on options for debt relief, supported with technical assistance from Northern NGOs like Oxfam. The results of this dialogue were then incorporated into the international debt campaign. Research has shown that NGO networks can achieve their policy goals, build capacity among NGOs in the South, *and* preserve accountability to grassroots constituents if they consciously plan to do so from the outset and are prepared to trade some amount of speed and convenience in order to negotiate a more democratic set of outcomes (Covey 1995; Fox and Brown 1998). Sadly, relatively few Northern NGOs seem willing to follow this approach.

From Campaign Slogans to Constituencies for Change

One of the consequences of globalization is that traditional answers to social and economic questions become redundant, or at least that the questions become more complex and the answers more uncertain. The theoretical underpinnings of pro- and anti-freetrade positions, for example, are highly contested. We cannot know in advance whether one course of action will be better than another, whatever the theory predicts. But this is far from a theoretical question: What if those NGOs who protested so loudly in

Seattle turn out to be wrong in their assumptions about the future benefits that flow from different trading strategies? Returning to the issue of accountability, who pays the price? Not the demonstrators, but people in the South who may suffer the consequences for generations. The same strictures apply to pro-freetraders too of course, but NGOs cannot use this as a defense. All protagonists must face up to the same, stark question: In an increasingly uncertain world, what does it mean to advocate responsibly for a predetermined position?

The contents of this book shed considerable light on this thorny problem. They emphasize the importance of greater humility among civic groups as well as more investment in research and learning so that policy alternatives are properly grounded, tested, and critiqued. One of the consequences of this dilemma is likely to be a switch from "conversion" strategies (the traditional view of advocacy) to "engagement" strategies, which aim to support a process of dialogue rather than simply lobbying for a fixed set of outcomes. This will take civic groups further into territory that may seem obvious ground for them—building public constituencies for policy reform—but which has largely been absent from their agenda.

A strong constituency in the industrialized world is a prerequisite for the success of more equitable global regimes, new forms of governance, and the sacrifices required to alter global patterns of consumption and trade. Codes of conduct to govern multinational corporations, for example, are of little use unless they are backed by large-scale consumer pressure to enforce them. Although governments and business can play an important role in building these constituencies, the major responsibility is likely to fall to civil society organizations, since it is they who have the public trust and international connections to talk plainly and convincingly about matters of global justice. NGOs have always talked of the need to build constituencies, but they have focused on problems in the South instead of lifestyle change at home, playing on the line that "your five dollars will make the difference." It rarely does, and what would make a difference (like mass-based public protest against Western indifference) is never given sufficient attention. Many NGOs have cut back their public education budgets in recent years, seeing this as an overhead instead of a core activity, while government spending is only slowly resurfacing after the insularity of the Thatcher/Reagan years. A deeper engagement in constituency building does not mean abandoning campaigns or surrendering the power of protest. But it does mean a different balance between traditional forms of citizen advocacy and slower, longer-term work on the causes of injustice. To support this shift, civic groups will need to develop a range of new skills and competencies in public communications, and they will need to work with academics, think tanks, trade unions, and others who can help them develop and articulate more nuanced positions on trade and labor issues, adapted to different country contexts.

The Structure of the Book

The first section of this book contains two chapters that help to lay out the conceptual ground for the empirical material that follows. "How can a campaign on global ethics not be ethical itself?" asks John Clark in Chapter 2, "Ethical Globalization." If one accepts that rules and standards are essential to govern the costs and benefits of the global economy, does it not follow that global civil society should also be subject to guidelines that govern its conduct and behavior? After recounting the challenges facing global citizen action, Clark goes on to provide a checklist of action points that civil society organizations might find useful in assessing where and how to put their house in order. As Ann Florini concludes in Chapter 3, this is far from a theoretical question: "It matters whether these problems are solved, because transnational civil society can serve humanity well." And they can serve even better, one assumes, if citizens groups can practice what they preach in terms of democracy, accountability, and the principle of equal voice. Florini brings together the results of a worldwide research program on civil society and global governance to answer two fundamental questions: Is global civil society a reality or a romantic and convenient myth? And if it *is* a reality (or at least a real emerging force), then what are the likely costs and benefits of such a radical change in international relations?

Part 2 contains a series of essays on global citizen action in relation to the international financial institutions (IFIs, especially the World Bank and the International Monetary Fund, or IMF). Arguably, this is the area in which NGOs and others have made the most visible progress in their lobbying efforts over the past ten years, though the contributors also acknowledge the dangers of cooptation, and the huge, incomplete agenda for change that remains. Jonathan Fox and L. David Brown and Paul Nelson survey a broad range of campaigns and campaigning styles against the World Bank, looking for common patterns and conclusions in terms of effectiveness and internal democracy. "Will civil society reproduce existing lines of authority and inequality," they ask, going on to compare and contrast project and policy-based advocacy work and different forms of regional civil society structure. Some of these structures—like the Lead Regional Partners model of the Democratizing Bretton Woods Project—seem to be both more influential and more accountable because they build from existing regional structures in the South such as the Association of Popular Organizations in Latin America (ALOP) and Red Bancos in Latin America.

A broad social base, a coalition that can bridge project and policy-based campaigns, together with an emphasis on building local, national, and transnational capacities to monitor "non compliance with reform commitments" turn out to be important ingredients for success. These conclusions are shared and elaborated by the Southern contributors to Part 2. In Chapter 6, Manuel Chiriboga (the executive secretary of ALOP) traces the history of the NGO Working Group on the World Bank and outlines the rationale for the group's recent decision to decentralize its operations to the regional level. This move, he believes, opens up important possibilities for greater effectiveness and a much more genuine dialogue between ordinary citizens and World Bank officials. In their comparative study of multilateral lending institutions in Latin America, discussed in Chapter 8, Diana Tussie and María Fernanda Tuozzo confirm the importance of building stronger civil society organizations at the local and national levels to create a firm foundation for global citizen action and the need for NGOs to develop stronger links with other groups in civil society such as labor unions. This, Tussie and Tuozzo argue, will help them to influence the strategic decisions of the World Bank and the Inter-American Development Bank as well as the shape and character of their operational work. The lessons of these early campaigns should help to inform the tactics of civic groups that now wish to influence the International Monetary Fund. As Jan Aart Scholte shows in Chapter 7, the IMF is some years behind the World Bank in its relations with civil society groups; and civil society groups have yet to come to grips with the challenge of engaging with the IMF. This is extremely difficult for both sides, yet—given the enormous importance of the IMF's resources and policy advice to countries under economic stress—a closer and more creative dialogue is urgently needed.

Part 3 provides case studies from each of the major global social movements of the last ten years. Matthew Scott looks in Chapter 9 at the International Campaign to Ban Landmines (ICBL), christened as the "harbinger of the new multilateralism" by former Canadian Foreign Minister Lloyd Axworthy. The ICBL and a number of middle-power governments scored a spectacular success in gaining the assent of 122 countries to the Ottawa Treaty against antipersonnel mines. Yet much less has been achieved in clearing landmines or providing assistance to their victims, areas in which donor rhetoric has not been matched by concrete commitments. This causes Scott to raise an important question that echoes through many of the other case studies: "Who will build the broad-based constituency that might ensure that gains made on paper will be translated into results at the grassroots?" Jubilee 2000, the global campaign against "unpayable debt" analyzed by Carole Collins, Zie Gariyo, and Tony Burdon in Chapter 10, goes some way to answering this question. Although the global effort has focused its attention on the G7 (since Western governments were in the best position to secure deep debt relief and changes in the practice of economic policymaking), Jubilee 2000 has made a serious attempt to support strong national campaigns in both the South and the North and to give them space to articulate their own campaign demands. The experience of citizen organizing around trade has been somewhat similar. John Cavanagh, Sarah Anderson, and Karen Hansen-Kuhn show in Chapter 11 how groups from Canada, Mexico, and the United States developed a collective agenda for trade reform and alternative economic policy through a series of crossnational dialogues stretching back ten years or more. This was an intensive and difficult process, but it may now provide a democratic basis for turning the backlash against globalization into a "frontlash" that can push viable alternatives into the economic and political mainstream.

Holding disparate civic groups together long enough for a global campaign to have any impact on its targets is a difficult task. As Chapters 12 and 13 demonstrate, an overarching framework of shared values and ideology can be critical in this respect, allowing flexibility and room to maneuver at the national and local levels while generating coherence for the movement as a whole. Roy Trivedy and Tom Lent show in Chapter 12 how the UN Convention on the Rights of the Child facilitated connections between national coalitions and international NGOs, helping to root the global movement for children's rights in diverse local polities. Similarly, Kamal Singh demonstrates in Chapter 13 how a strong belief in participatory approaches provided a unifying framework that held together "a scattering of local network processes all linking and sharing with each other, as and when the need arises," in a movement that changed development policy and practice across the world. The environmental movement can claim to have been one of the most successful global campaigns in terms of shifting the public and political consciousness, and Part 3 ends with two case studies that explore contrasting reasons for the environmentalists' success. In Chapter 14 Peter Newell explores the widely varying strategies adopted by environmental NGOs in campaigns against global corporations, concluding that both informal norms and formal standards are important in regulating business behavior—civil society groups having a major role to play in both. The notion of self-regulation is central to Felix Dodds's chapter too, though in a very different sense. Dodds provides a detailed account of the NGO Steering Committee on the UN Commission on Sustainable Development, one of the few global civil society networks that has implemented its own code of conduct to answer criticisms about legitimacy and accountability. The bureaucratic nature of these arrangements is not to every NGO's taste, but in the absence of concrete alternatives, codes of conduct and formal criteria for NGO involvement will probably spread to other areas of global governance over the next ten years.

Part 4 contains four chapters that reflect more broadly on the lessons learned from global citizen action in recent times, plus a wide-ranging conclusion from John Gaventa. Charlotte Bunch and her cowriters show in Chapter 16 how the global movement for women's human rights avoided sacrificing "diversity for universality," by organizing around a broad vision and dispensing with centralized, hierarchical governance structures and a fixed membership. Taking "urban transformation" as an example, Diana Mitlin, Sheela Patel, and Joel Bolnick take these structural insights further by focusing in Chapter 17 on the importance of horizontal exchanges among grassroots groups as a basic organizing principle for the future. In a challenge to the largely Northern NGOs who have dominated many campaigns to date, they show how over 650,000 people in eleven countries have become directly involved in helping each other to reshape policy and practice locally, nationally, and globally. The importance of grassroots involvement to results on the ground is one of the conclusions identified by Jenny Chapman in her overview of lessons learned and a theme taken up by Caroline Harper in her assessment of the analytical content of global campaigns. "Armed only with highly contested anecdotal evidence," as she puts it, civil society groups have found it difficult to blend analysis and activism together in a more effective and responsible way. This is especially difficult in global citizen action because freedom and spontaneity are two of the essential characteristics of civil society, yet a greater element of self-discipline is the essential ingredient in assuaging the criticisms that might otherwise erode political support for greater civil society involvement. In this constantly evolving set of structures and processes—dynamic, fluid, multilayered, and difficult to capture—lies both the promise and the challenge of global citizen action.

Notes

The editors are grateful to the UK Department for International Development (DFID), the Swedish International Development Authority (SIDA), and the Institute of Development Studies (IDS) at the University of Sussex for generous financial assistance toward the cost of producing and disseminating this book.

PART I

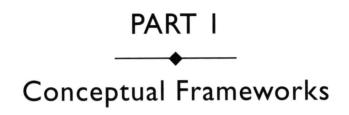

Conceptual Frameworks

2

Ethical Globalization: The Dilemmas and Challenges of Internationalizing Civil Society

John D. Clark

Global interdependence was the theme of the Brandt Commission report in 1980, but few political leaders of the day took this theme seriously or allowed their policies to be influenced by the North-South polarization described by that august group of elder statesmen and women. Now, however, economic globalization has changed the political climate completely. Stockbrokers in Europe check the East Asian markets before breakfast, and political turmoil in Indonesia and Malaysia filters swiftly through as a domestic economic issue in the United States. Almost $400 billion is exchanged in the world currency markets every six hours—more than the World Bank has lent in its entire history. As capital markets have become deregulated, allowing for the free flow of both capital and crisis, growing attention has been given to the ethical issues associated with neoliberal economics (Lockwood and Madden 1997). No one in high office today would deny that we live in an interdependent world, though policy responses largely remain focused on immediate national interests.

Less dramatic, though potentially as profound in terms of repainting the political landscape, has been the gradual emergence of a different form of globalism—that of citizen action. True, there are earlier examples of this trend, such as the antislavery movement or trade unionism, but it was the peace protests that emanated from opposition to the Vietnam War in the late 1960s, plus the mounting popular fear of nuclear war, that signaled a new age of global peoples' movements. These movements—for peace, the environment, human rights, economic justice, and equal rights for women— have important characteristics in common (Clark 1991). They

- Address political issues that were largely ignored (or opposed) by all the mainstream political parties at the time; growing popular concern could not therefore be channeled through conventional political routes.

- Address issues that are truly global and that concern large-scale disparities of power.
- Seek three goals: to influence public policy, reform institutions, and change public attitudes.
- Pursue two strategies: constituency-based campaigns and the use of the mass media to demonstrate force of numbers and win hearts and skillful research and advocacy to win the intellectual case.
- Constitute global movements; they deliberately seek to create international networks and derive enhanced legitimacy from them, promote an ethos of internationalism, and favor simultaneous action at the local, national, and international levels.

It is this last point that has become a defining feature of contemporary citizen movements and a source of their growing influence. Up to the 1990s, participants in social movements were typically exhorted to read about the global consequences of the issues at hand, to replicate actions that had been effective in other countries, but to plan their activities at the national or local levels. Now, they are encouraged to compile evidence through careful study of local context and share this through the Internet with fellow activists across the world, to argue on the basis of pooled information, and to help plan and implement a global campaign strategy. The old peace movement slogan "Think globally, act locally" has been reversed to read "Think locally, act globally"—or even "Think locally *and* globally; act locally *and* globally together" (Clark 1991).

Salamon (1994) celebrates the evolution of citizen power as a "global associational revolution that may prove to be as significant to the latter 20th century as the rise of the nation-state was to the latter 19th century." This chapter addresses Salamon's claim by tracing why global movements have become such a powerful force and analyzing the internal dilemmas and tensions they face. I will also suggest that the time is ripe for a new phase of development in these movements—called "ethical globalization"—in which the moral underpinnings of citizens' networks are consolidated into a more systematically articulated political philosophy that is genuinely international in character and in which movements expose their strategies to more rigorous, ethical road testing.

Why Global Movements?

The growing strength and number of global movements is due to a variety of factors. First, recent decades have seen the emergence of global issues of popular concern including environmental issues, HIV/AIDS, the drug trade, third-world debt, nuclear testing, and the social ramifications of economic globalization.[1] In that these issues cannot be effectively addressed without concerted action by governments throughout the world, they lend themselves to international citizens' action. The globalization of market fundamentalism has become a particular bête noir of civil society throughout the world (Soros 1998). Trade unions, NGOs, churches, networks of intellectuals, and others have come to believe that the current economic crisis in large parts of the global South demonstrates the need for a new financial order, including curbs on the mobility of capital. Civil society is increasingly seen as a vehicle for injecting values and moral pressure into the global marketplace.

Second, enhanced communication facilitates global movements. At the start of international campaigning on the Narmada dam fifteen years ago, it took at least ten days for a letter from Indian activists to reach their partners in the headquarters of NGOs in the North. Now, even grassroots organizations are equipped with fax machines, mobile phones, and electronic mail, and may even be able to post the latest news on their own web site. Information exchange is instantaneous, and international discussion on campaign strategy can be achieved at modest expense. Movement leaders also have more opportunity to meet counterparts in other countries, at conferences organized by international organizations and major NGOs, underwritten by much cheaper air travel. When the World Health Organization (WHO) and the United Nations Children's Fund (UNICEF) organized a conference on the marketing of breast-milk substitutes in 1979, they gave campaigners in different countries their first opportunity to meet face to face. At the close of the meeting this small group held a press conference to announce the launch of the International Baby Foods Action Network, and within a year over a hundred NGOs had joined, representing every populated continent (Clark 1991; New Economics Foundation 1997). This was the birth of the first multinational campaign targeted at multinational corporations. The network's founders had coordinated strategy and shared information by mail for some years previously, but the physical coming together was the catalyst required for the formation of a global movement.

Third, as countries have aggregated into political, trading, and economic blocs, civic leaders have had to coordinate their activities with counterparts within the same regions. For example, human rights campaigners in Malaysia and Indonesia see the Association of Southeast Asian Nations (ASEAN) and the Asia-Pacific Economic Community (APEC) as significant forums for eliciting support for their cause from more liberal governments in the region. At the same time, cynicism about politicians and political parties has increased in many Western countries, evidenced by a fall in voter turnout and active party membership, and mainstream political parties have been slow to change with the times, often remaining locked into traditional left-right domestic divides while the public's interests have become more diverse and international. Pressure groups and social movements have moved into this gap in the political marketplace. For example, by 1990, Greenpeace UK had more members than the British Labour Party (Clark 1991), though this may no longer be true.

Fourth, the rise of the idea of "good governance" has encouraged global movements. As citizens have become more confident, skepticism and mistrust of politicians and officials have turned from complaints to organized action. Citizens rights groups, service users' councils, parliamentary lobbies, and campaigns for freedom of information have all sought to make government more accountable, transparent, efficient, and responsive. Similar campaigns linking citizens' groups from the North with those in the South have focused on international organizations such as the World Bank, the International Monetary Fund (IMF), the UN, the WTO, and the European Commission (Fox and Brown 1998).

Fifth, the growth of civil society continues at an unprecedented rate. Global movements are one manifestation of the growth and diversity of civil society in most countries as well as of the conjunction of civil society concerns across the world. Salamon and Anheier (1998) reveal that for 1995, the size of the nonprofit sector (including government contributions, fees, and voluntary donations of funds and time) was estimated at U.S.$1.3 trillion in the five largest economies alone—approximately the same as the publicly guaranteed debt burden of all developing countries or the combined gross domestic product (GDP) of the fifty lowest-income countries, including China and India. The same study reveals that in these five largest economies, the nonprofit sector averaged 4.7 percent of GDP (more than the agriculture or defense sectors) and employed 7.1 percent of the nonagricultural workforce. Wuthrow (1994) shows that 40 percent of the U.S. population belong to at least one small group that meets regularly, and that nearly 20 percent of the British population engages in some form of voluntary work, half of whom do so on a weekly basis. According to Salamon and Anheier (1998),

> The existence of a vibrant non-profit sector is increasingly being viewed not as a luxury, but as a necessity, for peoples throughout the world. Such institutions can give expression to citizen concerns, hold governments accountable, promote community, address unmet needs, and generally improve the quality of life.

Dilemmas and Tensions

When David kills Goliath, it is a cause for celebration, but by the time he has killed several Goliaths, people start questioning who the aggressor really is. Since 1990, international citizens' movements have grown in size, sharpened their goals and strategies, and defeated many giants in the global arena. With their success comes growing criticism from both within and outside (Edwards and Hulme 1992). It is important for civic leaders to face these criticisms squarely, for, if ignored, they may become the bane of global citizen action. I will mention five of the most common dilemmas.

First are the charges of Western imperialism. Developing country elites often dismiss social movements as little more than latter-day cultural imperialism. They regard these campaigns as orchestrated either by Westerners or by nationals who have become Westernized through education and travel overseas. These campaigns, they contend, are insensitive both to their country's traditions and to its stage of industrialization. Sometimes such arguments are lame excuses for controversial traditions (such as summary executions or the genital mutilation of girls), but at other times they carry significant truth. Lectures from well-heeled Americans about the urgency of reducing carbon dioxide emissions must offend nationals of developing countries enjoying only one-twentieth the per-capita consumption of fossil fuels.

Second, oversimplification elicits criticism from campaign targets. Combining high level advocacy with mass campaigns presents an inherent dilemma for NGOs. What works for rallying the troops can be alienating to the policymakers, while the facts required for detailed policy work are of little interest to the public. The history of debt campaigning illustrates this well. When Oxfam started writing about third world debt in 1984, the UK Treasury and high street banks responded politely but perfunctorily, and the British public were not moved. In 1986, the agency launched a high profile campaign proclaiming the scandal of African countries gripped by famine that were paying twice as much to service their debts as they received in famine relief. As a result, the public was shocked into action: They protested and demanded change. Suddenly, what had been a dry, technical issue became a national issue to which the government had to respond. The response (Chancellor of the Exchequer Nigel Lawson's "Toronto Terms") was largely ineffective, but it opened the door for future campaigning and further concessions (Black 1992). Paradoxically, the mass letter writing and simplified presentation of arguments (without which there would have been no political climate for change) alienated and distracted senior Treasury officials who were allies in the cause of African debt relief. They had to cope with thousands of letters, scores of parliamentary questions, and the burden of briefing ministers for copious media interviews. As rigorous economists, they considered it misleading to compare famine assistance with debt relief—two unrelated financial flows. Asked some years later about Oxfam's efforts, the Treasury undersecretary who was the brains behind successive debt-reduction initiatives said that "the campaign was well placed, and shameless."

Debt campaigning today often implies that third world debt should simply be written off. Officials respond that this simplistic position ignores some basic questions: How would such bookkeeping losses be accounted for? How would the debtors ever get credit again? Why should profligate governments and elites be so easily let off the hook? Bald statements about children dying at the hands of "heartless debt collectors" make them angry, since they know that the campaign leaders realize it isn't as simple as that. This is a difficult trade off. How can a campaign on global ethics not be ethical itself? On the other hand, without galvanizing public concern the campaign would have little chance of success. The Jubilee 2000 campaign for debt relief has found a skillful balance between these imperatives (Collins et al., Chapter 10; Jubilee 2000 1999). Drawing as it does on the biblical Jubilee theme (the forgiveness of debts, the freeing of slaves, and the redistribution of land), it has a popular appeal, built on the outright cancellation of third world debt. But the text of its petition and campaign literature speak of reducing debts to levels that countries can afford, describing different ways of achieving this that are not dissimilar to some of the ideas promoted by the World Bank and other creditors.

Third, citizens' movements often draw criticism because they have the luxury of thinking only about their supporters and a single issue. Governments have to think about the entire population and have to balance competing issues, just as international organizations must respond to their member governments' constraints. As campaigning organizations move closer to real power, they must face up to these trade offs in order to retain their credibility. For example, now that the German Green Party shares political power they have become much more nuanced about economic growth and energy needs. On the other hand, too much realism dulls the sharp edge of idealism needed to carve out new approaches in the policy arena.

Fourth, effective movements are often driven by leaders who are relentless in their cause and who instruct their followers what to do and what to say. But true citizen pressure results from the spontaneous voice of people, typically with multiple and shifting leaders. These two realities can be incompatible. The first is a clarion call, the second a cacophony. The first may be more likely to cause the walls of Jericho to crack, but the second may be more authentic. International campaigns driven by centralized leadership are prone to internal dissent, but they do hit their mark—even if they may lose touch with the grassroots as they become more skilled at advocacy (Miller 1994). Inevitably, as the movement matures its messages become more diverse, but it can be difficult to focus the message as a result.

Fifth, issues of accountability are increasingly pushed to the fore. Determining who has the right to speak on behalf of the third world poor is an increasingly vexed issue within North-South NGO relations. Some Northern campaigners have built up communications and debating skills that are the envy of political spin-doctors, yet their arguments may be untrammeled by on-the-ground realities. In drawing raw facts from their Southern partners for use in advocacy strategies that are not based on consultation with those partners, the Northern NGOs can be faulted as insensitive and extractive. Hence there is a growing call from Southern NGOs for Northern groups to surrender power and allow Southern civil society to speak for Southern citizens (Tandon 1995).

This is not easy to achieve in practice. "Voice" may shift to the South, but do the poor get to participate? National NGOs in the South may criticize their Northern counterparts, but they themselves are often criticized by more grassroots NGOs. In addition, there is the question of whether organizations can have true independence without financial independence. If Northern NGOs finance a large proportion of the budget of Southern NGOs, they will continue to call the shots. They may agree that their partners' voices should be heard in international forums, but since it is Northern funding, they select which voices are heard.

The campaign against World Bank financing of the Arun III dam in Nepal illustrates these dilemmas. The issues around the dam were first flagged internationally by a Nepali NGO that had an exemplary record in micro-hydroelectricity production. Opponents argued that such a large dam was inappropriate to the country's energy needs and would obliterate the potential for small-scale schemes. However, their efforts achieved relatively little attention until international lobbyists took up the campaign and stressed the social and environmental damage the project would cause in the valley in which the dam would be located (Fox and Brown 1998). The image of "innocent tribal people" and their Himalayan Arcadia being bulldozed to make way for a megadam captured the attention of the international media and public, promoting congressional discussions in the United States and parliamentary debates in Germany and the UK. Paradoxically, most of the inhabitants of the valley who did speak out did not do so against the dam but against a decision to change the original plans for the road leading to it, and they criticized the lack of benefits destined for local people. They were not averse to the project so long as the road passed close to their villages, brought employment, and made it easier for them to market their crops. Indeed, an NGO evaluation of the campaign concluded that the main NGO network in Nepal "acted more on the international arena and significantly at the national level, but perhaps very little where the dam was to be built and the people were to be affected" (Participatory Research in Asia 1997). In deciding not to finance the project, the World Bank probably arrived at the right decision, though its own independent review concluded that the Bank had failed to follow its own policies in many respects (Inspection Panel of the World Bank 1998). But the Bank's decision to withdraw had more to do with economics and overall development priorities at the national level than with the needs of the valley inhabitants, as they themselves had voiced them.

This example raises a crucial question: Who has the right to speak for poor countries on such topics? The Nepali government stressed that they had been elected democratically and thus were the only officials with a mandate to speak for citizens. They objected that legislators in other countries were discussing, still less opposing, a domestic political decision for Nepalis. But their focus was the aggregate: the national desire for faster growth and more electricity. Being closer to the ground, Nepali civil society organizations might have represented potential micro-hydro producers and the valley inhabitants much more effectively. And though this was to be a project of a sovereign government, it was to have been financed out of taxpayers' money contributed to the World Bank, which itself could justify an international debate on the matter. It is also true that those who have seen the social consequences of development in remote areas can make an important contribution to the debate. The time is right for a much more honest discussion about the accountability of advocacy organizations and citizens movements (Covey 1994; Fox and Brown 1998). Such tensions will remain until all countries have unfettered and robust civil societies, which are fully engaged in major development decisions.

Principles for Ethical Globalization and How to Achieve Them

Neoliberalism and information technology have fostered an economic transformation over the last decade, as market forces have become relatively unrestrained by national boundaries. For the reasons already described, a similar transformation is allowing the forces of civil society to act at the global level. But just as economic globalization requires a clear (albeit light) framework of international regulations, coordinated policies, and international institutions, so too ethical globalization requires a more clearly defined framework of norms and values, greater attention to accountability and legitimacy within civil society, and international structures that allow for more equitable partnerships and the more honest delineation of roles.

As Fowler (1997) points out, although NGOs are proud to describe themselves as "values-driven," few have taken the trouble to define their ethical foundation with much precision. It is even harder for loosely structured networks to do so, but it may be even more important. Feminists and born-again Christians may seek common cause in fighting pornography, for example, but the two camps are worlds apart on questions of gender. Movements that target a narrow cause without putting that cause into a broader ethical context might lose their chance to help shape the new architecture of global citizen ethics. Governments have their core values (such as national sovereignty, national security, the rule of law, and public service) and so does the private sector (profit, a duty to shareholders, customer loyalty, and competitive edge). What might be the comparable cornerstones of a global civil society? Likely candidates include

- the eradication of poverty (spiritual as well as economic);
- inclusion, that is, a voice in decisionmaking, and economic equity;
- social justice, that is, gender equity, labor and human rights, the rights of speech and association, and a fair and independent judicial system;
- respect for nature and culture; and
- citizens' involvement in governance, in other words, greater public disclosure and accountability for all in public office and institutionalized popular participation.

Legitimacy and Accountability

It is increasingly recognized that national and international NGO networks must devote much more attention to ethical and governance issues within civil society. This is not just a question of fiduciary responsibility but of the right to exercise trusteeship of citizen voice and civic values. Do NGOs achieve what they claim to achieve? Do they coordinate with others, or do they undermine each other's efforts? Are they transparent? Are their public statements a fair reflection of their constituencies' views and experience? Are these statements accurate and objective? Are they ethical in their fundraising? Do they treat gender and environmental issues seriously (both in their programs and within their own organization)? Does their assistance to one population group cause any problems for other groups? Do they have just labor practices themselves? Do they have adequate mechanisms for listening to the views of their members or their constituencies? And do they take notice of the signals of such views?

The leadership of any significant NGO should be accountable on such issues, but to whom and through what mechanisms should these leaders report? The World Bank (1998) argues in favor of self-regulation by the NGO sector and cautions governments against over-regulation and micromanagement. For self-regulation to be convincing, however, NGOs need to be reasonably transparent (there can be a debate about how much transparency is "reasonable"), and they need to have mechanisms in place for peer review. This is rarely the case. NGOs are reluctant to criticize each other publicly, except when at polar extremes on a particular issue. But there are some examples to build on, such as score cards on nonprofit organizations, which survey issues of ethics and performance (National Charities Information Bureau 1996). In the Philippines, CODE-NGO now expels and publishes the names of members who don't come up to its governance standards. Also, the Philippine Revenue Department has delegated an NGO Certification Committee (an NGO body) to decide which NGOs get tax privileges (CODE-NGO 1997). In Bangladesh, the Association of Development Agencies sometimes advises donors on which NGOs to support. However, these are fairly isolated examples.

Except for genuinely democratic membership organizations, in most cases, members and supporters apply little pressure for accountability. The major funders (bilateral agencies, foundations, and major international NGOs) are in a position to ask more questions, but in practice few probe beyond routine accounting matters such as the proportion of funding spent on administration. It is unhealthy to rely on such a "caveat donor" approach to accountability. Civil society is not a commodity sold by NGOs to donor agencies but a public good—to some measure held in trust by NGOs and donors. True accountability should reside as closely as possible to the citizens of the country in question.

This puts the onus on NGO networks to follow the few pioneering examples that do exist and give much more attention to frank, objective assessments of the strengths and weaknesses of member groups. If the networks find this too sensitive, they might consider independent monitoring and evaluation, perhaps within an academic institution, to provide such functions. The critical determinants of NGO legitimacy in speaking for the poor include:

- demonstration (whether the agency can show that its activities have made a positive difference to the poor);
- local knowledge;
- representation (whether the organization has members or functions according to participatory decisionmaking predecures);
- partnerships (if the group cannot claim representation directly, can it do so indirectly, through its partnerships?);
- values base, and whether the organization is accurate in its research and objective in its analysis.

Funders, journalists, politicians, the church, and other popularizers of social concerns pursue these questions. Only the issue of representation brings accountability anywhere near the poor themselves, and this is the least developed, least focused-on question. Social movements can be highly skilled in communications and advocacy but weakly organized and poorly accountable at the grassroots level (New Economics Foundation 1997). This is far from healthy.

In addressing this situation, NGOs in the North and the South must develop more effective partnerships with each other and with the grassroots whose voices they claim to represent. Partnership implies a basic equality, but this is not possible when the relationship is characterized by money flowing in one direction and accountability in the other. Donor agencies, foundations, and NGOs in the North have much more access to funds than Southern counterparts, and that may be their chief comparative advantage. But at least as important is the comparative advantage of being close to the people concerned. Few Southern NGOs have been able to build a powerful international reputation on this score, but this can be an important factor in promoting greater equality in global alliances, especially if funders could relinquish power in five ways:

- Agree to expose themselves to more honest peer pressure within international networks. The establishment of the International Forum on Southern NGO Capacity Building (IFCB) might prove to be an interesting example in this regard;[2]
- Place greater emphasis within the South on self-monitoring and peer evaluation with funders agreeing to use and support these channels rather than relying on their own evaluations;
- Allow monitoring and evaluation to become a two-way street with Southern networks and institutes monitoring the activities of Northern funders and reporting on ethical, fiduciary, and governance issues;
- Establish decisionmaking, or at least advisory, bodies within recipient countries for funding decisions, monitoring and evaluation, and advocacy strategies;
- Agree with NGO networks on the most important indicators of progress to monitor as well as which aspects of institutional capacity need strengthening.

Such a renegotiation of roles would challenge Northern NGOs to expand their horizons. Currently, most are so preoccupied with their financial bottom line that they view their citizens as merely donors, neglecting their potential to act as educators (of their children and peers), advocates (for example through local newspapers or societies), voters, consumers (boycotting or favoring certain products), investors (making ethical choices), and—if all else fails—as troublemakers though demonstrations and direct action. Renegotiating roles in this way necessitates a leveling of the playing field for global citizen action. Capacity building and NGO support programs should be designed to erode the power differentials that exist between Northern and Southern NGOs and between organizations in the capital city and at the grassroots. More equal access to information and influence are critical. Unfortunately, in many campaigns, Northern advocacy groups have easier access to information about the country in question than organizations in the country themselves and tend to share that information more readily with Northern peers than with grassroots groups in the South. They also have better access to influential journalists, politicians, officials, and other policymakers and may not use their connections to provide platforms for grassroots activists, preferring to monopolize airtime themselves.

There are many laudable exceptions to this critique, but the issue needs to be stated starkly because it is *felt* starkly by many Southern NGO leaders. Their message is clear: It is not time for Northern NGOs to pack their bags and go home, but it is time for a new order. It is time to share the reins of influence, hand over the microphone, and make way for more democracy in global citizen action.

Notes

The opinions expressed in this chapter are the author's alone and are not necessarily shared by the World Bank.

1. International NGOs have been particularly powerful within global environmental debates. Their formal or semiformal role in some UN forums has been seen by some governments to threaten the one nation–one vote principle of international decisionmaking. (Cameron and MacKenzie 1995)

2. This forum (the IFCB) brings the supply side of capacity building programs (international NGOs, foundations, and donors) together with the intended users of such programs (the Southern NGOs and their networks) to listen to the demand side. The Society for Participatory Research in Asia, New Delhi, acts as the secretariat of the IFCB.

3

Transnational Civil Society

Ann M. Florini

From human rights to land mines, sustainable development, and democratization, global problemsolving is increasingly being left to an agglomeration of unelected, often unaccountable transnational civil society actors. Nongovernmental organizations, informal associations, and loose coalitions are linking up across borders to play a wide range of roles: participating in treaty negotiations and monitoring how well governments comply; creating broad new expectations about the responsibilities that states and corporations should bear; and altering, sometimes quite specifically, how countries can pursue their goals or corporations can seek their profits. The Union of International Associations lists over 15,000 internationally and regionally oriented nongovernmental organizations (Union of International Associations 1999). Will transnational civil society become a permanent and powerful contributor to solving the world's problems, and should it?

This chapter summarizes the findings of a project that addresses the dual questions of the extent and desirability of transnational civil society power. The project, sponsored by the Japan Center for International Exchange, brought together a multinational group of analysts to assess the growing role of transnational civil society in six case studies selected for their diversity, ranging from multilateral arms control, to a global anti-dam network, to the emerging global campaign against corruption. The project was born out of the conviction that transnational civil society is an increasingly important piece of the larger problem of global governance. In the absence of Cold War certainties about how the world should govern itself, a broad continuum of thought now stretches between two extremes. At one extreme are those who believe that nothing much has changed or is likely to change: the basic structure of world politics remains that of the nation-state system, with states the only actors that can make and enforce rules for the world and war as the ultimate arbiter. At the other extreme are those who believe everything has changed: that states are doomed to powerless irrelevance, and regional associations, large corporations, and civil society organizations are destined to fill the void (if we are fortunate) or end in chaos (if we are not). Neither endpoint seems plausible. The state system that has governed the world for centuries is neither divinely ordained nor easily swept away. It is, however, changing, and one of the most dramatic changes concerns the growing role of transnational civil society.

Writers who have examined the emergence of civil society organizations around the world make a strong case that civil society is playing a rapidly growing role in governance, and many of their writings hold out high hopes that civil society will help to solve problems that governments are unable or unwilling to address. But most of this literature examines civil society one country at a time or at most draws comparisons across countries about the status of national civil societies (CIVICUS 1997; CIVICUS 1994; James 1989; Fisher 1998; McCarthy 1992; Anheier and Salamon 1994; Anheier and Salamon 1998). Of the many analysts who have looked at the networks linking civil society organizations across territorial boundaries, most have examined just one case at a time.[1] Relatively few studies have compared transnational civil society networks to analyze the strengths and weaknesses of this emerging form of transnational collective action (Charnovitz 1997; Clark 1995; Keck and Sikkink 1998; Weiss and Gordenker 1996; Sinnar 1995-1996; Smith, Chatfield, and Pagnucco 1997). And only a handful have looked at a wide range of cases and issues to explore what, if anything, transnational civil society should do—and whether, and under what conditions, it is desirable for transnational civil society to play a significant part in making the decisions that shape the future for all of us (Clark 1991; Hulme and Edwards 1996; Fox and Brown 1998; Korten 1990; Mathews 1997; Simmons 1998; Spiro 1995).

Three Case Studies

This chapter provides a brief summary of three of the project's case studies: multilateral nuclear arms control, opposition to large dams, and the much-noted international land mines campaign (see Florini 2000 for more detailed versions of the cases).

Pool Games

The multilateral nuclear arms control case examines two related sets of treaty negotiations: the permanent extension of the Nonproliferation Treaty

(NPT) in 1995 and the agreement on the Comprehensive Test Ban Treaty (CTBT) in 1996.[2] The case is actually a single story because the two negotiations were closely connected. The NPT is a bargain in which nonnuclear states agree to renounce the acquisition of nuclear weapons, while nuclear weapons states agree to pursue nuclear disarmament. Many nonnuclear states have long seen the comprehensive test ban as the ultimate test of that commitment to disarmament, reasoning that it is hard to maintain an arms race without testing. In 1995, the NPT was due to expire unless renewed by its parties. Debate centered on whether the renewal should be temporary, to put pressure on nuclear states to conclude a test ban treaty, or permanent, as a valuable arms control accord in its own right.

This case study demonstrates that intergovernmental agreement on a nuclear test ban in 1996 came about only because of the continuing efforts of a wide range of civil society organizations, sometimes acting in concert and sometimes independently. Greenpeace, an international NGO, helped to create intense pressure on the French government to cease nuclear testing by sailing its boats so close to the French testing site that they were seized or, in one case, bombed, with large-scale publicity in the media. Meanwhile, a homegrown civil society movement in Ukraine linked up with activists overseas and forced the Soviet government to stop testing at its main test site at Semipalatinsk. U.S. Defense Department efforts to carve out an exemption for low-yield tests faltered under the onslaught of a vigorous civil society campaign. And China, the last holdout among the nuclear weapons states, found itself the target of an intense diplomatic campaign conducted by such nonnuclear states as Japan, Germany, and Australia working in concert with other civil society organizations.

The NPT extension was a much messier story, given the divisions within transnational civil society over whether the treaty's extension should be pursued at all. This chapter paints a picture of a deeply divided network of antinuclear activists and nongovernmental policy analysts, all ostensibly striving for the goal of a nuclear-free world but unable to agree on how to achieve it. Some NGOs regarded the NPT as the indispensable basis for promoting arms control and nonproliferation. Others viewed the treaty as a flawed and discriminatory instrument that validated the possession of nuclear weapons by a chosen few. The more activist organizations largely found themselves out in the cold. Analysts at think tanks and policy research institutes, alternately, proved critical to the ultimate outcome. Most notably, they sponsored games of pool that turned out to be crucial to the campaign negotiations.

Until shortly before the spring 1995 conference at which the vote to extend the NPT was taken, the prospects for indefinite extension looked bleak. The CTBT had not yet been signed (that happened the following year), and many of the nonnuclear states showed a reluctance to accept indefinite extension in view of what seemed to them to be inadequate progress toward disarmament. The official U.S. position favored indefinite extension, but the Clinton administration was not doing much to bring it about. Transnational civil society—or at least that part of it that wanted the NPT extended—stepped into the breach. Most important was the Programme for Promoting Nuclear Nonproliferation (PPNN), a group that coordinated unofficial meetings among governmental officials and independent experts. In the course of these meetings, diplomats from Canada, South Africa, and Finland discovered a common passion for playing pool. And during those pool games, they came up with the compromise that was eventually adopted at the 1995 NPT Review and Extension Conference, trading permanent extension for a much-strengthened process of treaty review conferences every five years to maintain pressure on the nuclear weapons states.

Dams

For decades, large dams were routinely built to provide water, irrigation, electricity, and flood control in scores of countries. Such needs remain unmet in many places. A billion people still lack adequate access to water, some two billion lack reliable electricity, and large-scale floods in China and elsewhere point to the still-unsatisfied demand for flood control. But the number of dams under construction has dropped precipitously, with a 74 percent decline in fact from the 1970s to the 1990s.[3] Since demand for water, irrigation, electricity, and flood control has not lessened, and potential sites for large dams remain plentiful, something else must account for this remarkable decline. That something else is civil society.

Opposition to large dams first arose between the 1950s and the 1970s in separate campaigns in Europe, the United States, India, and other parts of the world. In rich countries, opposition came from conservationists trying to preserve nature. In poor countries, opponents tended to be those who stood to lose their homes and livelihoods, along with environmentalists. In the 1980s, these domestic nodes began to link together. Civil society groups in Europe and the United States, enjoying increasing success in halting and reforming dam building in their own countries, saw equally objectionable projects arising in the South, along with vigorous but often ineffective domestic opposition. At the same time, a number of mostly U.S.-based environmental organizations initiated a campaign organized against the World Bank and other multilateral funders of large infrastructure projects. By the end of the decade, the loose anti-dam network was holding international meetings, issuing declarations and publications, and bringing large-scale publicity to anti-dam protests that made it difficult for dam construction to proceed. By the mid-1990s, it had forced substantial changes in

World Bank practice, crucial because the World Bank was for decades the most important source of funding for dams in developing countries.

In 1997, the broad anti-dam network accomplished something it had long pursued: agreement on an independent and comprehensive review of big dams. At a workshop sponsored by the World Bank and the IUCN, representatives of governments, international development agencies, transnational civil society, and private-sector dam builders agreed to establish the World Commission on Dams (WCD). This commission is most unusual. Its twelve members include four each from government, the private sector, and civil society. Should it meet its ambitious goals—a consensus assessment of dams and their alternatives, along with criteria for the making and decommissioning of dams—the WCD could provide a powerful model for partnerships across sectors in the management of global issues.

Landmines

In December 1997, 122 government delegations met in Ottawa, Canada, to sign a treaty banning antipersonnel landmines.[4] The Convention on the Prohibition of the Use, Stockpiling, Production, and Transfer of Antipersonnel Mines and on their Destruction set a limit of four years for the destruction of the stockpiles of antipersonnel mines and ten years to clear antipersonnel mines from the signing states' territories. Based on its potential humanitarian impact alone, the international landmine ban represents a momentous achievement. The millions of landmines in place in scores of countries around the world are responsible for injuring or killing 26,000 people a year. The vast majority of the victims are not combatants. They are civilians, often children, who stumble across the mines long after they have been forgotten by the fighters who put them there. The world has previously outlawed categories of weapons, finding chemical and biological weapons, for example, humanely unacceptable. But this time it was civil society, not governments, that took the lead, despite vehement objections from the world's major military powers. Without the International Campaign to Ban Landmines (ICBL), the treaty would not exist.

The campaign to ban landmines has a long history. The international community recognized the need to grapple with the landmine problem as early as 1980 when seventy-six states participated in the Conventional Weapons Convention (CWC) and agreed to a protocol to limit the use of antipersonnel mines. The protocol did little good—in 1997 landmines were still killing civilians at the rate of one every twenty minutes (CQ Researcher 1997). In the early 1990s, NGOs who were witnessing this devastation in their humanitarian work around the world, including the Vietnam Veterans of America Foundation, Medico International in Germany, and Human Rights Watch, jointly launched the ICBL to advocate a total ban on antipersonnel landmines. Throughout the 1990s, support for a global ban grew steadily. The antilandmine movement spread from a handful of NGOs that pioneered the ICBL in 1992 to over one thousand in more than sixty countries by 1999. The numbers of effective grassroots campaigns in a wide range of countries, loosely connected through an international network by email, faxes, and occasional conferences, shaped the ICBL into a force governments could not ignore. Indeed, some governments did not ignore the campaign; they actively welcomed it (see Chapter 9).

In contrast to the advances made by the NGO community throughout the first half of the 1990s, intergovernmental negotiations to ban landmines faltered. Frustrated with the stalled efforts to revise the CWC treaty, Canada, led by then Foreign Minister Lloyd Axworthy, officially called for the launching of a fast-track strategy, establishing December 1997 as a deadline for action on a total landmine ban. Freed from the necessity of pursuing consensus through the United Nations forum, Axworthy was able to employ some creative tools of diplomacy, including mounting an effective public relations campaign. At a Canadian-sponsored meeting held in Ottawa in October 1996, twenty-five government representatives were expected, but over seventy-five came. Many of the world's most powerful states, including the United States, China, Russia, the UK, and Japan, however, were not among the initial supporters of this Ottawa process, but the Canadians, like-minded governments, and the NGO coalition refused to be dissuaded.

The meeting in Ottawa in October 1996 confirmed that NGO activity had become linked to nation-state involvement; each side relied on the other. As Axworthy put it, the Ottawa process

> worked because new synergies were created. This was not simply a question of consulting NGOs or seeking their views. We have moved well beyond that. What I am talking about is a full working process between governments and civil groups. (Boswell 1997)

The success of that process was affirmed in October 1997 when the International Campaign to Ban Land Mines received the Nobel Peace Prize, awarded "as much for how it carried out its mission as for what it accomplished" (Frandsen 1997). The prize committee expressed its hope that the campaign, with its working partnership between governments and civil society, would serve as a diplomatic model in the future (Shimbun 1997).

Though a remarkable achievement, the signing of the treaty represents only the first step toward ridding the world of landmines. In this case, civil society, working with medium-sized states, was able to bring about a major international treaty without superpower support. Was this a unique occurrence, or does it represent the wave of the future? Landmines have some unusual features. They are a problem in nearly every region of the globe, making it easy to garner worldwide support for their removal, and they are an indiscriminate weapon. Victims are often innocent civilians caught at the wrong place at the wrong time, often years after the mines were planted. The campaign was able to build on the publicity following both the Nobel Peace Prize and the death of Princess Diana, an active and visible campaigner for the ban.

Even so, while an impressive number of nations have signed the ban, a number of the world's most powerful nations have not. Nonsignatories include China, Russia, and the United States, although all three have agreed to cooperate with the convention on demining and victim assistance. The landmine ban will only be effective if the nations that have ratified the treaty live up to its terms and if other nations agree to ratification. Moreover, most of the issues on the transnational governance agenda lack the compelling imagery of mutilated landmine victims. It is relatively easy to agree to rid the world of such a repugnant weapon. Civil society campaigns on issues like climate change or biodiversity have to contend with greater technical complexity. The new campaign against small arms, for example, a successor to the landmine campaign, has to contend with the legitimate security uses and cultural acceptability of such weapons. On the other hand, back in 1991 when the ICBL was forming, very few people dreamed that a total ban might come about within a mere seven years.

Lessons Learned

The first of the three questions this project set out to address was whether the growing attention to transnational civil society reflected a real shift in world power.[5] These case studies, along with many others published in recent years, make it clear that civil society actors are having increasing influence in global affairs. Civic groups caused nuclear weapons states to recalculate the costs and benefits of retaining the option of nuclear testing. Transnational civil society networks are even creating new issues for negotiation and persuading some states to act on those issues in the name of the global public good. It is hard to see, for instance, what particular Canadian national interest was served by Canada's forceful advocacy of the ICBL.

However, there are clear limits to the power of transnational civil society networks. For one thing, there is no single, coherent transnational civil society agenda. The vast array of civil society actors involved in efforts to control nuclear weapons found themselves sharply divided over the NPT extension. Moreover, it is not enough to accomplish the relatively straightforward goal of getting governmental negotiators to sign a treaty. Since the

1996 conclusion of the Comprehensive Test Ban Treaty, India and Pakistan have conducted their first nuclear weapons test, and the U.S. Senate has voted against ratification. Indeed, civil society may find its role in global governance is changing from that of gadfly to that of direct participant in the management of global issues. The World Commission on Dams is being closely watched as a potential model for a new type of tri-sectoral effort. Other models exist. Examples include the close cooperation between civil society and intergovernmental organizations evidenced between Transparency International and the World Bank in the global campaign against corruption as well as the rapidly proliferating codes of conduct promulgated by civil society groups for the edification of socially responsible businesses.

Since civil society does seem to be playing an increasingly powerful role in global affairs, the second question is, Why? Skeptics see the current period as a temporary lull between the end of the Cold War and the beginning of a new great-power conflict that will inevitably dominate global affairs. It is certainly true that the end of the Cold War loosened the international system and offered NGOs more space in which to speak out and be heard. But a less jaundiced view would discern broad trends that seem likely to foster a strong role for transnational civil society in the foreseeable future, trends that would be affected but not dissipated even by the renewal of ideological disputes between states. These trends include the growing strength of domestic civil society in many parts of the world; advances in technology that make communication cheaper and information access more decentralized; a large number of targets around which transnational civil society can coalesce; and a continued willingness of donor agencies to support domestic and transnational civil society.

In most regions of the world, increasingly vigorous domestic civil societies provide the nodes for transnational networks. With democratization has come the beginning of a broader acceptance around the world of the desirability, or at least inevitability, of a strong civil society. The wave of democratization that swept through Eastern Europe, Latin America, and Africa in the 1990s opened the way for stronger domestic civil societies that could participate in transnational networks. In many regions, governments are beginning to make it easier for civil society organizations to form and to act. The most striking change has appeared in the countries of the former Soviet Union and Eastern and Central Europe. The former communist governments had stifled civil society, allowing it to exist mostly in the form of government-controlled mandatory "voluntary" activities, although a few Eastern European countries managed to keep at least a rudimentary form of civil society alive. Since 1989, however, the growth of civil society in several of those countries has been nothing short of spectacular, reflecting both democratization and the strong support of Western donors, both of which have led to pressures on the new governments to allow independent civil societies to function. But governments in other parts of the world have also begun to change their attitudes toward, and laws governing, civil society. Japan, for example, passed a law in 1998 easing what had been onerous financial requirements for the registration of NGOs.

Even where governments are less than enthusiastic about the emergence of civil society, officials are having an increasingly hard time keeping civil society under control. Problems stem largely from ever-cheaper communications and transportation technologies that are making people in very different parts of the world not only aware that they share common interests and values but also able to act together to realize common goals. The Internet, particularly the exponential rise in the number of Internet users, poses a dilemma for governments. Although governments may want the business opportunities that enter their countries via the Internet's cross-border information highways, with those new highways come many unwanted travelers and ideas. In China, "Hactivists" have infiltrated government websites boasting progress in human rights, replacing official statements with claims that "China's people have no rights at all, never mind human rights." The Internet makes it possible for such political activism to take place outside the territorial control of governments.

Transnational civil society coalitions need a focal point around which to organize their efforts. Governments and intergovernmental organizations have frequently, if unwittingly, obliged by sponsoring conferences that draw representatives of civil society in addition to governments. Perhaps most important are the United Nations conferences on global issues that began in the 1970s, which both reflected and spurred the development of a stronger, more integrated transnational civil society. NGOs appeared in force at the 1972 UN Conference on the Human Environment, with accredited NGOs outnumbering governmental delegations two to one. By the time of the 1992 UN Conference on Environment and Development (UNCED) in Rio de Janeiro, Brazil, NGOs displayed striking influence over the agenda and outcome (see Chapter 15). At the 1995 Beijing Women's Conference, this enormously expanded role for NGOs had come to seem so normal that an uproar ensued when the Chinese government exiled the parallel nongovernmental forum to a site far from the official conference center. The heyday of UN megaconferences is over, undermined by budget constraints, general exhaustion, and, not least, the feeling on the part of some governments that civil society's role in them was getting out of hand. But the transnational networking made possible by the conferences has created or reinforced nongovernmental links involving all sorts of groups in a very wide range of countries.

Transnational civil society is relatively inexpensive, often relying heavily on the labor of committed volunteers, but its activities still cost money. Significant sources of funds have become available since the 1970s to both domestic nodes and transnational links. Such funding often comes from rich-country sources. The myth that someone in a log cabin in Vermont ran the landmines campaign on e-mail is already widespread, but in reality, the efforts of the ICBL were well financed by groups such as the Vietnam Veterans of America, enabling leaders to shuttle around the globe and organize a highly visible campaign via the mass media. As for multilateral nuclear arms control negotiations, most of the money supporting involved civil society groups came from Western foundations. The Climate Action Network, meanwhile, owes its origins in significant part to generous early support from the German Marshall Fund. As the Internet generation of billionaires moves to set up its own foundations, funds for such causes seem likely to increase.

Desirability

The hardest of the three questions posed in the study is a normative one: If transnational civil society is both strong and sustainable, is this good or bad? Or, to render the question more properly nuanced, what is good and bad about the emerging role of civil society, and what can be done to encourage the good and alleviate the bad? In one respect, the question is unanswerable in any objective sense. To victims of landmines, to villagers threatened with displacement and poverty because of large-scale dam projects, to business executives tired of being shaken down for bribes, transnational civil society may appear a very good thing indeed. Without organizations like the ICBL, the World Commission on Dams, and Transparency International, few of these people would have redress for their complaints. But to governments trying to protect national security through weapons programs they deem proper, or to owners of dam-building firms who believe they are providing a major public benefit through the development of much-needed infrastructure, and to politicians working within age-old customs, transnational civil society can seem disruptive, narrow-minded, and above all unaccountable.

Specific transnational civil society coalitions do indeed pursue narrow mandates, and they lack mechanisms for reaching broad agreement across peoples and issues. After all, their raison d'etre is usually a single issue or group, and they induce contributions from both their own members and from outsiders by claiming that their cause has the highest claim on those resources. Such claims can serve as a force for fragmentation. Even for those who share the goals of particular networks, troubling questions about legitimacy and accountability remain. Transnational civil society networks by definition operate at least in part beyond the reach of the specific governments, businesses, and individuals whom they most affect. They often consist of people in one place claiming to speak on behalf of people in another. To date, most have remained relatively immune to the growing pressure for transparency on the part of governments and the private sector. There are no easy means of imposing accountability. By its very nature, transnational civil society is not subject either to elections or to market tests. Yet to leave the issue unaddressed is to threaten the long-term legitimacy of an important contributor to global governance.

It matters whether this problem is solved, because transnational civil society can serve humanity well. Because the networks claim to speak on behalf of the global future, they provide a kind of competition for the public conscience. That competition prods government officials to consider broader perspectives than the immediate bureaucratic turf battle or the next election, or even the immediate national interest, and pushes corporate officials to consider more than the next quarter's bottom line. It also helps to keep attention on pressing transnational issues that worsen slowly and incrementally—just the sort of barely perceptible change that ordinarily does not register on the political radar screen. Since globalization leaves people everywhere more susceptible to the actions of others far away, it seems fitting that transnational civil society provides a mechanism for those people to have some say about those actions. For the large number of people whose governments are less than fully democratic (or less than fully responsive to the needs of those citizens unable to make large campaign donations), transnational civil society may provide the only meaningful way to participate in decisionmaking.

For all these reasons, it is highly desirable that ways are found to deal with the weaknesses of transnational civil society without unduly hampering its strength. Because there is no easy, one-size-fits-all measure for determining which of the thousands of clamoring voices are pursuing noble goals (or even which goals are truly noble), those means should not constrain the sector's vaunted flexibility. No one model serves for all of transnational civil society, just as no one model serves for the whole of the private sector.

The one very broad reform that transnational civil society *should* adopt is the same one that governments and businesses are increasingly being pressured to adopt in the name of good governance: transparency. By and large, civil society organizations are poor at providing information about their personnel, operations, funding sources, expenditures, and even, sometimes, their purposes. Sometimes that opacity is a deliberate effort to conceal nefarious activity. More often, it reflects a natural human tendency to see getting on with the job as more important than reporting on one's activities. But if transnational civil society networks are to flourish as significant contributors to the management and resolution of global problems, they will have to do better. There is a role for governments here in requiring reporting on funding sources and expenditures. But it is up to civil society to make its own case by reporting openly and honestly about purposes and activities as time and resources will permit.

Notes

1. There is a vast literature of single-issue case studies. A very useful bibliography that includes many types of movements can be found in Tarrow and Acostavalle (1999).

2. This section, "Pool Games," is drawn from Johnson 2000.

3. This section, "Dams," is based on Khagram 2000.

4. This section, "Landmines," draws from Mekata 2000.

5. This section, "Lessons Learned," is based on Florini 2000.

PART 2

◆

Global Civil Society and the International Financial Institutions

4

Transnational Civil Society Coalitions and the World Bank: Lessons from Project and Policy Influence Campaigns

L. David Brown and Jonathan Fox

For more than two decades, the World Bank has been a lightning rod for transnational civil society action. Coalitions of civil society organizations—nongovernmental organizations, churches, indigenous peoples movements, and international environment and human rights networks—have repeatedly challenged the World Bank's high profile promotion of socially and environmentally costly development strategies. Playing David to the Bank's Goliath is a particularly striking example of ambitious North-South civil society campaigning. In turn, the World Bank has responded in many different, sometimes contradictory, ways, ranging from short-term damage control, substantive policy reforms, and islands of innovation on the one hand to persistent gaps in meeting its own social and environmental reform commitments and a more-of-the-same approach for structural adjustment on the other. The diversity of Bank campaigns across countries and issues, together with the Bank's long track records, makes those campaigns especially rich sources of lessons for understanding transnational coalitions more generally.

The World Trade Organization's (WTO) debacle in Seattle in 1999 led the *Economist* to trace civil society protests in part back to the 50 Years Is Enough campaign against the World Bank and International Monetary Fund (IMF) in 1994. The *Economist* proceeded to congratulate the Bank for its subsequent effort, supposedly successful, to demobilize and coopt its NGO critics. The *Economist* observed that

> From environmental policy to debt relief, NGOs are at the center of World Bank policy. Often they determine it. The new World Bank is more transparent, but it is also more beholden to a new set of special interests.[1]

Is it possible that NGOs have gained this much influence? Have they really demobilized as much as is claimed?

While it is true that, since 1994, the IMF, the Multilateral Agreement on Investment (MAI), and the WTO superceded the Bank on some protesters' lists of top targets, many other advocacy groups and social organizations—especially those closer to the ground and further from the global media spotlight—remain deeply concerned with the issue of how to get the World Bank to live up to its social and environmental reform commitments.[2]

The analytical challenge implicit in the *Economist'*s assessment is how to disentangle cooptation from substantive concessions while recognizing that the difference is often in the eye of the beholder. There is, moreover, a basic contradiction in the *Economist'*s assessment: If NGOs really did determine World Bank policy, that would suggest that they have much more influence than the term *cooptation* implies. For example, if NGOs set Bank policy, then it would be difficult to explain why, for the first time in 1999, more than half of the Bank's lending went to quick-disbursing, nonproject macroeconomic adjustment loans (a category of loan inherently far removed from both civil society levers of influence and the Bank's own social and environmental reform policies). Even at the level of specific infrastructural investments, which offer critics more tangible targets, the World Bank continues to propose new projects that directly subsidize huge transnational corporations to carry out likely environmental disasters, as in the case of Exxon and the Chad-Cameroon pipeline.[3] Also in 1999, an international debate exploded over the discovery that the Bank was planning to fund a project called China Western Poverty Reduction, which turned out to threaten ethnic Tibetans. In spite of the Bank's well-known, sophisticated NGO engagement, involving extensive operational collaboration, policy consultations, and enlightened discourse, in the Tibet case, the institution unknowingly stumbled over one of world's most influential indigenous rights campaigns. The resulting mobilization was almost as intense as the previous peak of anti-Bank protest back in the early 1990s, leading to widespread press coverage, unusual "no" votes by the U.S. and German representatives on the Bank's board, high-level international diplomatic tensions with China, imprisonment and serious injury to NGO investigators, an ongoing investigation by the Bank's official inspection panel, and possible suspension of the project.[4]

At the same time, as powerful elements within the World Bank continue to ignore its own environmental and social reforms, in some sectors and in some countries, civil society actors perceive the Bank's enlightened discourse as an important partial opening, especially under regimes that are even less enlightened than the World Bank. Moreover, at least some controversial projects that once would have sailed through the approval process are now subjected to greater scrutiny in the design phase, both internally and externally. The Bank's involvement in postconflict situations also creates opportunities for constructive leadership, as in the case of East Timor. The overall result is a highly uneven, patchwork quilt of partial reforms combined with entrenched resistance to change. Transnational campaigns continue to challenge the World Bank, and they have had some degree of influence. In the process, with their long track record, these campaigns have helped to build ever more balanced partnerships between Northern and Southern civil society actors.

This chapter explores these patterns by drawing on a series of transnational coalition efforts aimed at influencing World Bank policies and projects. These case studies were carried out between 1992 and 2000 under the auspices of the Institute for Development Research.[5] We seek to extract from the cases lessons about what makes such efforts successful. More particularly, the chapter focuses on two questions:

1. What is required for transnational coalitions to influence institutions like the World Bank?
2. How can transnational coalition members be accountable to each other across large gaps of power, wealth, and culture?

The Transnational Coalitions Study

This study explores critical factors embedded in complex, long-term campaigns. We chose to develop in-depth case studies and then compared those cases to see what sorts of patterns emerged. The cases were written by individuals close to events on the ground with access to both the grassroots populations involved and decisionmakers at the World Bank and other agencies. Four cases focused on coalition efforts to influence specific development *projects*—a geothermal plant in the Philippines, a natural resource management project in Brazil, petroleum and land legislation linked to structural adjustment in Ecuador, and a dam in Indonesia.[6] Four other cases focused on coalition efforts to shape Bank *policies* on critical issues—indigenous peoples, water resources management, resettlement of populations ousted by projects, and information and inspection panel policy.[7] Tables 4.1 and 4.2 summarize major features of the project and policy cases.

In this chapter we present some important lessons suggested by the detailed analyses of these cases published elsewhere.[8] The next two sections present and illustrate eight lessons, four concerning coalition impacts

Table 4.1   Project Reform Campaigns

Projects and Key Actors	Critical Events in Alliance Evolution
Kedung Ombo Dam, Indonesia (1984–1994) GRO: Villagers; students NGO: Local and national legal aid; other local and national poverty and environmental NGOs BO: International NGO Group on Indonesia (INGI) INGO: Members of INGI from Northern countries	Most families were not aware of relocation plans until the dam was almost finished. Then some families asked local and national legal aid NGOs for help getting more compensation for their land. Some suits were eventually successful, but the Indonesian government invalidated the judgments. INGI began to lobby the World Bank via its international members in 1988. Popular protests by students and religious groups supported affected villagers after dam completion in 1989. INGI meetings with the World Bank led to government attacks on INGI for "washing dirty linen" in public. The government did make other land available to villagers. The Bank and other international actors agreed to avoid future "Kedung Ombos."
Mt. Apo Thermal Plant, Philippines (1987–1993) GRO: Indigenous peoples groups; local farmers NGO: Local, regional, national networks; Legal Resources Center BO: Philippine Development Forum (PDF); Bank Information Center (BIC) INGO: Environmental Defense Fund (EDF); Columban Fathers; Greenpeace	Indigenous groups and farmers began to organize local, regional, and national networks to challenge the project in 1987. Elders of local tribes swore to defend Mt. Apo to "the last drop of blood." Local coalitions built links to INGOs and the PDF. Two Bank missions drew contradictory conclusions about the project. In 1989, the Philippine Development Forum of NGOs and INGOs agreed to lobby the Bank on Mount Apo. The Government of the Philippines (GOP) certified the project for environmental compliance in spite of protests. National "solidarity conferences" among NGO networks agreed to emphasize indigenous rights and carefully monitor lobbying of PDF. PDF lobbying helped the World Bank reject the government's environmental impact assessment, and the GOP withdrew its loan request. In 1993, further solidarity conferences set strategies for lobbying export-import Banks.
Planafloro Natural Resources, Brazil (1989–1995) GRO: Rubber tappers; farmers NGO: Local and national NGOs and networks (e.g., Instituto de Antropologia e Meio Ambiente [IAMA]; National Council of Rubber Tappers [CNS]; Instituto de Estudos Amazonicos [IEA]; and others) BO: Rondônia NGO Forum, INGO: EDF; World Wildlife Federation; others	INGOs(such as the Environmental Defense Fund) protested the lack of local participation in the initial design in 1989, in part because few GROs were organized in the region. The Bank suspended the project until the Rondônia NGO Forum was created to enable local and international (but not national) NGOs to participate in project decisions in 1991. It became clear that state agencies would violate loan terms in spite of the forum, and forum protests carried little weight. The forum requested that the World Bank suspend disbursement in 1994 and asked the Bank Inspection Panel to review the project in 1995. Planafloro was accepted as a case by the panel that year.

(Table 4.1 Continues)

Table 4.1　Continued

Projects and Key Actors	Critical Events in Alliance Evolution
Ecuador Structural Adjustment, Ecuador (1986–1994) GRO: Indigenous peoples (IP) groups; environmental groups NGO: Federation of Indigenous Peoples (CONAIE); Accion Ecologica BO: Ecuador Network; BIC INGO: Rainforest Action Network; Oxfam	The Federation of Indigenous Peoples (CONAIE) mobilized indigenous peoples (IP) groups. In 1990 it helped organize an uprising against structural adjustment. In 1992 it allied with NGOs to challenge World Bank and government oil extraction initiatives that threatened indigenous groups. Negotiations with the Bank and the government altered the oil law. In 1994 CONAIE led a national "Mobilization for Life" coalition against a proposed land law that threatened access to communally held lands and paralyzed the country. CONAIE created the Ecuador Network with INGOs to influence Bank policymaking. Eventually, negotiations with government leaders and agribusiness interests produced a more acceptable land law and a larger policy role for CONAIE in the future.

Note: GRO means grassroots organization; NGO means local or national NGO; BO means bridging organization; INGO means international NGO.

and four concerning coalition organization and accountability. Then we comment briefly on the implications of these lessons for future international coalitions to influence global institutions and policies.

Lessons About the Impact of Coalitions

It is clear that influencing an institution like the World Bank is not a short-term, low-investment process. Making a difference requires a sustained, cohesive coalition capable of gathering and analyzing information relevant to Bank activities, making that information available to key actors, and mobilizing many sources of influence. The analysis of these cases suggests the first four lessons about effective transnational coalitions.

Lesson 1: Make the campaign fit the target.　We found that different patterns of coalitions emerged to deal with different issues. For some coalitions, the dominant issue was moderating or undoing harmful impacts of specific Bank projects on grassroots communities. In the Philippines, for example, the coalition challenged the building of a geothermal power plant that threatened indigenous peoples' sacred ancestral lands as well as the surrounding environment. In Ecuador, an agricultural development program involved legislation that threatened the communal lands of indigenous peoples. The new land law, passed with support from multilateral development banks as well as agribusiness interests, made it likely that communally held

Table 4.2   Policy Reform Campaigns

Policies and Key Actors	Critical Events in Alliance Evolution
Indigenous Peoples Policy (1981–1992) GROs: Indigenous peoples (IP) and environment movements in many countries NGOs: Linked to project alliances INGOs: International Survival; International Working Group on Indigenous Affairs (IWGIA); Cultural Survival WB: Social scientists; IP policy supporters	In 1981, indigenous groups at the Chico River in the Philippines won their first victory over a Bank dam project, leading to an initial Bank policy protecting indigenous rights in its projects. IP problems in Bank projects were highlighted in a series of projects (Polonoereste, Transmigration, etc.) and by the Bank's 1987 five-year review of environmental policies. Active local movements lobbied Bank projects successfully over the next five years. INGOs supporting indigenous peoples did not develop a common front, but GROs were quite successful in influencing local projects. The Bank's 1991 policy statement opened the door to further indigenous challenges.
Resettlement Policy (1986–1994) GROs: Affected villager movements in many projects NGOs: Allies of villagers like Narmada Bachao Andolan INGOs: Narmada Action Council; International NGO Group on Indonesia WB: Resettlement Review Task Force	The Resettlement Policy Review was in part inspired by the revelations of the Morse Commission about the controversial Narmada project. An internal team was authorized to assess implementation of the resettlement policy in Bank projects to respond to external campaigns. The review indicated that compliance with the Bank's 1986 policy was running at about 30 percent in the first five years. It improved rapidly under external and internal scrutiny, though the review team had to fight a guerilla war to get good information from reluctant task managers. Intense internal bargaining over the final report culminated in early publication in 1994 to forestall threats of leaks by external advocates.
Water Resources Management Policy (1991–1993) GROs: Not involved NGOs: Fifty volunteered to provide input to policy discussions INGOs: International Rivers Network; Environmental Defense Fund WB: Operations and engineering staff	In 1991, Bank staff organized a workshop for government officials on revising water resource management policy. NGOs were not invited, but INGOs collected comments from more than fifty NGOs. The Bank agreed to consult with NGOs and received substantial input. The INGOs found it difficult to maintain NGO interest in the policy process. Bank officials decided against further consultations, in part because of internal pressures to shape policies by economic considerations. Ultimately, the INGOs lobbied with executive directors to affect the policy. Though the policies adopted did include some NGO recommendations, the initiators were disappointed in the necessity for a retreat to advocacy.

(Table 4.2 Continues)

Table 4.2 Continued

Policies and Key Actors	Critical Events in Alliance Evolution
Information and Inspection Panel Policy (1989–1995) GROs: Not directly involved NGOs: Narmada; IDA-10 Campaign activists INGOs: EDF; BIC; others ank eform ampaigners; Fifty Years Is Enough WB: Allies of More Disclosure Others: U.S. Congressional Committee; U.S., Japanese, and European executive directors of the World Bank	The Bank has always limited access to project information. The struggle over the Narmada dams and the criticisms of the internal Wapenhans Report set the stage for many Bank reforms. The alliance among INGOs, NGOs, and GROs that carried out the Narmada and the IDA-10 replenishment campaigns pressed the Bank for policies making more project information available at early stages and for an inspection panel to investigate project abuses. With allies from within the Bank and the U.S. Congress, the alliance successfully lobbied for the new policy with threats to withhold future funding. The new panel was immediately asked to investigate the proposed Arun III dam in Nepal. Its report raised serious questions about the dam, and the new Bank president canceled the project soon after entering office.

Note: GRO means grassroots organization; NGO means national NGO; INGO means international NGO; WB means World Bank staff; the category Others refers to other alliance participants.

lands would become vulnerable to sale for commercial development. In both cases, the transnational coalition was spearheaded and sustained by grassroots movements that were directly threatened by the projects, together with national NGO allies who in turn sought international support. Because these campaigns were essentially the international wings of already-existing national movements, we called them national problem coalitions.

In other settings, the campaign coalition was primarily concerned with Bank failures to live up to its own policies. While impacts on local constituents provided evidence of Bank failures, the primary target was reform of the Bank itself. In Brazil's Planafloro case, for example, international NGOs challenged the Bank's failure to ensure local participation in the natural resources management project in a setting where grassroots groups were not yet sufficiently organized to mount a credible protest on their own initiative. Similarly, the campaign to expand public access to information on Bank projects and to create an institutional channel for responding to charges of noncompliance in reform policies succeeded in part because the involved NGOs concerned had the technical and policy skills, political influence with donor governments, and the organizational resources to maintain pressure across many projects. Furthermore, these NGO networks succeeded in spite of not having immediate stakes in each project. Such *transnational advocacy networks* can articulate principles, formulate alternative policies, and press for improved implementation and systemic reform over long periods of time and across many local instances of abuse.

In still other cases, coalition leadership came from within the Bank, as internal reformers worked with external groups to review Bank experience and articulate alternative policies. In the review of the resettlement policy, for example, an internal team designed and implemented a review that resulted in massive resistance from internal constituencies committed to preserving their autonomy. The existence of strong external coalitions that supported the internal review made it possible for that team to challenge powerful, entrenched interests in the review and ultimately to publish a very searching report despite the resistance. In essence, such *internal reform initiatives* make use of the special knowledge and access of insiders to marshal evidence and articulate plausible reforms.

Coalition tactics need to be defined in the context of their goals and targets. When the focus is controlling project damage or shaping implementation on the ground, the local actors to whom both the World Bank and international NGO critics should be accountable are often relatively clear-cut. When the focus is on articulating the broader policies that will shape future Bank interactions with grassroots actors, international NGOs, with their policy knowledge, media savvy, and lobbying skills, tend to play more prominent leadership roles. Where the target is fundamental change in Bank priorities or institutional arrangements, internal reform alliances, which unite internal staff holding special knowledge with sources of external leverage, may be needed to influence Bank policymakers who resist reforms.

Lesson 2: Open up the cracks in the system. It is easy to think of the World Bank and other large actors as monolithic institutions that present united fronts to external challengers. This assumption can focus coalition attention exclusively on allies outside the Bank. But these cases suggest that failure to engage with potential allies who emerge from intra-institutional politics can be a costly mistake.

In actuality, the Bank, like many other large institutions, includes staff with a wide range of political and social perspectives. In all the cases in this study, some Bank staff strongly favored reforms advanced by external coalitions, and those coalitions often benefited from the advice, information, and support given by internal actors. The most effective campaigns built coalitions among progressive groups in many different institutions. The campaign against the Philippines geothermal plant, for example, found that different Bank departments involved in the project had made conflicting recommendations for handling indigenous peoples' lands. In that case, the struggle among different constituencies within the Bank was an important asset to the external campaign. Identifying sympathetic Bank staff can help coalitions understand issues as they are perceived within the Bank, recognize plausible alternatives given Bank priorities, and build the internal support needed to implement reforms.

From the point of view of internal reformers, contacts with, or even the existence of, external coalitions concerned about an issue may strengthen their ability to deal with internal resistance. When senior management threatened to suppress the resettlement review as excessively controversial, the possibility that external challengers might publish early drafts eventually compelled publication to avoid public accusations of a cover-up of Bank failures to implement its own policies. Institutional change in an agency like the Bank is almost inevitably partial and slow, but these cases demonstrate that internal reformers often depend significantly on the existence of external pressure and scrutiny.

It should also be recognized that in certain issue areas, both internal reformers and external pressure groups clearly lack the leverage needed to outweigh influential interest groups and their donor government allies. For example, the contrast between NGO impact on the Bank's environmental and social policies and its sharply increased emphasis on structural adjustment and financial sector bailouts is quite notable. While Bank policies now officially encourage the empowerment of the poor, gender-sensitive policy design, and the greening of industry, most of its funding now goes to conventional macroeconomic policy-based lending.

Lesson 3: Impact comes in different forms. It is easy for coalition members to focus on a few campaign goals—change the policy, stop the project, enhance the resettlement program—to measure success. Such criteria, however, obscure important complexities and possibilities. In these campaigns, definitions of "success" often shifted over time as new strategies came into play or new actors joined the effort. The more effective coalitions recognized that the campaigns could succeed or fail on several dimensions, including strengthening local organizations, building links for future campaigns, increasing awareness and skills for policy influence, evolving strategies and tactics for policy participation, shaping public awareness of critical issues, and encouraging target institution reforms, in addition to shaping specific project and policy outcomes.

Campaigns that do not succeed with direct influence may still be considered to have had significant impact when measured by more indirect indicators. The Indonesian campaign to defend the rights of villagers affected by the Kedung Ombo dam did not take off until the project was already well under way and the campaigners' legal strategy won court decisions that the government managed to ignore. This was a classic case of an advocacy campaign that extracted very limited tangible concessions for those most directly affected but had important indirect effects by making subsequent international funding for Indonesian dams much less likely in the future. On the other hand, the campaign enhanced the reputation of the association of national and international NGOs that lobbied the Bank and donor governments on the issue. The network of national and international NGOs that participated in the campaign built relationships and capacities that served them well in subsequent campaigns. The campaign also led to informal commitments by several donor agencies to avoid such projects in the future.

Making good judgments about tradeoffs among objectives may require a broad historical and societal perspective. In the Philippines, for example, the campaign to stop the Mount Apo thermal plant focused on the project's violation of the rights of indigenous peoples, in part because that issue was, at the time, more publicly visible and politically potent than the parallel concerns of farmers and environmentalists. While some environmentalists and farmers disagreed with the decision to de-emphasize their interests and grievances, the focus on indigenous people's rights helped to mobilize support from national indigenous networks and their allies at a time when indigenous concerns were at the center of political attention—and so helped raise widespread awareness about the Mt. Apo issue.

Lesson 4: Create footholds that give a leg up to those who follow. The interests of grassroots constituencies are often focused on the immediate impact of projects, but changes in policies and other institutional arrangements may have significant effect in the long run. Individual project campaigns focus on specific issues affecting particular countries. It's important to remember, however, that a combination of campaigns may add up to a force that changes institutional arrangements affecting many future activities.

Changes in Bank policies, for example, reshape the institutional context within which project managers operate. Many transnational campaigns have been focused on establishing or refining the organizational policies that guide Bank projects. The adoption of a new policy does not guarantee its implementation, of course. This reality has been amply demonstrated by the review of compliance with the resettlement policy. But the existence of a policy standard does create leverage when external coalitions can demonstrate that Bank projects have failed to comply with it. Bank staff have become sensitized to the embarrassment created by failures to meet their own policies. Thus project compliance with the resettlement policy improved dramatically as it became clear that the review process was going to make noncompliance highly visible. So observers, activists, and project staff can create leverage for confronting future abuses by promoting policies that protect indigenous peoples or resettled populations.

Campaigns promoting accountability may have even bigger impacts. Policies that make project information available early in the project cycle can enable early challenge of problematic programs. It is much easier to influence projects in the design stage than it is to revise them after a variety of national and international interests are vested in project completion. Influence at early stages is difficult if no information is available, however. Mechanisms for wider and earlier sharing of project information are essential to early, and thereby meaningful, project revision. Of course feedback also helps institutions to enrich future campaigns.

Coalition Organization and Accountability

Transnational coalitions often span great differences in cultural backgrounds, economic wealth, and political power. Rubber tappers in Brazil and indigenous farmers in the Philippines can be as organizationally distant from the Washington-based leaders of the Environmental Defense Fund as they are from World Bank policymakers. For coalitions to be effective over years of under-resourced struggle, they need to build shared strategies, bonds of trust, and recognition of each other's resources, all of which can sustain collective action in spite of the conflicts and misunderstanding inherent in the gaps that separate them. Our study also asked how transnational coalitions could be organized to enable mutual influence and accountability in spite of these differences. The results of this analysis are briefly described in the next four lessons.

Lesson 5: Leveraging accountability requires specifying accountability to whom. Broad social bases enable credible representation and local voice. Transnational coalitions are sometimes initiated by grassroots movements seeking to pursue their goals through international links. The Ecuador Network, for example, was initiated by the federation of indigenous organizations that led the national campaign against the new, probusiness Ecuadoran "land-development" law. But it is more common for grassroots constituencies to be poorly connected with each other and consequently to have difficulty in speaking to powerful opponents with a united voice. In the Indonesian and Brazilian cases, for example, few credible voices emerged to speak for grassroots interests. Transnational coalitions often seek to represent grassroots interests to national and international decisionmakers, but they have difficulty in establishing exactly which voices are genuinely representative of local constituencies.

These cases suggest that coalition organizers are wise to find or foster horizontal connections among constituencies in order to enable credible local voices. Where social capital, in the form of grassroots federations, already exists, as in the Philippines and Ecuador cases, the coalition can build on genuine local representation. The local, regional, and national coalitions and shared decisionmaking in the Philippines enabled ongoing consultations with indigenous interests to maintain coalition legitimacy. In Ecuador, the coalition of indigenous groups was seen as providing genuine representation to the majority of their members. In other situations, a coalition with genuine grassroots representation may depend on local organization building. In the Brazil case, for example, an alliance of local NGOs and grassroots groups did not emerge until relatively late in the project, although the Rondônia NGO Forum—founded in 1991 as an umbrella organization of NGOs and grassroots organizations to encourage the World Bank and Brazilian government to pursue sustainable development policies—became an important actor in subsequent years (Rodrigues 2000).

While grassroots voices are often particularly difficult to mobilize, similar problems may affect the participation of other coalition members. The effort to shape policy on water resource management, for example, found it difficult to mobilize national NGOs, given the expense of transportation and the lack of immediate impacts of policy decisions. Ironically, the press to keep directly affected constituencies involved in the coalition comes in part from the Bank. Bank staff have frequently challenged civil society coalitions for not representing real grassroots constituencies, and so pressed transnational coalitions to attend to their own legitimacy and accountability.

Lesson 6: Power and communication gaps within civil society need bridges. Coalitions across geographic, cultural, economic, and political differences may require substantial investments in order to build the mutual influence and trust that enables a quick and cohesive response to changing circumstances. The challenge of building such relationships between a Washington-based lobbyist and a Brazilian rubber tapper, separated by language, economic fate, political perspective, and cultural values, may be formidable. Constructing and maintaining such transnational social capital can be difficult and expensive, but it is central to creating and maintaining effective coalitions.

In the cases we studied, coalitions seldom depended on bonds across such great organizational distances. More common were organizational "chains" of relatively short links that spanned great organizational distances. Thus, in the Philippines coalition, the elders of the indigenous groups connected horizontally with local NGOs, church groups, and other local network members and vertically with the regional indigenous leaders and regional campaign representatives. Those regional representatives, in turn, were connected vertically with the national network. National network representatives worked with members of the Philippine Development Forum, a Washington-based group of Philippine and international NGOs.

The resulting chain spanned the smaller gaps from local to regional to national to international—more manageable organizational distances than the gap from local to international.

In addition to building new links for these chains, in these cases coalitions built in part on previously existing social capital. The national to international link in the Philippines coalition, for example, was the Philippine Development Forum, a pre-existing network of national and international NGOs. Likewise, the link between Indonesian national NGOs and international actors was provided by the Indonesian NGO Forum for International Development (INFID), a pre-existing forum of large Indonesian NGOs and international actors that support them. The nucleus of the national to international coalition on the information and inspection panel policy drew on relationships built during the international campaign against the Narmada dam in India. These chains, once forged, can be used for other purposes. Investments in such linkages may be productive long after their initial impetus has passed away.

Lesson 7: The Internet is not enough to build trust across cultures. Coalitions evolve over time in response to external and internal forces. At the outset, most transnational coalitions are loosely organized around shared values and visions rather than detailed strategies and responsibilities. But policy influence campaigns often require systematic articulation of goals, development of strategies and plans, and agreement on how to implement those plans. Without agreement on who is responsible for what, it is difficult to hold partners accountable, or even to know how or where influence might be exerted to shape coalition activities.

Transnational coalitions are by definition geographically dispersed; consequently they face difficulties in negotiating shared expectations. To some extent, modern information technology enables interactive decision-making. For instance, the coalition to reform the information and inspection panel policy made extensive use of electronic communications. But there is no substitute for face-to-face negotiations in creating trust and mutual influence in these coalitions. Members of the Narmada Action Council report that visits to the valley were essential to building their relationships and strengthening their commitment to the campaign (Udall 1998). The director of the Philippine Development Forum, meanwhile, attributed her loyalty to the indigenous elders to her personal contacts with them (Royo 1998). Face-to-face engagements among key individuals shape the coalition's social capital, influence patterns, and membership.

Lesson 8: Small links can make strong chains. The most visible actors in these cases are national governments, large international institutions, and social movements composed of thousands of members. The stakes involve millions of dollars, thousands of lives, and scores of countries. Given these stakes, it is striking what pivotal roles a few key individuals and organizations play in bridging the chasms that separate many of the actors.

The effectiveness of transnational coalitions depends on trust and mutual influence among individuals and organizations along the chain. Conflicting pressures and incentives can easily pull apart coalitions, and coalitions are difficult to reassemble once disintegrated. The Narmada Action Council, composed of a small number of organizational representatives from Northern countries as well as key leaders in India, coordinated lobbying activities around the globe that eventually played a central role in forcing the Bank's reluctant withdrawal from the Narmada dam project. Some of the council's members then acted as the nucleus for the campaign to reform the Bank's policies on information and inspection panels. In effect, a virtual organization of less than twenty people played a central role in reshaping the institutional characteristics of the world's most influential development organization. In this way, key individuals and organizations—acting as bridges in a global network—can have influence wildly disproportionate to their wealth or formal power.

Transnational Coalitions and Global Influence

When we began this study in 1992, very little had been published on the roles of transnational coalitions in shaping global policies. Between 1995 and 2000, however, the research available on this topic grew rapidly.[9] Coalitions are essential to civil society organizations seeking to influence events beyond the ordinary scope of small, often disenfranchised, locally based actors. But building trust and understanding across gaps of wealth, power, and culture does not come easily to civil society leaders, who are more accustomed to influencing those who share their values, aspirations, and expectations. The David-and-Goliath encounters between civil society coalitions and the World Bank described in this chapter suggest that civil society actors can have wider influence if they can build bridges across their differences, understand their institutional targets, and learn from both failure and success.

One of the most important lessons of the World Bank campaign experience for other civil society efforts to hold powerful transnational actors accountable points to a shifting North-to-South center of gravity. In the early years of the Bank campaigns, Southern coalition partners provided the credibility while Northern NGOs had the media influence and political clout with donor governments critical for extracting commitments to environmental and social policy reform. These policy reforms set important benchmark standards but have proven to be limited in terms of their capacity to change what the World Bank and its national government partners actually do in practice most of the time. Reform promises from the World Bank are no substitute for democratizing nation-state development aid strategies in both the North and the South.

More generally, whether the issue is Bank reform, human rights, or corporate accountability, local-global partnerships can be quite successful at "damage control," or at extracting *promises* of reform. But then what? Tangibly changing the ways powerful institutions actually behave requires more than campaigns. Only by bolstering local, national, and transnational capacities to monitor, target, and impose sanctions for noncompliance with reform commitments can coalitions translate their apparent campaign victories into sustained accountability.

Notes

1. This quote is from "Citizen's Groups: The Non-Governmental Order," *Economist,* 11 December 1999.

2. For example, broad-based civil society networks in Brazil, Mexico, Indonesia, and India continue to focus significant attention on the World Bank.

3. In this case, embarrassing internal memos revealed that the Bank's senior environmental policymakers planned a deliberate greenwashing strategy. See Paul Brown, "World Bank Pushes Chad Pipeline," *The Guardian,* 11 October 1999.

4. For details, see the NGO Center for International Environmental Law web site at http://www.ciel.org and the NGO Bank Information Center web site at http://www.bicusa.org.

5. The Institute for Development Research undertook these studies as part of a program of research on the roles of civil society organizations in shaping national and international policies. The results of these studies are available online at http://www.jsi.com/idr.

6. For the project studies, see Antoinette Royo, "The Philippines: Against the Peoples' Wishes: The Mt. Apo Story," in Fox and Brown 1998, pp. 151–180; Margaret E. Keck, "Planafloro in Rondônia: The Limits of Leverage," in Fox and Brown, 1998, pp. 181–218; Kay Treakle, "Ecuador: Structural Adjustment and Indigenous and Environmentalist Resistance," in Fox and Brown, 1998, pp. 219–264; and Augustinus Rumansara, "Indonesia: The Struggle of the People of Kedung Ombo," Fox and Brown, 1998, 123–150.

7. For the policy studies see Andrew Gray, "Development Policy—Development Protest: The World Bank, Indigenous Peoples, and NGOs," in Fox and Brown, 1998, pp. 267–302; Deborah Moore and Leonard Sklar, "Reforming the World Bank's Lending for Water: The Process and Outcome of Developing a Water Resources Management Policy," in Fox and Brown, 1998, pp. 345–390; Jonathan A. Fox, "When Does Reform Policy Influence Practice? Lessons from the Bankwide Resettlement Review," in Fox and Brown, 1998, pp. 303–344; and Lori Udall, "The World Bank and Public Accountability: Has Anything Changed," in Fox and Brown, 1998, pp. 391–236.

8. See L. David Brown and Jonathan Fox, "Accountability within Transnational Coalitions," in Fox and Brown, 1998, pp. 439–484 for a comparative analysis of coalition dynamics across the eight cases. See Jonathan Fox and L.

David Brown, "Assessing the Impact of NGO Advocacy Campaigns on World Bank Projects and Policies," in Fox and Brown, 1998, pp. 485–551, for an analysis of the impacts on the Bank.

9. See, for example, Keck and Sikkink, 1998; Smith, et al. (eds.) 1997; Boli and Thomas (eds.), 1999; Khagram, Riker, and Sikkink, *Reconstructing World Politics,* forthcoming; and Khagram, *Dams, Development and Democracy,* forthcoming.

5

◆

Information, Location, and Legitimacy: The Changing Bases of Civil Society Involvement in International Economic Policy

◆

Paul Nelson

The successes of NGOs in challenging the exclusive right of states to govern the international system have produced significant policy changes and a revised political landscape. NGOs and civil society organizations (CSOs) are acknowledged and often consulted by international organizations in a wide range of policy fields, notably development, relief, environment, and human rights. These consultations have been highly visible at the international financial institutions (IFIs)—the World Bank Group, the regional development banks, and, to a much more limited extent, the International Monetary Fund (IMF). With these successes, particularly at the World Bank, have come new challenges for the NGOs concerned, who struggle daily with issues of coordination, governance, accountability, learning, and political strategy as well as with choices about organizational priorities. The stakes are high, because civil societies are being formed and reshaped, and their global and regional links are being created in the process of their advocacy and other work. Will civil society organizations become empowering, emancipatory vehicles for influential participation in the wealth and the decisionmaking of the planet, or will they reproduce existing lines of authority and inequality?

In the wake of the 1999 Seattle Ministerial meetings of the World Trade Organization (WTO), charges have intensified that much of the NGO agenda is, like the agendas of consumer organizations and organized labor, an agenda of societies in the global North. Commentators and some participants ask how networks are representative of concerns in the South, to whom they are accountable, and whether their continued location in the capitals of the industrialized world is consistent with their global claims. Responses to these concerns, including organizational changes in the self-governance of NGO networks, the regionalization of advocacy networks, and measures to increase Southern NGO leadership, have been uneven and tentative. They are experiments in the governance of networks and coalitions of diffuse political actors, a field that lacks formal governance structures or even clearly defined norms. These changes remain experiments, and they are not well documented. But if the prominence of the NGO networks that have lobbied the World Bank makes them models for further civil society organization and strategy, then their approach and the changes discussed in this chapter may have an impact beyond the particulars of the networks' individual engagement with the IFIs.

The remainder of this chapter takes up, in turn, the critique of international NGO advocacy and four experiments with regional advocacy networks as well as some of the implications of these efforts. The new models suggested by regional networks are significant, although networks managed by international NGOs based in the industrialized world remain predominant. With respect to the IFIs, new forms of structure may present NGOs with a choice between emphasizing openness and broad participation in leadership on the one hand, and rapid, politically agile action on the other. The potential implications for NGO participation in economic policy beyond the IFIs are even greater. If, as some have argued, NGOs should and will de-emphasize the IFIs in favor of increased attention to debt, trade, and finance issues, the experiment in regionalization may be appropriate to the World Bank but not well suited to global financial issues. There is as yet no clear indication of how the NGO models of the 1980s and 1990s will be transformed for advocacy on the international financial architecture. This chapter invites attention to this issue and to new network approaches that challenge the political relationships embedded in current NGO partnerships.

Critique: Challenging the
Heroism of Civil Society Advocacy

The heroic treatment sometimes given to civil society advocates, and those advocates' highly public strategies, have made it inevitable that criticism of their work and impact would surface. The critique has been articulated by their opponents and individuals within the target institutions, by affected governments, occasionally by scholars and, most significantly, by practitioners themselves. From all of these quarters one can assemble the outlines of a critique and reflective self-critique of the politics and impacts of civil society advocacy with the IFIs.

Most of this criticism has been aimed at NGOs based in industrialized countries, which coordinate most campaigning. Critics raise issues concerning decisionmaking within networks; class identity and the international NGOs' legitimacy as advocates; and the tendency to push policy issues into the international political arena. Recent trade and investment negotiations have provoked the sharpest comments, as in the following from the *Financial Times*: "the claims of NGOs to represent civil society as a whole and, as such, to possess legitimacy rivaling—perhaps even exceeding—that of elected governments is outrageous" (Wolf 1999). My objective here is not primarily to evaluate the validity of this critique but to establish that the criticism is real and sufficiently credible or politically damaging to attract the attention of NGO participants. This review is the basis for an analysis, in the second part of the chapter, of trends and innovations that have the potential to reshape civil society participation in economic policy.

Legitimacy: Northern Domination

The best-known and best-financed advocacy work at the IFIs has been directed by NGOs based in the industrialized world, especially in cities such as Washington, London, Oxford, and Brussels. Whether NGOs claim explicitly or only implicitly to represent excluded populations from the global South, the most frequent comments on their legitimacy address the question of representation: Do INGOs accurately represent the priorities and demands of poor communities in countries affected by the IFIs? And is this form of representation appropriate?

The issue is a lively theme in North-South NGO discussions. The 1998 Harare Declaration by twenty NGOs from seven African countries is but one example. The declaration called for Southern NGO initiative and direction in organizational, program, and advocacy work; it also urged Northern NGOs to accept greater accountability to Southern partners and recognize their "legitimacy and autonomy" as actors who will "take control of the development agenda in their own countries" (Transform 1998). The criticism is sharpened by trends in the World Bank to decentralize some aspects of the design of national programs, which makes the division between Washington-based advocates, focused on transforming the Bank's structures and policies, and national organizations concerned with the impact of those policies in their countries more tangible. Woods (1999) argues that the significant input NGOs had in the policymaking process within World Bank governing bodies in the 1990s has reinforced the disadvantage of loan-seeking governments in internal debates and negotiations. This influence, she argues, distorts the World Bank's governance by focusing the board's attention on an NGO agenda rather than a potential borrowing government's agenda for procedural, policy, and governance reforms.

Internationalizing Economic Policy Debates

A coalition involving international NGOs and NGOs based in the World Bank's borrowing countries must choose between and balance strategies that target national and international authorities. International NGOs (INGOs) have tended to target international organizations as a source of influence over governments. When they do so, they may contribute to larger trends that are shifting key policy decisions and authority into the international arena. NGOs themselves have been among the most vocal advocates of local control and devolution of authority in debates over the World Trade Organization and international investment agreements, yet NGO advocacy with the World Bank has arguably pushed more authority into international arenas in environmental policy (Nelson 1996) and social and antipoverty policy (Toye 1999).

Whether decisionmaking has actually shifted to the international arena or NGOs have simply helped to encourage the perception that authority rests there is an important question, but either the actual shift or the mere perception can reduce the significance of participation in national debates by eroding the policy-setting power of borrowing governments. For example, environmental safeguards that were proposed to restrain the World Bank's lending for environmentally questionable projects have also justified an increasingly intrusive approach to lending and conditionality (Nelson 1996). NGOs are only secondarily responsible for this internationalizing trend since increased external influence on national decisionmaking is an artifact of larger trends. But NGO advocates should carefully weigh any strategies that increase international agencies' leverage over borrowing governments.

Northern Policy Elites or Populist Advocates?

Are international NGOs part of a global policymaking elite, critics of such an elite, or both? Roe (1995) criticizes international NGO environmental advocacy as a debating exercise between members of a "new managerial class." Lawyers, scientists, economists, and anthropologists based in the offices of NGOs in the industrial capitals are, by virtue of class origin and academic training, part of the same elite as the staff of the World Bank. NGOs are loyal to different theories of development, argues Roe, but participants on both sides of the debate begin from the premise that they know best in how to promote economic and social change. The objects of their attention—poor communities and polities of the global South—should in Roe's view be liberated from the guidance of global managers, whether they work in governmental or nongovernmental agencies.

Roe's concerns should be heard. They should also be refined and sharpened by giving more detailed attention to important differences among the INGOs based in industrial capitals and the networks in which these INGOs are enmeshed. INGOs vary widely in the extent and success of their efforts to ground their advocacy agendas in continuous consultation with poor communities or their representatives. With small and praiseworthy exceptions, IFI dialogue with civil society gravitates toward individuals who speak the language of international development policy (in either Washington or in the borrowing countries). Indeed, professionals in borrowing countries are likely to be at least as susceptible to the tendency to take their place at the table in consultative processes constructed in the language of the international development industry.

Learning: The Information Base

NGOs' specialization and passionate focus on single issue areas are often cited among their strengths as political actors. A group of NGOs with a well-defined issue focus (on forestry policy, debt relief, land mines, rivers, or gender) can deploy limited resources to substantial effect. Such a focus requires that the NGO use information selectively and strategically, sustain the intensity of focus, and create and sustain a consistent and motivating image of the world. NGOs maintain their world views and inform their constituencies based on carefully chosen information. NGO partners in the industrial countries often rely on Southern partners for information and expertise about the partner's immediate environment and its field of work, and these ties are a source of legitimacy to international NGOs.

The objective of being a "learning organization," universally praised in discussions of program development, monitoring, and evaluation, may not be as widely accepted in the more adversarial field of policy advocacy, where selectivity and tenacity are more highly valued. As NGO agendas embrace debt and other issues that lie outside of NGO field experience, NGOs have developed internal expertise and relationships with researchers who share their concerns. Critics and observers within and outside the NGOs are making it clear that simply invoking the term *NGO* no longer protects international policy advocates from close scrutiny. Issues of governance, agenda, information, legitimacy, strategy, and identity are surfacing and have begun to provoke change within NGOs. The World Bank's shift of some program authority to country directors based in the national capitals may add strategic motivation for change. The following section examines a series of adaptations that give NGO advocacy a regional basis. These regional initiatives address some of the above concerns, while raising new strategic and theoretical issues of their own.

Adaptation: Regionalization and Governance

NGOs have tended to rely on established patterns of advocacy, and funders have generally been willing to continue to finance World Bank–focused campaigns centered in the industrial capitals. But there is also evidence of change and adaptation in governance and strategy. What follows are profiles of four initiatives that expand the regional base of NGO advocacy. There is insufficient evidence to suggest that NGO advocates in general are transforming their work and self-governance, and there is probably more continuity than change in NGO agenda setting, governance, and management of information. Most of these models involve important roles for INGOs in the industrial capitals, so the INGOs are not abandoning their networking roles but reshaping them. However, the cases analyzed below do indicate a growing awareness and concern among NGO activists and suggest the potential (and limitations) of self-transformation within civil society organizations. These regional adaptations involve a somewhat distinct model of decisionmaking, information movement, authority, and strategic action, each of which is analyzed below.

From a Global Committee to a Federation of Regional Assemblies: The NGO Working Group on the World Bank (NGOWG)

The NGOWG functioned from 1982 until the mid-1990s almost solely as a global working group. With some twenty-five members, the NGOWG served as a forum for Northern, international, and Southern NGO discussion of development policy and institutional reform with the World Bank. It was active through the 1990s on participation, IDA financing, capacity building for policy advocacy among Southern NGOs, and the critique of Social Investment Funds.

The NGOWG's lack of strong links to NGOs in the various regions was one of several themes in an ongoing critique by some NGO activists and observers (Nelson 1995; Covey 1998). The NGOWG lacked a consistent agenda and often served essentially as a consultative body for the World Bank. It missed opportunities to support NGO initiatives that originated outside of the group that would have advanced its popular participation agenda.[1] The global NGOWG often found it difficult to sustain the energy, motivation, and coordination required to prepare for its semiannual discussions with the Bank. Without strong links to other NGOs in their regions, NGO participants, who were usually managers or policy advocates with broad responsibilities, were essentially uncoordinated, engaging a sophisticated international financial institution in policy discussions, usually with little preparation or coordination.

In 1994, the NGOWG began to confront changes in its political environment. Important new debates and discussions had surfaced between the World Bank and NGOs, and the NGOWG was now one among several NGO consultative fora. Encouraged by the Bank and some NGOs, the NGOWG began a shift toward essentially regional operation. Decisive structural change came in 1997 when the NGOWG reshaped its structure and governance, shifting initiative and decisionmaking to the regional level and creating regional structures that promote broader engagement with the Bank by civil society. Its global body, previously a self-elected working group, now consists of representatives elected by the regional assemblies.

This shift is intended to build NGOWG members' relations to NGOs and civil society organizations in their regions, strengthen relationships with other advocacy networks, broaden NGO participation in advocacy, and continue to promote Southern NGO leadership and voice in global debates. Still in process in 1999, the restructuring involves the creation of stronger regional bodies in each of eight subregions: Africa (Southern, Eastern, Western), Asia (Southeast, South), Eastern Europe and Central Asia, Latin America and the Caribbean, Middle East and Northern Africa (MENA), Europe, the Pacific, and North America.

The regional groups were to establish agendas and build links to the region's civil societies through annual regional assemblies, information dissemination, and education and training activities for NGOs and civil society. Each region elects a regional steering committee and convenes an annual assembly of interested NGO representatives. Regional networks have adopted work plans emphasizing capacity building of NGOs (Africa); broadened participation of NGOs in regional advocacy with the World Bank (East Asia and the Pacific); and increased monitoring of and participation in Bank projects (Latin America and the Caribbean) (Bankwatch 1999).

Strengthening Southern Regional Networks:
Examples from Latin America and the Caribbean

The NGOWG's regional groups often find themselves alongside flourishing regional NGO coalitions with related agendas. In the Latin America and Caribbean region, for example, the Latin American Association of Popular Organizations (ALOP) is a regional network of development NGOs with a variety of coordinating functions, which has been active in advocacy with the World Bank (see Chapter 6). Red Bancos, based in Montevideo, Uruguay, is a specialized network monitoring the regional work of the World Bank and the Inter-American Development Bank (IDB). It has strong ties to the global Third World Network (based in Malaysia) and to the Washington-based Bank Information Center (BIC), but it is, like ALOP, a network of NGOs in the region.

The Washington-based working group on the IDB is an informal group of NGOs that has worked to increase NGO attention to the IDB throughout the hemisphere. Working group members have, for example, facilitated comment by Latin American and Caribbean CSOs on draft sector policy directives from the IDB. The sector policy statements themselves may not be of great strategic significance, but the process opens a channel for further and perhaps more influential CSO advocacy in relation to the IDB, which has largely escaped the intensive attention given to the World Bank.

Red Bancos and ALOP are the Western Hemisphere's manifestation of a regional phenomenon with worldwide importance. Leaders have moved from global NGOs located in the North to global NGOs based in the South, such as Focus on the Global South in Thailand, which gives voice to a regional critique of official development practice in Southeast Asia. They joined with the long-standing Asian NGO Coalition for Agrarian Reform in Manila, much of whose advocacy work in the 1990s focused on the Asian Development Bank.

(Partial) Devolution of a Global Dialogue:
The Structural Adjustment Participatory Review Initiative

An ongoing global dialogue among NGOs, governments, and the World Bank offers another possible approach to integrating the national and international dialogue. The Structural Adjustment Participatory Review Initiative (SAPRI) is an experiment with national advocacy, coordinated internationally. Growing out of negotiations in Washington, SAPRI now involves governments, NGOs, and the World Bank in national discussions and investigations of adjustment policy. Under SAPRI, tripartite discussions have been officially sanctioned by seven governments: Ghana, Hungary, Uganda, Zimbabwe, the Philippines, Ecuador, and Bangladesh. Actual discussions in these countries have varied considerably, but the model, developed by a global committee of NGOs, calls for national investigations and debates that include evidence and views from civil society organizations as well as from government and the World Bank.

The international effort is coordinated by an NGO committee, with representation from every region. In participating countries, activities are planned and coordinated by joint committees involving NGO and government participants. The SAPRI model is an important innovation in NGO advocacy on adjustment. NGO advocacy at the global level has tended to focus responsibility on the World Bank, treating governments as either unwilling or hapless victims of the IFIs. In contrast, SAPRI's organizational design challenges international and national NGOs to confront governments' views and policies, making governments party to the debates. The

World Bank and international NGOs take the roles of facilitators, research supporters, and global rapporteurs.

SAPRI is not likely to force a decisive change in the World Bank's economic planning and thinking. But the model has the potential to strengthen the national debates on economic policy and link the national and global levels more strongly. In Ecuador, for example, a national SAPRI investigation and debate is being coordinated by the Instituto de Ecologia y Desarrollo de las Comunidades Andinas (IEDECA). In the first formal stage of the national investigation, IEDECA and its steering committee cooperated with the Ministry of Finance and the Central Bank in Ecuador, as well as with World Bank officials from Quito and Washington, to convene a two-day national forum in January 1999. According to the SAPRI international coordinators, "200 people representing indigenous and peasant organizations, unions, small-business associations, NGOs, urban neighborhood organizations and a wide variety of other sectors" met after months of organizing and networking across the country (Ecuador Opening National SAPRI Forum 1999).

Parties agreed to a program of investigation with the overarching objective of improving "living standards of the poor and middle income groups," together with four more focused themes relating to the income and consumption effects of fiscal reform, trade and investment liberalization, labor reform, and monetary and financial reform. These issues were investigated through a series of regional meetings during the year 2000.

Regional Learning and Research Networks: Democratizing Bretton Woods Reform

In 1997 the Washington-based Center of Concern (CoC) initiated an effort to strengthen North-South links and expand participation by Southern policy experts in debates over the IFIs.[2] The project encouraged economic and legal professionals in borrowing countries to communicate among themselves through electronic networks, to make use of documents and information supplied by the project, and to make their research and recommendations accessible to NGO activists. The project raises many issues for NGO advocates regarding their knowledge base, their willingness and capacity to entertain agendas and positions that diverge from their own, and the strengths and failings of the Internet as a democratic forum. For present purposes, I focus on the project's regional structure.

The key to the project's operation are nine lead regional partners (LRPs), organizations of economic and legal professionals in Africa, Latin America and the Caribbean, and South Asia that serve as hubs for information dissemination and exchange. Each LRP receives information from the

Center of Concern on issues designated as high priority by either the LRP or the Center of Concern. The nine LRPs are

- African Economic Research Consortium (AERC), Nairobi, Kenya;
- African Society for International and Comparative Law (ASICL), Accra, Ghana;
- Association of African Women for Research and Development (AAWORD), Dakar, Senegal;
- Facultad Latinoamericana de Ciencias Sociales (FLACSO), Buenos Aires, Argentina;
- Instituto Latinoamericano de Servicios Legales Alternativos (ILSA), Bogotá, Colombia;
- Instituto Interamericano de Derechos Humanos (IIDH), San Jose, Costa Rica;
- Bangladesh Centre for Advanced Studies (BCAS), Dhaka, Bangladesh;
- University of India, National Law School, Bangalore, India;
- Development Alternatives with Women for a New Era (DAWN), University of the West Indies, Barbados.

LRPs initiated or tapped into networks with diverse memberships. In Latin America, for example, ILSA enrolled organizations ranging from grassroots human rights networks to the Andean Commission of Jurists, university institutes, and labor organizations. FLACSO created a list including academic institutions, NGOs, grassroots organizations, political officials, and parliamentary staff. IIDH's eighty subscribers include mainly human rights NGOs and networks (Nelson 1999).

Collectively, LRPs give highest priority to the issues of participation and trade. Three LRPs make gender a priority issue, and the other issues receiving coverage include judicial reform; social, cultural, and economic rights; debt; sustainable development; parliamentary oversight; indigenous rights; democratization of the IFIs; and child labor and social causes (Nelson 1999). The well-established and purposively selective information networks of NGOs assign special importance to the knowledge and views of NGO partners. As a result, LRP priorities do not closely match the present NGO advocacy agenda at the World Bank; this relatively weak alignment may have limited the project's short-term influence. However imperfect these partnerships may be as a means of representation for Southern institutions and opinion, they are an important guide for INGOs in forming policy priorities (Nelson 1997). Regional partners in the project make no claim to be representative, but they accept responsibility to build broad networks and respond to intellectual and political interests as they develop among their network participants.

The Regional Models

The full significance of these regional initiatives cannot yet be known, but we can note the patterns and variations they display. The four models have in common an expanded role for regional participants in decisionmaking and advocacy, but they diverge in important ways. NGOWG and the Democratizing Bretton Woods networks make the region the unit for organizing, while SAPRI links global to national. The LRPs of the Democratizing Bretton Woods project seek to bridge the gaps between practitioner and scholar, North and South; SAPRI aims to bring civil societies and their national governments more directly into debate; and the NGOWG seeks to increase the volume and diversity of civil society advocacy with the World Bank.

These models address the criticisms of NGO advocacy partially at best. The important contribution that each makes is to challenge the notion that the most important dialogue about the roles of the IFIs only happens at and around their headquarters. Some key characteristics of these efforts are summarized in Table 5.1.

Implications, Prospects, and Conclusions

CSO Influence Is Limited

A handful of the IFIs' largest shareholding governments have very broad powers over the governance of these institutions. Shareholder views and priorities are influenced at times by NGO campaigns, but NGO influence is focused on a handful of policy issues, and their victories have come in carefully, strategically chosen campaigns. In this context, is it appropriate to ask searching questions about NGO governance, accountability, and strategies in lobbying the IFIs? The more powerful actors—the U.S. government and the major corporations and financial institutions—might pay attention to criticism of their substantial powers in the IFIs, but they surely won't fundamentally alter their strategies or goals for influence when they are criticized.

Civil society organizations are—and should be—more attentive to criticism concerning influence. NGOs have proclaimed themselves part of a distinctively democratic political movement in the international order, and they demand accountability and democracy from public institutions. They

Table 5.1   Regional Advocacy Initiatives

	NGO Working Group on the World Bank (NGOWG)	Structural Adjustment Participatory Review Initiative (SAPRI)	Democratizing Bretton Woods	Existing Southern Networks
Purpose	NGO/CSO dialogue with World Bank	Investigation, debate on national structural adjustment	Information exchange among researchers and activists, North & South	Varied
Agenda setting	Regional assemblies, called by member NGOs	Global: assembly in July 1997; national meetings; committee of NGOs and government	Annual meetings of lead regional partners; LRPs set and manage network priorities	At regional level
Participants	Regional: participation open. Global: elected by regions.	Global NGO committee negotiates with World Bank; national NGOs and governments also involved	Information network subscribers	National and regional NGOs and CSOs
Global links	At annual global assembly; ongoing through secretariat	Through coordinating committee and secretariat	LRPs meet annually; ongoing electronic exchange	Ad hoc partnerships, funding agreements, coalitions

therefore have the double burden of winning influence while being attentive to the inclusiveness, legitimacy, and governance of their own coalitions.

Washington-Based Organizations Remain Dominant

Is the weight of significant dialogue between the World Bank and CSOs shifting? Would it be possible to map the trend, to evaluate, over the com-

ing decade, whose voices are heard most influentially by international decisionmakers and governing institutions? NGO efforts to broaden their voice
have produced some significant results. But the main flow of information,
opinion, funds, and contracts between the Bank and NGOs continues to be
processed through U.S.- and European-based NGOs. They coordinate
coalitions on participation, gender, education, structural adjustment, debt,
involuntary resettlement, rainforests, river basins, pesticides, judicial
reform, and a dozen other topics. They operate at a global level and address
the World Bank and IMF directly, through the influence of their governments as well as through the international media. And the new prominence
that student, consumer, and labor organizations have won, through street
demonstrations at the 2000 Bank and IMF meetings in Washington and
Prague, suggest Northern voices may grow to be even more influential—
but also more diverse.

If it is desirable that this discussion include Southern organizations and
communities as fully as possible, then coalition structure and governance
does matter. International NGOs could encourage more informed discussion if they began to report, among their accomplishments, on how poor
communities directly influence the INGO agenda and strategy as well as on
the circumstances under which people in poor communities were enabled to
speak directly to government, IFI, or corporate officials. Observers could
give particular attention, in addition to these questions, to how regional
coalitions differ from their global counterparts, that is, how regional agendas are determined, work coordinated, and differences reconciled. Finally,
NGOs and their observers need to continually test the belief that Southern-
based NGOs in fact learn and articulate the views of people in poor communities (Nyamugasira 1998).

High-Impact Strategic Advocacy and Regionalization

Do NGOs have to choose between maximum impact, through centralized,
politically alert leadership on the one hand, and decentralized, democratized Southern-led advocacy, which might respond more slowly to political
openings at the IFIs, on the other? The experience of increasing Southern
voice in existing lobbying campaigns seems to suggest that there is such a
trade off. An advocacy campaign focused on World Bank or IMF policy
that consults frequently with participants around the world must often wait
for Southern opinions on strategy, while political exigencies in Washington
require quick action. Moreover, NGOs based North and South won't
always agree on strategy choices, as evidenced by disputes over the use of
IDA funding as leverage over the World Bank, money for the IMF's
Enhanced Structural Adjustment Facility, trade side agreements, or the
attachment of antipoverty conditions to debt relief measures. In each of
these areas the leading Northern participants have been more prepared to

challenge Bank and IMF funding (Nelson 1997b) and to attach labor rights or environmental conditions to any trade or debt concessions.

Is less centralized leadership desirable, if it compromises the political agility and unity of NGOs? The answer depends on NGO priorities and may require some rethinking. If the strategic focus is on policy change at the World Bank and IMF, as with debt relief, strong central initiative may remain important. But if the priority is to win widespread changes in practice—increased participation or gender sensitivity in Bank-financed projects—the focus may shift from global capitals to national governments and corporations. This shift should imply another change, from central coordination to nationally based advocacy. Advocacy focused on the IFIs has been used to shape the climate for national policy by influencing an important investor that sets norms and rules for government planning and administration. But persistent, repeated use of this international strategy may diminish its effectiveness by increasing Southern governments' resistance to World Bank regulation and conditions.

Trade and Finance: Global and Regional Agendas

The regional models developed in the 1980s and 1990s were created for advocacy and dialogue with the World Bank, a usually willing international interlocutor, and with the regional development banks, also increasingly open to discussion with NGOs. What application do they have to the emerging round of advocacy on debt relief, trade, and financial regulation, in which there is not a single agency already convinced of the value or need to talk with NGOs? In these debates the international authority (or target) is less open (as is the case with the IMF), more diffuse (as with corporate decisionmakers), or less able to exert regulatory influence (for example, the WTO and regional trade organizations). These debates may also attract broader participation by consumer and labor organizations. Nevertheless, the lessons learned from early attempts to root NGO advocacy in the South via regional structures do have much to teach the next generation of global campaigns.

Notes

1. The author was a North American NGO representative on the NGOWG from 1992 to 1995, representing Church World Service.
2. This section is based on a report on the project, Center of Concern, *Democratizing Reform of the Bretton Woods Institutions: Networking Priorities Among NGO Activists and Scholars* (Washington, DC: Center of Concern, July 1999), available at the Center of Concern website, http://www.coc.org.

6

Constructing a Southern Constituency for Global Advocacy: The Experience of Latin American NGOs and the World Bank

Manuel Chiriboga V.

This chapter discusses the challenges that Southern NGOs face when they begin to participate in global NGO advocacy activities and to build a constituency for such work. As newcomers to an already densely established system of transnational coalitions and networks, Southern NGOs have to develop their own agendas, establish alliances, and develop analytical and communications capacities. At the same time, they need to go through their own learning processes, build relationships with their governments, and become accountable to their members and regional groups.

I argue that Southern NGO networks can be important channels for NGO advocacy and for more sustainable policy alliances with Northern NGO groups and coalitions. They are better placed to build collective capacities than individual Southern NGOs; they can foster the comparative research required for advocacy and develop policy dialogue capabilities. They also bring with them a membership generally constructed around a broad spectrum of development issues rather than a single issue or campaign. Transnational NGOs can strongly benefit from alliances with Southern NGO networks: They help to level the field among global campaigners; strengthen accountability structures and practices; and present a stronger front to the organizations they seek to influence than Northern groups acting alone.

More often, however, Southern NGOs are unequal partners. Transnational NGO networks appear strongly biased toward Northern leadership and concerns, information does not flow adequately from the North to South, accountability to Southern members is limited, and the risks incurred in global campaigns are not distributed equally, with Southern NGOs more exposed to potential sanctions or other reactions from their governments (Jordan and van Tuijl 1997; Fox and Brown 1998; Nelson 1997b).

This chapter draws on the example of the Latin American Association of Popular Organizations (ALOP), a Southern NGO network established by Latin American development NGOs in 1979, and its participation in the NGO Working Group on the World Bank (NGOWG) and the NGO World Bank Committee (WBNGOC). ALOP joined the latter in 1994 and served as global and regional chair from 1996 to 1998. In this chapter I also discuss the broader experiences of these international NGO groups with regard to advocacy with the World Bank. The chapter is organized into four sections. Section 1 discusses major trends within Latin American development NGOs, particularly regarding advocacy. Section 2 describes ALOP's experience of advocacy within the NGOWG. Section 3 analyzes the broader experience of the NGOWG, and section 4 returns to critical elements in the construction of an NGO constituency for global advocacy.

Latin American Development NGOs and Advocacy

Even though Southern NGOs had been participating in international campaigns such as on the environment, debt, or aid flows since the mid-1980s, traditionally global advocacy had been led and resourced by Northern NGOs or individuals. These campaigns were of interest to Southern groups more as an opportunity to advance activities at the national level than because of their global agendas. It was only when neoliberal adjustment policies were implemented in Latin America under the so-called Washington Consensus that Latino NGOs began to pay attention to global affairs. Moreover, as democracy began to spread throughout the region, disenchantment with traditional political parties encouraged citizen rights and democratic accountability in NGO political culture.

The experience of Southern NGOs in global campaigning up until the 1990s had been limited to providing project information and political legitimacy to campaigns designed, structured, and developed in the North and directed toward an audience of Northern government decisionmakers (see Chapter 4). This was due not only to differences between the political systems and the availability, or otherwise, of public officials to respond to citizens' demands but even more to the global economic power divide between North and South.

When NGO networks in Latin America began advocacy activities, they confronted many challenges, especially because these efforts coincided with a period of rapid change in NGO ideology, focus, alliances, and financial strategies. These changes were a reaction to the new political and economic environment and the diminishing support of Northern partners. They can be summarized as follows (Valderramo 1998):

- The traditional relationship between NGO networks and people's organizations such as trade unions and peasant federations was being replaced by links to a more diverse set of social actors, including women, ethnic groups, and a new proliferation of NGOs as social actors in their own right.
- The guiding principles and paradigms that guide NGOs continued to change. Radical social change and socialism dominated ideology in the 1960s and 1970s, while inclusive and sustainable development, consensus building, and democracy have preoccupied NGOs since the late 1980s.
- Program composition also began to change, whereby action lines such as popular education and trade union political assistance diminished and others, such as microfinance, technical assistance, and local development emerged more strongly.
- Social and economic research was replaced by action-oriented programs.
- The market-oriented activities of the poor began to be supported through innovative forms of association, through the training and establishment of financial and service provision enterprises, and, in some cases, through contracting with the business sector.
- NGOs began to establish contracts with governments, both national and local, for social service provision.
- NGOs developed new strategies for fundraising, including the development of commercial activities, cost recovery, and local fund-raising.

As Eduardo Ballon has observed, these shifts transformed Latin American NGOs in three main ways: in their visions of development; in changes regarding legitimacy and accountability; and in the relationships with other actors and organizations, such as businesses and the state, which emerged from the search for new sources of funding (Valderrama 1998). I believe that these changes, both in the regional context and within NGOs themselves, have created new opportunities to influence social, political, and economic processes and to construct coalitions with other social actors.

At the same time new processes and structures have been initiated recently by Latin American NGOs at country, subregional, and regional levels. At the national level, citizen initiatives and accountability struggles have appeared throughout the region. Some are purely national processes and others are linked to more global concerns. In Nicaragua, for example,

El Grupo de Cabildeo e Incidencia—a coalition of NGOs and social groups—has become a voice for Nicaraguan groups to influence discussions with donors about foreign aid. In Colombia, Viva la Ciudadania was established by a coalition of NGOs to advance citizen participation in the Constitutional Assembly and in national debates about the peace process. In Mexico, groups such as Ciudadanos Frente al Libre Comercio and, more recently, Accion Ciudadana en Relacion a la Union Europea, Ciudadanos por la Democracia, and Convergencia have mobilized citizens and social groups around trade, human rights, and accountability and transparency on internal affairs (Reygadas 1998). In Peru, Propuesta Ciudadana and in Ecuador El Foro de la Ciudadanía are further examples of NGO national advocacy initiatives (GPC 1997; Verdesoto 1996). On World Bank issues, meanwhile, a Mexican people's and NGO coalition recently organized Citizen Evaluation of Structural Adjustment (CASA) to analyze and influence government structural adjustment policy.

In Brazil such NGO initiatives have proliferated and become influential. The Rede Brasilera Frente a la Banca Multilateral (REDE) and the Campaña Nacional Contra el Hambre, la Miseria y la Vida have been very successful in influencing country-level policies through broad social mobilization and dialogue with decisionmakers. REDE, a coalition of NGOs, people's organizations, and research institutes at the national and state levels has been involved not only with the banks but also with government and the Brazilian congress. It works both on national policies and in support of people affected by particular Bank activities (Leroy and Couto Soares 1998).

In the 1990s, a number of new regional or subregional advocacy-oriented NGO coalitions and networks also appeared in the region. The most important are the Central American networks: Concertacion, which links NGO regional associations; Iniciativa Civil para la Integración Centroamericana (ICIC), an alliance of regional civil society networks that seeks to influence the Central American Integration System; and the Greater Caribbean Forum, which includes a variety of civil society groups from Mexico, Central America, the Caribbean, Venezuela, and Colombia (Morales and Cranshaw 1997; CRIES-INVESP 1997). Other examples of regional groups are: El Banco Mundial en la Mira de las Mujeres, which has a strong gender perspective on multilateral development bank (MDB) issues; the Continental Social Alliance on Trade, which links NGOs, trade unions, and farmer and peasant organizations from Mexico, Brazil, Chile, Central America, the United States, and Canada on free trade issues; and, in the arena of human rights, the Plataforma Sudamericana Sobre Derechos Humanos.

ALOP is involved through its members in many of these national and subregional campaigns. At the same time, it has itself been responsible for a number of advocacy initiatives: on international financial institutions and multilateral development banks; on regional trade and integration agreements such as Mercosur (Common Market of the Southern Cone); the Andean Community and the Central American Integration System; on relations between the European Union and regional trade agreements; and on aid and cooperation, becoming the regional member of the Reality of Aid Coalition.

These examples have a number of features in common: the collective definition of goals and strategies by this coalition of NGOs; the pooling of human and financial resources; a definition of collective organizing and direction mechanisms as well as procedures for accountability; and the merging of different types of civil society organizations—people's and grassroots organizations, NGOs, and cultural groups. Although it is difficult to find examples of sustained Southern campaigns on transnational or global policy issues, or on the reform of global institutions, these initiatives are still potential partners for transnational coalitions seeking to influence the process of international institutional reform.

ALOP and the NGO Working Group on the World Bank: The Regional Experience

ALOP is a Latin American development NGO network established in 1979 out of initiatives linked to the hunger campaigns of the 1970s. By 1999 it included around fifty NGOs from twenty countries equally distributed among the main subregions: the southern cone, Andean region and Mexico, Central America, and the Caribbean. Potential members are strictly scrutinized for the compatibility of their mission and their institutional and financial soundness. Geographical representation is also considered, seeking an adequate regional and country balance. On the activity side, although the majority of original members came from the rural development area, ALOP actively sought to diversify from 1990 onward and find new members from among the NGOs working on urban affairs, microenterprise, sustainability, etc. Most ALOP members are action oriented, although a number have research capabilities, particularly in the social sciences.

Most of the founding members are the historic development NGOs of the region, established in the 1970s and 1980s and working closely with peasant federations, trade unions, and the organizations of poor urban dwellers. Up until 1990, most of ALOP's activities were centered on experience exchange, training, and fundraising, mostly from their Northern European partners. Although differences existed among members, most saw as their role serving those popular organizations believed to be central actors in the struggle for radical change. Their activities were organized around sociopolitical education, popular organization, and leadership development.

However, by the early 1990s regional changes had created a climate for a strategic shift in ALOP's mission. It aspired to become a regional civil society actor. Although this new role and the arenas in which it would be constructed had not been defined fully at this stage, ALOP's leadership initiated a dialogue with various social, business, and state actors, including intergovernmental organizations. It also began to monitor a number of new policies that had appeared by then, such as social investment funds (SIFs). By 1994, ALOP had broadly defined an agenda for action: It wanted to influence multilateral development banks, regional trade and integration agreements, and aid and cooperation efforts as well as the structures of development—the NGOWG concerning international finance institutions issues and the International Council of Voluntary Agencies (ICVA) on aid and cooperation issues.

In the Latin American region, the NGOWG organized four meetings in which some two hundred NGO groups participated. The criteria used to invite groups helped to expand the constituency of the group considerably: national or regional NGO networks with an interest in Bank issues (including representative groups such as the Colombian Confederacion and the Peruvian Asociacion or more specialized groups such as the Brazilian REDE and the Nicaraguan Grupo de Cabildeo) and more specialized NGO networks such as the El Banco Mundial en la Mira de las Mujeres. At the Montego Bay meeting the group elected a geographically balanced regional steering committee to represent the diversity of this constituency.

All of the regional meetings of the NGOWG occurred in the presence of the Bank vice president, a critical demand from the NGO side. Each meeting included a set of policy discussions chosen by NGOs working through panels, reports from monitoring exercises, and agreements between the Bank and NGOs, to be followed up at the next meeting. These agreements developed incrementally with each of the four meetings and included

- The contracting of NGO specialists to all resident missions of the Bank in the region;
- The launch of a regional workshop and research group on urban poverty;
- The translation of Bank loans synthesis and policy documents;
- The decision to push for participatory country assistance strategy (CAS) exercises in a number of countries;[1]
- The development of a regional gender action plan with strong NGO participation;
- The establishment of a Bank steering committee to deal with NGOs as well as the development of a regional work plan.

Although these agreements have been implemented with varied success so far, the regional working group has the potential to become a strong player. Its agenda includes advocacy on general issues such as gender and participation but also regional policy issues such as second generation reforms.[2] Nonetheless, the NGOWG faces dilemmas: the balance of its constituency between operational representative NGO networks and policy- and issue-oriented groups; the importance of policy discussions vis-à-vis project collaboration; the role and influence of non-NGO members; and the nature of its global agenda. If it fails to resolve such challenges and find new means to advance NGO advocacy, other emerging NGO structures will replace it.

The type of relationship that the NGOWG has established with the Bank can be defined as one of critical engagement. It includes elements of conflict and cooperation, an appropriate strategy since the parties desire both a substantial outcome and a constructive relationship (Covey 1998). This strategy differs from conflict and protest strategies or from mere cooptation. As Jane Covey has observed, this type of collaboration requires a learning process during which both parties must accept the notion of mutual influence and evolve the capacities to achieve this goal (Covey 1998: 110). This type of Bank-NGO relationship does not preclude conflict. On the contrary, some Bank loans and policies demand a more adversarial approach, such as certain dam construction and resettlement programs and loans and certain sector and global structural adjustment programs.

What has been the outcome of the first four years of critical collaboration between Latin American NGOs and the Bank vice presidency? It has been a mutual learning process, with important results in the three main areas of Bank activity: regional policies, country portfolios, and impact on projects. Although it is difficult to assess results objectively, a difference can be observed between process and substantive results. The process areas include access to information, consultation, and influence on decisionmaking. The substantive areas include the definition of concepts and strategies as distinct from actual implementation.

I would argue that the majority of measurable results have appeared in the area of process but that opportunities have emerged for more substantive results. If we look at regional projects that have NGO involvement, developments in Latin America are noticeable although not as significant as in South Asia. NGO participation has increased in the social sector and in the areas of the environment and agricultural loans, but it is nonexistent on multisector projects (normally the adjustment programs), electricity, and urban development (1997 loans). Provisions for involvement by NGOs and community-based organizations (CBOs) were strongest in Brazil (20 percent of projects between 1973 and 1997), Mexico (14 percent), and Bolivia (26 percent). Nonetheless, the level of involvement in most projects was minimal. There is no information readily available on the level of involvement for the region as a whole, but it is probably increasing slightly. Involvement occurs mostly at the implementation phase of projects, but some increase is also noticeable at the design phase (Gibbs, Fumo, Kuby 1998: 7–9)

As recent monitoring of participation in a limited number of regional projects has shown, the extent of NGO involvement has varied considerably from country to country, depending on overall NGO policy, the enthusiasm of task managers, the attitude of government agencies, the political environment, and the more or less adversarial character of the project. What regional projects need are policies and guidelines promoting NGO involvement, incentives for task managers, and objective procedures that limit government political influences.

It is also noticeable that up until 1997 the Bank had been moving away from adjustment loans and toward second generation reforms and social sector and human resources development loans, although the recent financial crisis in the region has wiped out most of the gains from this trend. However, 1998 and 1999 showed a return to an increase in structural adjustment loans as a consequence of the Asian-Brazilian financial crisis, increasing the vulnerability of the region.

In policy areas advances have been slight—in the urban poverty policy development area and SIFs, in the willingness to work on second-generation reform policies and projects, and in advances in participatory CAS in Colombia, El Salvador, and Peru. Further progress will require NGOs to take a more proactive approach to policy development, increase their analytical skills, and work with university and think tank specialists. Many projects will still continue to benefit most from adversarial strategies, as the experience in the Brazilian CAS has shown (Leroy and Couto Soares 1998).

The NGO Working Group on the World Bank: The Global Experience

The NGOWG and the formal interaction structure, the WBNGOC, were established in 1981 in order to expand operational collaboration between the Bank and operational NGOs, especially those in the North. Their mission and membership changed over time. Membership grew to include development policy–oriented NGOs, regional and country federations and networks, and stronger representation from the South. When ALOP joined, there were twenty-six members: two international NGOs; five NGOs from Africa, Asia, Latin America, and Europe; and four from North America and the Pacific. Membership included representatives from regional, national, issue-based, or church-related networks such as Interaction, EUROSTEP,

the Association of Protestant Development Agencies in Europe
(APRODEV), Oxfam, CIDSE (the Catholic equivalent of APRODEV),
ALOP, and the Asian NGO coalition (ANGOC), all with a generally progressive approach. Their mission evolved from one of operational collaboration to a policy advocacy agenda through a process of so-called critical
collaboration. This explicitly included discussions on structural adjustment
and participation (Covey 1998).

Up until 1994, the working group's dialogue with the Bank on the main
policy items was limited. The impact of structural adjustment in Mexico,
Sri Lanka, and Senegal had gone without serious consideration by the
Bank. A more constructive dialogue on participation had taken place but
had been limited in its institutional impact. Neither the participation action
plan approved by the Bank Board of Directors nor a Bank document on
participation had fully considered NGO perspectives. However, this situation began to change significantly due to the following variables:

- The International Development Agency (IDA) replenishment discussion caused a break with other Bank campaigners; the NGOWG
  decided to support the Bank in its dealings with the U.S. Congress
  against the background of a general commitment by the Bank to
  IDA policy reform.[3]
- The working group decided to decentralize and expand its constituency, which led it to organize meetings in every developing
  region and increase its exposure to NGOs.
- The working group decided to broaden dialogue with Bank management, including the Bank's president, the regional vice presidents,
  the Bank's economic vice president, and managers of critical
  departments of the Bank. More importantly, the working group
  decided to seek direct discussions with the Bank's Board of
  Directors.
- The working group began to include participation on its global policy advocacy agenda but also new subjects such as capacity building
  of Southern NGOs and SIFs. Regional dialogues opened up the
  agenda to regionally specific policies, which in many cases brought
  in other actors, including donors, governments, foundations, and
  NGOs.
- The Bank strengthened its reformist positions as a result of James
  Wolfensohn's presidency. Progressive staff were introduced into
  harder areas of Bank operations but also—as a result of political
  changes in Europe—onto the board.

While this fifth variable was a decision of member governments, the NGOs
working within the group were largely responsible for the first four.

Southern NGOs played a significant role in these strategic changes as they were responsible both for critical political decisions, such as IDA, but also for the structure and agenda. New members introduced accountability requirements that had been almost completely absent in the past. They also democratized the group, altering its self-selecting character. This process evolved toward a formal restructuring of the group approved at the last two general meetings of the working group and the committee. The restructuring included decentralization, the creation of a smaller global working group, and the decision to work more closely with other Bank campaigners.

The NGOWG has been increasingly challenged on its global agenda and leadership as its groups have become preoccupied with regional issues, as membership has included more operational NGOs, as the role of Northern NGOs within the coalition has proven ill defined, and as the Bank has evolved toward decentralization. How it resolves these challenges will determine whether the NGOWG is able to rebuild itself as an agent of Bank reform.

Many of the results achieved at the regional level would have been impossible if the NGOWG had not also achieved significant results at the global level. For this, the group engaged a two-pronged strategy. One, it took advantage of the Bank's decision to decentralize and pushed for regional dialogues with the vice presidencies on specific agendas. At the same time, it initiated a dialogue with the Bank's board and the central decisionmaking levels of the institution, thereby introducing a global agenda partially constructed out of regional processes.

Immediately following the election of President Wolfensohn, the committee was able to advance its agenda by a cumulative strategy of increasing influence on the various decisionmaking levels at the Bank. This was accomplished by taking advantage of the reformist opportunity created by the new presidency and of political changes in Northern countries. This allowed the committee to broaden its proposal on participation, to promote the opening of the CAS to civil society participation, to strengthen its public accountability, and to support reforms to the IDA and the efforts of other alliances, such as the European Network on Debt and Development (EURODAD) and the Bank Information Center (BIC) on the inspection panel.[4]

These achievements resulted from the prestige accumulated during the previous phase and from teamwork among the members of the coordinating group. To succeed, the NGOWG maintained its focus on the periodic revision of IDA; it carried out advocacy activities in the parliaments of Northern countries when the Republican Congress sought to reduce U.S. contributions; and it continued to promote participation both at the project level and in relation to the CAS. Regarding participation, increased levels of consultation were promoted and project monitoring was introduced into the regions in which the Bank operates. Monitoring allowed NGOs from the South to discuss specific projects and participation and dissemination issues on the CAS with the regional vice presidencies. Finally, the group emerged from a more comprehensive discussion of the Bank's policies in this area with a complete set of participation policy and guideline proposals.

The dialogue with the Bank's Board allowed NGOs from the South to establish discussions with an institution with which they had had little previous contact. Besides functioning as an assessment of Bank-NGO relations, these meetings helped the NGOWG promote its agenda on participation and reform of the IDA as well as progress initiatives from other coalitions such as BIC, EURODAD, and SAPRI. This enhanced the reputation of the group among those coalitions and alliances with whom it had been in conflict previously.

Internally, the NGOWG steering committee resolved to modify its structure and expand its membership. To achieve this, it decided that members of the global committee must be selected by the regional assemblies of NGOs, and it resolved to include other regions in which the Bank operates—the Middle East, Central Asia, and Central Europe—as well as the developed regions. It also proposed establishing relationships with other alliances and groups that work on banking issues.

Finally, a crucial aspect of working group activity was its contribution to the development of the institutional capacities of Southern NGOs to monitor Bank activities and engage in policy dialogues. The working group backed training and education, and it supported specific monitoring experiences and the preparation of policy discussion documents. ALOP, which had little previous experience of global advocacy, benefited from the education of its members in this area; the consolidation of an internal working group with members from all over the region; the definition of its own strategy; and alliances with national groups working in this area (not to mention support for the creation of such groups where they did not already exist). A similar process took place with NGOs in Asia and Africa. These experiences allowed, in some instances, a new type of relationship with the regional counterparts of NGOs and with global alliances.

Conclusions

Much of what was achieved can be attributed to the particular character of the NGOWG, especially its steering committee at the time. Its members included representatives of NGO networks and support organizations with both a regional and a global vision and strategy. Their vision embraced a political understanding of the Bank's role as a global actor and the power structures underpinning it as well as what NGOs could achieve through advocacy, policy engagement, and campaigning. It is most likely that it was this vision that helped the group understand how campaigning for IDA could support policy and institutional reform and how the group could take advantage of the reformist environment in Northern governments and the Bank to pursue specific objectives.

The other important strength of the NGOWG was its representative membership. Organizations such as ALOP, ANGOC, APRODEV, CCC, CIDSE, EUROSTEP, INTERACTION, the InterAfrica Group, Save the Children, Oxfam, and Participatory Research in Asia (PRIA) gave it a representational strength that few other NGO structures could match. The fact that Southern NGO coalitions and support organizations were involved helped to level the advocacy field and structure it as a real North-South endeavor. These characteristics also helped to build bridges with other groups with conflicting agendas. Finally, the steering committee and members of the NGOWG learned to work together and support each other as a global team through face-to-face meetings and encounters at regional meetings and program activities, as well as through teleconferencing and e-mail exchange.

Was this an exceptional period, a reformist context coinciding with the existence of a group of regional NGO leaders with a global perspective willing to work as a team? It is difficult to judge as insufficient time has passed. Moreover, there are trends in the NGOWG that could jeopardize the experience: the difficulty of finding a global agenda to act as an umbrella for regional issues; the disengagement of part of the Northern constituency because of inadequate definition of its role; the need to reach out to other civil society actors; and the difficulty of establishing a cohesive new team formed by regional leaders with a global focus. Many Bank staff feel that the NGOWG has evolved toward a set of regional dialogues not necessarily linked to a global agenda, thus reinforcing some of these trends. It is possible that these trends result from a process that evolved too quickly. The global team disbanded rapidly without ensuring a proper transition; insufficient attention was given to the role of Northern NGOs in the new structure; and operational aspects took precedence over political agendas.

Other more general conclusions can be drawn from the ALOP-NGOWG experience. International advocacy coalitions, whose main purpose is the institutional and policy reform of global organizations, gain from including Southern NGO networks. One of the most interesting trends in recent NGO development in the South is the growth of regional networks that strive for global and regional policy dialogue and reform and that define themselves as regional actors. Northern NGOs need to work constructively with such networks, abandoning the ad hoc structures (which in many instances have encouraged patron-client behavior) that are so disruptive of these trends. Greater balance in North-South transnational NGO coalitions will also help counter Southern governments' arguments that NGO advocacy is mostly a Northern concern.

Nonetheless, Southern NGOs face complex challenges as they embark upon global advocacy activities, juggling the different arenas in which they must work, implementing the new accountability requirements, and developing their capacities for global advocacy. Southern NGO networks have to balance their work on global issues with their work at country and regional levels. They need not only to balance time and resources but also to create political balance. They have to ensure that global organizations such as the World Bank become more transparent, accountable, and committed to an inclusive development, at the same time that governments (including those segments that are in charge of multilateral development banks) do so. The failure to do this will reinforce the asymmetric trends of globalization that give international financial institutions greater power vis-a-vis Southern governments and societies.

Southern NGOs and NGO networks have been struggling to find ways to achieve this balance. Efforts such as those of REDE appear to achieve this balance—involving the Brazilian Congress in demanding more accountability from their government's relations with the World Bank and the Interamerican Development Bank, while at the same time bringing dubious projects to the attention of the inspection panel. Unfortunately there are few other similar examples. NGO networks need to strengthen their members' capacity to engage with government policies and accountability procedures as much as support their global advocacy missions. Northern NGOs need to reinforce such efforts.

Southern NGOs must strengthen their accountability to their own membership but also to other social groups, including grassroots organizations and popular movements. This requires particular attention to the following: (a) creating and reviewing advocacy agendas as participatory processes that involve members and other civil society allies; (b) constantly circulating information, both horizontally and vertically, among the membership, the external groups who share the agenda, and other critical stakeholders; (c) increasing accountability procedures for members and allies on advocacy issues and establishing a division of responsibilities on advocacy at national and international levels (Jordan and van Tuijl 1997). Southern NGO networks have made advances in many of these areas, of which their Northern counterparts may not always be aware.

Finally, Southern NGOs need to pay special attention to building their members' capacity for global advocacy. This includes expert and technical capacities, communication and networking techniques and procedures, coalition and alliance building, monitoring, and leadership (Valderrama 1998). Regarding policy discussion and dialogue, Southern NGOs need to look to the expertise of universities and research centers as NGO research capabilities have decreased due to changes in the priorities of their Northern partners. On the communication skills side, while there has been a significant growth in the use of computers and e-mail, communication is still not seen as a policy tool. It is probably in the areas of coalition and alliance building that most effort has been placed by Southern NGOs, yet there has been little emphasis on extracting lessons and examples of best practice for a more collective learning process. However, the leadership issue is perhaps the most important as it pulls together the diverse elements of global advocacy: collective effort, global and regional vision, the ability to relate to different levels and organizations, initiative and innovation, commitment, and organizational support.

Notes

This chapter was originally a paper presented at the NGOs in the Global Future Conference, University of Birmingham, UK, 11–13 January, 1999.

1. The CAS is the main document by which the Bank defines its policy and lending priorities for a specific country. There has been a strong demand by NGOs to make CAS efforts participatory and public. Limited participatory CAS exercises were held in Colombia, El Salvador, Peru, and Ecuador. REDE (Brazil) successfully worked through the National Congress to ensure that the CAS was disclosed.

2. Second generation reforms were intended initially to ensure that the state, executive, parliament, and judiciary fulfill their roles in a market economy. More recently these reform efforts have considered other issues linked to governance (Wood 1997).

3. The IDA is the concessional arm of the Bank that deals with the poorest countries.

4. The inspection panel was created by the Bank board to assess if the Bank, regarding its loans and projects, has abided by its own operational directives when an affected party brings a claim to it. Its creation was the result of international NGO pressure, after the Narmada campaign, on the U.S. Congress to link its funding of IDA to the creation of such an instrument.

7

The IMF and Civil Society:
An Interim Progress Report

Jan Aart Scholte

This chapter examines the promises and the pitfalls of civil society involvement in global economic governance through the International Monetary Fund (IMF). The first section describes the changing context of governance that has prompted a growth of relations between civic associations and global regulatory agencies such as the IMF. The second section surveys the contacts that have developed to date between the IMF and civil society. The third section assesses the benefits that these relationships have had for more effective and democratic governance through the IMF, while the fourth section examines the negative repercussions that have detracted from global financial governance. The general argument advanced is that while civil society has made some valuable contributions to the organization and operations of the IMF, much potential remains unrealized.

New Dynamics of Governance

Governance of the world economy is not what it used to be. Production and exchange have since the 1960s acquired substantial global and regional dimensions in addition to existing national and local contexts. Regulation has altered correspondingly with the growth of suprastate laws and institutions at regional and transworld levels. To be sure, national states remain key regulatory agents in current circumstances of regionalization and globalization. However, state centrism of the so-called Westphalian international system has given way to multilayered postsovereign world politics. (I have treated this general transition more extensively in Scholte 1997; 2000b: chapter 6.)

This broad trend of contemporary history has been reflected inter alia in the growth of global economic governance through agencies such as the IMF. The first-generation of IMF programs, those of the Bretton Woods period, concentrated on stabilization measures for short-term corrections of a member country's balance of payments. Since the 1970s the IMF has in addition designed and monitored structural adjustment programs for far-reaching economic reorganization in over one hundred countries. These second-generation programs have included comprehensive and detailed surveillance, both of the economic performance of individual member states and of the world economy as a whole. The IMF has also undertaken training and technical assistance activities on a large scale, chiefly in order to provide poorly equipped states with staff and tools that can, purportedly, better handle the policy challenges of globalization. More recently, the IMF has pursued various initiatives to promote stability in global capital markets. To the extent that the IMF has acted as a lender of last resort and addressed questions concerning the supervision of global finance, it has acquired certain features of a suprastate central bank.

Concurrently with the expansion of global economic governance, contemporary world politics has also witnessed large-scale growth of civil society. All countries have, albeit in different ways and to differing extents, experienced a proliferation of nonofficial and not-for-profit activities that seek either to reinforce or to change prevailing rules, norms, and deeper social structures. Civil society actors include religious institutions, labor unions, farmer groups, business lobbies, academic bodies, nongovernmental organizations (NGOs), and community associations. (My conception of civil society is elaborated in Scholte 2000a.)

These two trends—the expansion of suprastate governance agencies and the proliferation of civic associations—have converged in recent decades as the two sets of actors have begun to work together. Civil society groups have recognized that regulation and public authority now rest in suprastate as well as state organs. Civic associations have therefore increasingly sought to gain information, to develop policy ideas, and to exert influence by pursuing direct exchanges with regional and transworld regulatory bodies, often bypassing national governments in the process.

At the same time, these suprastate institutions have recognized that their relations with people are often not effective and democratic when those connections only move via national governments. To be sure, bodies like the IMF remain careful not to offend their member states. Nevertheless, these agencies have increasingly sought to obtain information, to gather feedback, to counter criticism, and to enhance their legitimacy by developing direct links with civic groups.

Owing to these developments, governance in the contemporary globalizing world involves more complex networks. Older links between state and civil society and between state and multilateral agencies have been supplemented with additional exchanges that directly connect suprastate institutions with civic associations. This emergent new multilateralism makes policy processes more complicated—but also potentially more rich.

Contacts between civil society and suprastate agencies hold at least eight general promises for better governance, that is, regulation that advances human security, social justice, and democracy. First, these interchanges can enrich civic education, thereby increasing public understanding of the dynamics of globalization and what it means for governance. Second, the exchanges allow stakeholders to provide regional and transworld governance agencies with information, testimony, and analysis. Third, relations between civic associations and suprastate institutions can stimulate critical and creative policy debates, discussions that can enhance the clarity and effectiveness of policy. Fourth, these contacts can bring greater transparency and accountability to global governance, whereby citizens are able to make more informed judgments about suprastate bodies and whereby governance institutions are compelled to explain and defend their policies to the public more effectively. Fifth, dialogue between suprastate agencies and civic groups can help to legitimate regional and global regulatory institutions (albeit that the governance bodies may have to alter their policies and processes before they can attain such a social consensus). Sixth, relations between civil society and suprastate agencies can reverberate to have broader democratizing effects. For example, civic groups might link lobbying of a regional or global body with a democratization of their state. Seventh, relations with civil society can push suprastate governance agencies to counter arbitrary social inequalities and exclusions and thereby contribute to greater social integration and community. Eighth, contacts with civic associations can encourage suprastate institutions to promote ecologically sustainable development. In short (and as later details in this chapter confirm), there are significant positive reasons for nurturing relations between civic associations and suprastate agencies.

However, this trend in contemporary governance should not be unconditionally welcomed. The positive potentials just reviewed do not flow automatically. On the contrary, if handled poorly, relations between a suprastate body and civil society can have at least five general detrimental effects. First, the initiatives taken by suprastate institutions and civic groups to engage with one another may be of a low quality: vaguely conceived, poorly informed, and ineptly executed. At best such ill-considered activities are a waste of time; at worst they can disrupt sound policy with destructive consequences. Second, contacts between suprastate institutions and civil society may be a dialogue of the deaf, wherein neither party is prepared to move from pre-established positions. Third, suprastate agencies and civic associations may engage in selective listening, focussing contacts on their supporters and neglecting their challengers. Fourth, civil society may involve only limited parts of a population, so that relations with suprastate agencies confirm or even enlarge structural inequalities and arbitrary privileges connected with class, gender, nationality, race, and so on. Fifth, the internal practices of civic associations themselves may be democratically deficient, in terms of inadequate consultation of constituents, peremptory constraints on debate, lack of transparency, and insufficient accountability.

In sum, then, much can go right and much can go wrong in relations between civil society and suprastate governance agencies like the IMF. Present indications are that these interchanges will persist and expand. The challenge is therefore to develop the relations between suprastate bodies and civil society in ways that minimize their potential pitfalls and maximize their potential benefits for effective, equitable, and democratic governance. This research is meant to contribute to that objective.

Proliferating Contacts

Before assessing to what extent relations between civil society and the IMF have either fulfilled the promises or slipped into the traps described above, it is useful briefly to survey the various contacts that have developed thus far. Most of these exchanges have emerged quite recently. The IMF and civic associations made no noteworthy attempts to develop relations until the 1980s. This decade saw inter alia early initiatives by policy research institutes, development and environment NGOs, and trade unions to engage with the IMF. For its part, the IMF set up its Public Affairs Division in 1989 with a specific brief to liaise with civil society groups.

Contacts between civil society actors and the IMF have taken various forms. Few of the interchanges have consisted of formally institutionalized meetings at prescribed regular intervals. However, many ad hoc encounters have occurred in the context of interviews, briefings, seminars, conferences, and social events. In addition, a host of indirect contacts have developed where civic associations and the IMF attempt to influence each other through third parties like national governments, other suprastate agencies, the mass media, and the general public.

The IMF has a number of institutional points of contact with civil society. At the most senior level, the current managing director of the IMF and his three deputies have undertaken various outreach activities aimed at civic groups. In addition, the twenty-four executive directors' offices at the IMF have developed various contacts with civic associations. The IMF has a substantial External Relations Department, including a Public Affairs Division with officials specifically designated for liaison with labor groups, churches, and NGOs. Operational departments of the IMF developed increasing—albeit on the whole still relatively incidental—links with civic groups in the 1990s. For the rest, many exchanges between IMF officials and civil society organizations have transpired in the field, through frequent staff missions as well as the resident representative offices that the IMF now maintains in over seventy countries.

Several sectors of civil society have shown particular inclinations to engage with the IMF. For example, business associations have frequently sought to represent their members' commercial interests to the two global governance agencies. In general, associations of banks and other financial institutions have figured more prominently in relations with the IMF than industrial and trade lobbies. Global labor organizations like the International Confederation of Free Trade Unions (ICFTU) and the International Trade Secretariats have pursued persistent campaigns for reform of the global financial regime. Regional, national, and local labor groups have tended to take more sporadic initiatives in respect of the IMF. Research institutions have—through both individual academics and economic policy think tanks—maintained quite a few contacts with the IMF. With respect to religious organizations, Western Christian bodies have lobbied the IMF quite intensely on debt and development issues. Finally, the IMF has, particularly in the 1990s, developed some relations with NGOs. Development cooperation groups and environmental campaigns have figured most prominently in these exchanges, with consumer groups, human rights lobbies, and women's associations also critiquing current frameworks of global economic governance.

As the brief survey just given intimates, civil society groups have adopted significantly different positions toward the IMF. On the one hand, many business associations and mainstream think tanks have broadly endorsed the existing aims and activities of the IMF. These conformists might disagree with one or the other rule, procedure, analysis, or decision of the IMF, but they accept the dominant established discourse of neoliberal global economic governance. In contrast, circles like the mainstream trade union movement, some research bodies, the Christian churches, and many NGOs have pursued a reformist line. Reformists accept the need for agencies like the IMF but argue that changes are needed toward something of a global Keynesianism in suprastate economic institutions. Then there are radicals who regard existing global economic governance as incorrigible. These circles advocate a contraction of the IMF (for example, moving back to the original Bretton Woods parameters) or even a complete abolition of the institution.

In sum, when comparing the IMF of the late 1990s to the organization in earlier decades, one clear change is the growing involvement of civil society. The IMF still maintains most of its contacts with member states, but governments no longer hold a monopoly position. Indeed, discussions began at the IMF in the late 1990s to consider whether its Articles of Agreement should be amended to acknowledge the agency's substantial exchanges with civil society.

Contributions and Their Limits

Earlier it was suggested that relations between suprastate agencies and civic groups in principle offer eight kinds of potential benefits to global governance. Yet to what extent have these promises been realized when it comes to the actual contacts that have (and have not) developed between civil society and the IMF? On each of the eight counts observers note some positive developments, but in each case the extent of these contributions must also not be exaggerated.

Civic Education

In regard to civic education, contacts with the IMF have helped civil society activists to become better informed about the agency's purpose, institutional organization, and activities. For example, the IMF has sponsored or cosponsored numerous symposia concerning its operations, especially for academics and trade unionists, though also occasionally for development campaigners, environmentalists, and religious groups. Certain resident representatives have made considerable efforts to impart information about the IMF to civic associations in their country of work, both directly and through the mass media. In the 1990s, the IMF also distributed a hugely increased quantity of publications to numerous civic groups, including via a mailing list of some 700 correspondents worldwide. The IMF has moreover produced several films about its work, opened a Visitors' Center in 1986, and launched an elaborate website in 1995. In addition, the External Relations Department has organized information missions to several member countries and sponsored seminars for journalists both in Washington and overseas.

Meanwhile some civil society associations have promoted civic education by making efforts to impart their knowledge of the IMF to the wider public. For example, think tanks and NGOs have made most of their research (apart from certain consultancy reports) publicly available in books, journal articles, and newspaper columns. Some civic organizations have also prepared fact sheets, pamphlets, and hand books about the IMF that interested citizens may acquire at little or no cost. A number of civic associations (such as the Institute of International Finance, or IIF; the ICFTU; and Oxfam) have constructed websites that provide regularly updated information concerning the IMF free of charge. Moreover, several civic organizations (including the Center of Concern, Fifty Years Is Enough, and Latin America Faculty of Social Sciences [FLACSO]–Argentina) have launched publicly accessible listservs concerning global financial issues. A few NGOs have sponsored public symposia and workshops on questions related to the IMF, while some clergy have used the pulpit to inform their congregations about Highly Indebted Poor Countries (HIPC), the IMF/World Bank program (started in 1996) of debt relief.

That said, far more could be done in the area of civic education about the IMF. Although the IMF has increased its outreach to civil society in the 1990s, the scale of these initiatives remains relatively small. Many IMF missions and resident representatives still give little attention to liaison with civic groups. Likewise, civil society bodies have on the whole executed only limited civic education programs about the IMF. Most of the world's citizens are still largely if not completely unaware of this key governance agency.

Giving Voice

Through relations with the IMF, civil society organizations can serve as a conduit for various constituencies to relay information, testimony, and analysis to policymakers. Significantly, civic associations may convey different inputs than those that the IMF receives from states. For instance, officials from national finance ministries are unlikely to discuss, let alone have expertise in, questions such as social exclusion, cultural mores, and ecological integrity. Similarly, business associations and economic research institutes can frequently provide market information and analysis that is unavailable in, or different from, the data supplied by states. Direct contact with representatives of workers, bankers, women, and minorities can give staff of the IMF a keener sense of the various perspectives and interests involved in policy debates.

The IMF has taken some initiatives since the 1980s to invite civil society input to policy, albeit not to the extent recently observed at the World Bank. For example, the IMF managing director and his deputies have often booked meetings with civil society representatives into their country visits. Likewise, the executive directors have since 1996 made a few site visits to program countries, in part to consult with civic groups. Certain IMF missions and resident representatives have made notable efforts to gather information for, and gauge opinions on, IMF-sponsored policies from a variety of civic circles. Since the late 1980s the IMF has allowed some NGOs to attend its annual meetings. More recently the IMF has through its website invited public comment on several of its policies, including the Enhanced Structural Adjustment Facility (ESAF) and the HIPC initiative.

On other occasions civic associations have undertaken pointed initiatives to put their constituents' concerns before the IMF. For example, the pope and other leaders of the Roman Catholic Church have convened meetings with the managing director of the IMF to discuss issues of debt and poverty. The ICFTU has in the 1990s organized several visits to IMF headquarters by trade unionists from Africa, Asia, and Central Europe. Likewise, a few Northern-based development NGOs have sponsored visits by their partners in the South to IMF offices in Washington, D.C. Several national and local business associations have also dispatched delegations to Washington to call at Nineteenth Street. Many other civic groups have sought appointments in-country with the resident representative of the IMF or the IMF mission team. As an alternative or complement to face-to-face meetings with officials, some advocacy groups have organized street marches, prayer vigils, and other public airings of views about IMF policies. For example, such demonstrations have accompanied the IMF and World Bank annual meetings since 1986.

In sum, both civil society organizations and the IMF have begun since the 1990s to establish a dialogue in which citizens are able to convey information, experiences, and analyses to suprastate authorities. That said, such exchanges remain on the whole underdeveloped. Countless potentially valuable contacts have not been pursued. For example, the IMF has not regularized consultations with civil society, say, through liaison committees or through permanent accreditation of civil society organizations (as opposed to ad hoc admission to specific events). The institution has not systematically involved civic groups in policy formulation and review. Overall, IMF consultations with civil society have remained relatively infrequent and unsystematic.

Stimulating Debate

High-quality and democratic governance rests in part on vigorous debate, not only within policymaking circles, but also between regulatory agencies and the wider public. Uninhibited discussion of diverse perspectives brings a wealth of propositions and experience to the table. Moreover, the process of debate itself can generate innovative analyses and policy suggestions.

Relations with civil society have indeed served as an engine of debate around the IMF. For one thing, scores of think tanks across the world have over the years held conferences wherein diverse policy directions are debated, sometimes with the participation of policymakers from the IMF. Prominent hosts of such meetings include the Institute for International Economics (IIE) in Washington, the Overseas Development Institute (ODI) in London, and Focus on the Global South in Bangkok. Certain business groups like the IIF, the Japan Center for International Finance, and the Bretton Woods Committee have also injected provocative ideas into policy circles. As noted earlier, many trade unions, church bodies, and NGOs have persistently challenged the IMF with calls for reform or even dissolution of the organization.

In addition to offering policy proposals, civic groups have stimulated debate regarding global economic governance by broadening the scope of issues under discussion in respect to the IMF. Thanks in particular to churches, development NGOs, environmental groups, trade unions, and women's associations, the scope of public debate concerning economic restructuring in the face of globalization has widened beyond efficiency concerns to incorporate questions of poverty alleviation, gender equity, employment security, ecological integrity, cultural preservation, and more.

While advancing this larger agenda, input from civil society has also frequently broadened the methodologies that inform discussions of global economic governance. For example, churches and NGOs have often tried to enlarge the definition of *evidence* beyond the statistical data that has usually predominated in macroeconomic policymaking. For example, civil society groups have injected much qualitative material into the Structural Adjustment Participatory Review Initiative (SAPRI) pursued by the World Bank since 1995 (with the IMF involved as an observer). Certain critical civic groups have also introduced alternative modes of calculating statistics. For example, EURODAD has compiled several editions of its *World Credit Tables*, which have focused on the accountability of the lenders as an alternative to the IMF's usual emphasis on borrower obligations.

Although these civic stimuli to searching debate about global economic governance have been important, their significance should not be overplayed. Most discussion of IMF policies has continued to transpire within the organization itself and among officials in finance ministries and central banks. Debates with civic bodies have generally remained peripheral to internal decisionmaking. Moreover, the IMF has normally favored debate with counterparts in mainstream think tanks and business associations who speak the same language of neoclassical economic analysis. Civic groups that pursue a deeper critique—by questioning the theories and methodologies that underpin IMF policies—have consistently had more limited access to, and a less attentive audience in, the IMF.

Increasing Transparency and Accountability

Relations between civil society and the IMF have made further positive contributions by reducing the secrecy that has traditionally enveloped global economic governance. To be sure, there are good arguments for discretion about certain macroeconomic policy decisions. For example, advance publicity for exchange rate adjustments and certain tax changes could frustrate the attainment of the pursued objectives. However, global financial institutions like the IMF have tended to drape the cloak of secrecy over much more than sensitive matters. The resulting shortfalls in transparency and accountability can have dangerous consequences for policy effectiveness, social justice, and democracy.

Pressures from civil society have done much to increase the public visibility of IMF activities in the 1990s. Thanks in part to civic campaigning, the IMF executive board has taken a number of steps since 1994 to increase disclosure, particularly after the U.S. Congress withheld three-quarters of a requested $100 million appropriation for replenishment of ESAF, subject to additional information from the IMF (Congressional Quarterly Almanac 1994). The IMF now issues many more—and considerably more detailed—press releases. Management has also urged governments to publish their program agreements with the IMF and to allow it to publish the documents that serve as background for surveillance operations. Since 1997 increasing numbers of governments have permitted the IMF also to release a public information notice (PIN) that contains a summary of the executive board's deliberations on a given state's economic policies in the context of surveillance. In recent years the executive board has furthermore issued public summaries of many of its decisions, and visitors to IMF headquarters have been able to consult a staff list.

Along with greater attention to issues of transparency, the IMF has also answered calls from some civic groups for greater accountability in its operations (Wood and Welch 1998; IMF Study Group 1998). Here, too, civic associations have lobbied Capitol Hill quite effectively in the context of U.S. allocations to the IMF. In particular the IMF has taken steps to develop a program of policy evaluations. Most of these reviews have been in-house, but since the late 1990s, following pressure from NGOs and the Group of Seven governments, the IMF has begun to supplement internal evaluations with external assessments. The first outside review, undertaken in 1997–1998, examined ESAF programs, with particular reference to issues such as social provisions and policy ownership that reform campaigners in civil society have long emphasized (IMF 1998). Other external evaluations have considered IMF research and surveillance activities.

These advances noted, various additional moves toward more openness and accountability could still be pursued. Many IMF program agreements, country reports, and conclusions of surveillance operations are still not published. The IMF has thus far not followed the World Bank example of establishing public information centers in a number of member countries. Evaluation of IMF policies is still a relative novelty.

Legitimation

Next to transparency and accountability, a further key criterion for effective and democratic governance is legitimacy. That is, policy is more likely to achieve its aims and serve the public good if citizens judge that the governance institutions concerned have the right to rule and that people have a duty to obey those rulings. In other words, the IMF will tend to attain its objectives better to the extent that it carries a social consensus behind the policies that it promotes. Lacking such legitimation—and in some cases indeed facing active resistance—the organization will find it harder to implement policies and more difficult to obtain resources (including funds from taxpayers) to run its operations.

Since the 1990s, management and staff of the IMF have become increasingly alert to the issue of legitimacy. Many an official can today be heard to declare that "a broad-based social consensus is needed to sustain an IMF package" and "we have to persuade the population that an adjustment package is legitimate" (interviews with the author, October 1996 and April 1998). "Ownership" has become the rhetoric of the day at the IMF because, in the words of one executive director, "if governments don't have a solid base of support for an IMF-sponsored program, it won't work" (interview with the author, November 1996).

Contacts with civil society can help the IMF to forge positive social support for the policies that it promotes. Indeed, officials had hoped that the previously mentioned public information efforts and consultations with civic groups would enhance their organization's legitimacy. However, far more extensive public affairs activities and several key changes in approach (detailed in the next section) would be necessary to consolidate this support. Most citizens still do not positively endorse policies sponsored by the IMF. Implementation is mainly pursued in situations where the general public is passive and ignorant, resigned and acquiescent, or in many cases openly hostile.

Civil society associations have on the whole not done much to advance the legitimacy of the IMF either. Those civic groups that tend to sympathize with the existing aims and activities of the IMF (especially business lobbies and economics think tanks) have generally not tried to rally the public at large behind the institution. The work of the Washington-based Bretton Woods Committee vis-à-vis the American public has been an exception in this regard. A number of reformist critics and radical opponents in civil society have taken their cases against the IMF to a wider public, but these attacks have aimed to undermine rather than promote the legitimacy of the organization.

Broader Democratization

Thus far we have considered the benefits of relations between civil society and the IMF only in terms of the direct remit of the institution. However, the gains can also extend more widely, for example, to a broader democratization of social life. This is by no means to endorse the neoliberal premise that market liberalization and political democratization go hand in hand as a matter of logical necessity. Nevertheless, contacts between civic groups and the IMF can promote wider democracy in other ways.

For instance, civic initiatives in relation to the IMF have frequently reflected—and at the same time reinforced and enlarged—a general mobilization of civil society for democratic change. Such a situation was especially evident during 1997–1998 in the three principal countries of IMF intervention in the Asia crisis: Indonesia, Korea, and Thailand. Likewise, NGOs in Uganda have made overtures to the IMF in the context of a vibrant general NGO movement in the country under the National Resistance Movement (NRM) government.

Second, exchanges with the IMF can encourage civic groups to widen their activities into other areas that promote democracy. For example, the Uganda Debt Network has used the knowledge and confidence gained in its efforts to improve the terms of the HIPC arrangement for Uganda as a basis to launch a campaign for greater transparency of the national budget (Uganda Debt Network 2001).

Third, wider democracy can be advanced when suprastate institutions give audience to civic groups that national and local authorities refuse to acknowledge. For example, in Thailand the IMF has since early 1998 maintained regular meetings with the State Enterprise Workers Relations Confederation, a labor union that the Royal Thai Government has declined to recognize as such. Similarly, in April 1998, at the height of public protest that was to topple Suharto as president of Indonesia, a team of IMF officials, among them the first deputy managing director, met with a group of trade unionists that included representatives of the then-outlawed Indonesian Prosperous Workers Union (SBSI) labor organization. On another occasion the IMF successfully pressed for the release of tortured trade unionists in an African country.

Fourth, with the encouragement of civic groups like Transparency International, the IMF has since 1996 explicitly added the issue of good governance to its agenda. Under this banner the IMF has included "ensuring the rule of law, improving the efficiency and accountability of the public sector, and tackling corruption" (IMF 1997: 209). In concrete terms, the IMF has halted the disbursement of a few credits (for example to Kenya and Cambodia) until corruption issues were addressed. Such interventions could in principle contribute to a general democratization of the state.

Interesting as these scenarios may be, it must be stressed that they have to date been relatively rare. My research on IMF–civil society relations has uncovered no further instances of wider democratization beyond those mentioned above in Indonesia, Thailand, and Uganda. I have encountered none at all during work in Argentina, Mexico, Romania, and Russia.

Indeed, experiences of an unresponsive IMF have discouraged many civic associations from further efforts to increase democracy in macroeconomic policymaking.

Building Social Cohesion

Policies that undermine social integration—by excluding vulnerable groups and otherwise reinforcing or widening structural inequities—are morally and often also politically unsustainable. With regard to the IMF, many observers have expressed concern about globalization when it is paired with policies of stabilization, liberalization, privatization, and deregulation that fail to address questions of attendant social costs. Civil society contacts with the IMF can therefore serve another positive purpose if these relations advance the cause of social justice.

Persistent pressure since the early 1980s from trade unions, NGOs, churches, institutes of development studies, and other civil society actors has encouraged the IMF in recent years to give greater attention to the so-called social dimension of structural adjustment. Since around 1994, IMF-supported policy packages have regularly incorporated so-called social safety nets. These measures have addressed matters including food security, preventive and basic health care, primary and secondary education, and (less often) unemployment problems and the protection of old-age pensions (IMF 1995; Chu and Gupta 1998). When the Asia crisis hit in 1997, social welfare concerns had been sufficiently integrated into IMF thinking that they were immediately among the top priorities of the structural adjustment programs concluded with the governments of Thailand, Indonesia, and Korea.[1] Pressure from civil society critics also figured in the IMF's decision in 1996, after many years of rejecting calls for debt relief, to embark on the HIPC program of debt reduction connected to increased social spending. Subsequent lobbying by a number of civic associations has had some effect in relaxing the eligibility criteria for HIPC relief and in increasing the degree of concessionality included in individual HIPC agreements.

That said, the rise of social policy issues at the IMF should not be overestimated. On the whole, questions related to food security, employment, health, education, gender equity, youth, and the elderly have remained secondary concerns. The sums designated for social safety nets in IMF-supported programs have generally been small, and the record of implementation has at best been mixed.

Promoting Ecological Integrity

Exponential increases in environmental damage have raised sustainable development to considerable prominence on the contemporary policy agenda. Not only have various suprastate conventions and institutions been created to address questions of environmental degradation, but worries have grown that existing global regimes often contribute to the damage. Environmental NGOs in particular have argued that prevailing approaches to structural adjustment through the IMF undermine ecological integrity, with possible dire consequences for human and other life on earth.

In the context of a substantial environmental movement—in particular pressures since the early 1980s from a large green lobby in Washington—the IMF has in the 1990s at least recognized the issue of ecological integrity. In early 1991 the executive board enjoined IMF staff to develop greater understanding of the interplay between economic policy and environmental change (Osunsade and Gleason 1992: 21). Fund officials have in this spirit produced several studies of macroeconomics and the environment.

Yet, as with questions of democracy and social cohesion, initiatives by the IMF in respect to ecological integrity have thus far remained fairly modest. Only a minority of the Fund's structural adjustment programs have made any reference at all to environmental degradation, let alone set specific targets. Indeed, executive directors have often expressed positive reluctance to bring the promotion of environmental sustainability within the IMF's mandate.

Taking the above points in sum, what can observers conclude regarding the positive effects of civil society involvement with the IMF? As the preceding pages have indicated, some welcome contributions have clearly been made, particularly in relation to educating citizens, giving voice to constituents, stimulating policy debate, and increasing the transparency of policy processes. However, these gains have remained modest to date. Moreover, still less potential has been realized in respect to increasing the accountability and legitimacy of the IMF, furthering general democratization, building social cohesion, and advancing ecological integrity.

Damages

Problems with relations between the IMF and civic associations go beyond a failure to realize adequately positive possibilities. As noted in the first section of this paper, contacts between civil society and global governance agencies have the potential in some ways actually to prolong or even deepen existing social ills. Thus the effects cannot be neutral but are actually damaging for human security, social justice, and democracy. The challenge is therefore not merely to increase the positive contributions of IMF exchanges with civil society but also eliminate the negative aspects, for example, the issues of South-North imbalance and accuracy in campaign information explored in other chapters in this volume. These detrimental effects include the following:

Poor Grounding

In order to contribute positively to global economic governance, exchanges between the IMF and civic associations must be well grounded. Both sides need to accord sufficient priority to building up relations. The parties need to be thoroughly briefed about each other, and they need to sustain their contacts over time. On the whole the IMF has not grounded its engagement with civil society particularly well. True, managerial staff have become convinced in general terms of the importance of civil society in emergent global governance. However, the IMF has not formulated clear objectives for its interchanges with civic groups. Nor has the organization carefully constructed channels of communication with civil society. Furthermore, the IMF has not hired staff who are specifically qualified to develop relations with civic associations. The institution has also failed to research carefully the civil society contexts with which it becomes involved. The IMF has rarely gone beyond ad hoc encounters to regular consultation with civic groups; nor has it built up a systematic archive of its relations with civil society. In short, policy has tended to run very largely on improvization. As one executive director has acknowledged, "When it comes to managing 'participation' we are only in the foothills—and some people want us back in the valleys" (interview with the author, May 1998).

Lack of Dialogue

Contacts between civil society and the IMF are also negative if they do not involve sufficient dialogue. For example, staff may treat encounters with civic groups as no more than a public relations exercise, where those in authority seek to convince subjects of the correctness of established policies. Likewise, activists may treat meetings with the IMF as merely an occasion to pronounce from their pulpit. A conversation marked by unquestioned preconceptions, entrenched positions, easy slogans, and self-righteous posturing on either or both sides is unlikely to lead to constructive dialogue.

Selective Dialogue

Compounding the lack of dialogue, the IMF and civil society actors may concentrate their relations on supportive groups and neglect challengers as a result. In consequence, the organization fails to gain much potentially interesting and useful information and insight. In addition, by preaching to the converted and avoiding critics, the parties are not pushed as much as they should be to clarify, specify, and critically examine their respective positions. Moreover, selective dialogue may cause governance agencies and civic groups to misjudge seriously the general political climate. In particular, by talking only or mainly to allies, officials and civic activists may overestimate the extent to which their positions enjoy wider popular support.

Underrepresentation

Miscalculations of the political context are especially likely when the civil society that interacts with the IMF does not suitably reflect the wider citizenry. This collection of civic associations may overrepresent certain interests and underrepresent or even completely exclude others. In particular, civil society relations with suprastate institutions like the IMF may unwittingly reproduce existing social inequalities in respect to age, class, gender, nationality, race, religion, and urban/rural divides. To date exchanges between civil society and the IMF have indeed been heavily biased in favor of more powerful and privileged social circles. Democracy suffers as a result, and the needs of vulnerable circles may become marginalized in policy.

Deficient Civic Democracy

The shaky democratic credentials of civil society extend beyond questions of representation to other criteria as well. Civil society is by no means inherently participatory, consultative, transparent, and accountable. Civic associations are not immune from malice, deceit, intolerance, and the arbitrary exercise of power. As a result of such democratic deficits, the IMF is given an excuse, partly justified, to limit its contacts with civic associations. Civil society has to clean up its own act as—and preferably before—it promotes better governance in the IMF.

Conclusions

From the preceding discussion it is clear that civil society contacts with the IMF are problematic. Much can go right, but much can also go wrong. Many advances have been made since the 1990s in exchanges between civil society and the IMF, particularly with respect to civic education, broadening policy inputs, stimulating debate, and increasing transparency. Yet much more can be done on each of these fronts, and other potential advances have thus far largely failed to materialize. In addition, relations between the IMF and civic bodies have positively detracted from governance when the contacts have been poorly prepared and executed, selective, unrepresentative, and otherwise undemocratic.

In view of the scale of these challenges, it can be tempting to abandon the new multilateralism of relations between civil society and global governance agencies. The statist conditions of Westphalian world politics seem so simple and manageable by comparison. However, large-scale globalization of recent decades has made the old international system of sovereign states impracticable. Global economic institutions like the IMF will stay and in all likelihood grow more important. Citizens will understandably and rightly seek to engage more and more with these institutions. The task is to shape new policy dynamics for better rather than for worse.

Notes

This chapter builds on Scholte 2000c and O'Brien et al. 2000. I am grateful for support under grant L120251027 from the Economic and Social Research Council in the UK.

1. The relevant Letters of Intent can be found by searching the IMF website, http://www.imf.org.

8

◆

Opportunities and Constraints for Civil Society Participation in Multilateral Lending Operations: Lessons from Latin America

◆

Diana Tussie and María Fernanda Tuozzo

At the dawn of a new century, the international system is witnessing increasing intervention by nongovernmental actors in national and global policy processes. The expanding activism of domestic and international civic actors in Latin America signals the beginning of a new phase of politics in the region. Democratization and liberalization in the developing world have spurred the rediscovery of civil society and its capacity to provide services that were previously supplied by the state. Parallel to this course of events, and partly as a result of these changes, the World Bank and the Inter-American Development Bank (IDB) have taken up a reform agenda that has furthered civil society consultation and participation. Their operations now increasingly include the application of mechanisms to involve NGOs and grassroots organizations. This is a welcome development since it engenders more legitimate and sustainable policy processes, yet at the same time it challenges the standard Bank tendency to design or implement policies in a top-down fashion. The involvement of civil society organizations in matters of public policy has become a source of tension for both governments and the multilateral development banks (MDBs).

This scenario is reshaping the boundaries of domestic and international politics, realigning the actors involved, and stimulating the emergence of new coalitions. New cleavages now cut across Latin America, characterized by rising internal inequalities instead of the traditional international-domestic divide. On one hand, Latin American governments, businesses, bureaucracies, and the international financial institutions have rallied together to support neoliberal economic reforms. On the other, civil society organizations are increasingly sharing their concerns and strategies with international networks. In this chapter we aim to explore the extent to which the participatory reforms of the MDBs have affected the relationship between governments and civil society in Latin America. We analyze the opportunities and constraints that these changes provide for civil society participation in second generation reforms, and we look at if and how participatory practices have influenced the nature of policy processes in the region. We attempt to answer the question, Is participation, however weak, altering these processes and the wider relationship between governments and civil society in order to consolidate more democratic patterns of decisionmaking?

The analysis is divided into three sections and draws from five country studies in Latin America: Argentina, Brazil, Colombia, Mexico, and Peru.[1] The first section explores the evolving nature of the relationships between MDBs and governments and describes the background against which reforms have been implemented. The second part of the chapter analyzes participatory practices in the MDBs as well as their most important results. The third section studies the impact of these reforms on the relationships among governments, MDBs, and civil society in the region, highlighting both positive and negative effects and analyzing the opportunities and constraints they generate for new and traditional social actors.

MDBs and Governments: A Changing Relationship

The presence of the World Bank and the Inter-American Development Bank in Latin America has expanded over the last ten years, and their roles have changed substantially. The volume of lending is no longer the sole or even most important determinant of their relevance (Culpeper 1997). Financial flows from the MDBs have increased, but so have policy recommendations that have greatly influenced the nature of the policy processes undertaken in the region. The MDBs have become key trendsetters, not only in the area of macroeconomic policy but in health, education, labor market reforms, and governance, that is, in the so-called second generation reforms.

Since new loans are directed at modifying health, education, and judicial systems, the reforms that go with them touch on values and traditions that are deeply entrenched in each society. Despite the intrusiveness of these new reforms, the recommendations of the MDBs seem to converge with the policies of borrowing countries. For governments, this has presented new challenges at the domestic level where support was needed to enforce policy changes. "Economic diplomacy" was used to persuade business groups to buy into the need to transform the economy. By the early 1990s, the reforms were strongly supported by technocratic elites and business groups but were rejected to the same extent by large sectors of civil society and opposition parties. The political opposition has repeatedly criticized the damaging effects of structural adjustment programs (SAPs) on the poorest and most vulnerable groups and has cautioned against the impact of widening inequality. Growing levels of poverty, inequality, and exclusion have obliged governments to implement compensatory policies (such as social safety nets) to make the economic model politically sustainable. As part of these programs, MDBs and governments are increasing the volume of social and poverty alleviation programs and promoting cooperation with civil society organizations to provide social services. This is the context in which new mandates of transparency, participation, and accountability have been introduced into the lending strategies of the MDBs, gradually changing the nature of their operations in the region.

What Role for Civil Society Participation in the MDBs?

Civil society engagement with the MDBs is an important component of the reforms these institutions are undergoing in order to become more transparent, participatory, and accountable. These reforms have been introduced as a result of lobbying by Northern civil society organizations and the weak performance of their respective portfolios (Nelson 1997 and 2000).[2] Public information offices and web sites have been set up to provide data in compliance with disclosure policies. Participatory mechanisms have been partially introduced into bank lending portfolios, and accountability is increasingly enforced through the creation of mechanisms such as the World Bank Inspection Panel and the Independent Investigation Mechanism in the IDB.

This internal reform agenda has furthered civil society intervention in MDB operations by introducing participatory mechanisms into the design and implementation of projects. Participation improves delivery but also strengthens monitoring and transparency. If participatory mechanisms can be introduced into decisionmaking processes, a new model of public policy formulation and implementation could emerge. Hence, participatory mechanisms provide a window for civil society involvement in decisionmaking. However, civil society participation is not always seen as desirable. At the very least, the record is uneven. Involvement is highly restricted, both in terms of the circumstances in which participation is applied and in terms of who is invited to participate. The MDBs' main areas of action in a country involve two different levels of decisionmaking. *Strategic* decisions are related to the general plans and policies of the MDBs, while *operational* decisions are related to their programs and projects.

Strategic decisions are translated into the country assistance strategy (CAS) in the World Bank and the country programming paper in the IDB. These documents constitute the lending strategies that MDBs formulate for a country for a certain period of time, and they set out the relevant budgetary implications. They include reports on the economic and political performance of the country, a risk investment analysis, and an assessment of the priority lending areas set by each MDB. The documents are discussed widely with governments but are ultimately drawn up by the multilateral institutions. The IDB considers the country programming paper an internal document, and therefore no consultation is deemed necessary. The World Bank used to follow a similar approach with the CAS but has recently changed its policy to include limited civil society participation, tested in a few countries in Latin America to assess the impact of this innovation.

At the operational level, a distinction can be made between *reform or adjustment programs* and *compensatory programs*. The first category is mainly directed at sectoral reforms and at modifying regulations and public sector management; the second is largely focused on social assistance. Patterns of civil society involvement depend on the character of the loan in question. MDB portfolios reveal that participation becomes more and more restricted as one moves from operations to decisionmaking. Neither the World Bank nor the Inter-American Development Bank have binding commitments for the application of participatory mechanisms. The official reports on good practices include only the quality of recommendations (World Bank 1998). Consultation is obligatory only in certain areas where visible negative impacts on affected groups must be avoided, such as in the resettlement of communities and indigenous peoples.[3] In all other areas, participation is introduced in a selective and ad hoc fashion, and MDBs introduce different degrees of participation at different levels of policy implementation and decisionmaking. As Table 8.1 shows, the application of participatory mechanisms is concentrated in operational decisionmaking where compensatory programs prevail, in contrast to a lack of participation in general strategies such as the CAS.

In most Latin American countries, decisionmaking in general strategies is restricted to the government and the MDBs, though the World Bank has shown more flexibility. The Brazilian experience provides a particularly interesting case. Even though the Brazilian government and the MDBs did not support the opening of the CAS and the country programming paper, both of these general strategies became public. Civil society organizations (acting through a network that monitors MDB operations) were successful in pushing through the publication of the strategy documents as a result of joint action with the Brazilian Congress—the first time that these two sets of actors had collaborated in challenging the restricted nature of the negotiations between the executive branch of government and the MDBs.[4] This experience contrasts distinctly from the involvement of civil society in other participatory experiences in the region.

At the end of 1996 the World Bank started a consultation process for

Table 8.1 Mechanisms for Civil Society Participation in MDBs

	Actors Involved		Degree and Nature of Participation	
	World Bank	IDB	World Bank	IDB
Strategic decisionmaking:	Chiefly MDBs and governments (executive)		Only limited consultation was conducted with selected NGOs and other grassroots organizations.	No consultation with civil society was carried out.
General strategies	The World Bank has carried out a few pilot "participatory" experiences in the drafting of the country assistance strategy (CAS) where selected NGOs (peasant organizations, indigenous peoples) were invited to participate.	The IDB and governments (executive)	Civil society has had no involvement in decision-making.	
Operational decision-making:				
Reform/ adjustment programs	Governments and MDBs	Governments and MDBs	Consultation with civil society is almost nonexistent	Consultation with civil society is almost nonexistent
Compensatory programs	Governments, MDBs, primary stakeholders, and technical NGOs	Governments, MDBs, primary stakeholders, and technical NGOs	Participation was mainly focused on the diagnosis of needs and implementation of projects.	Participation was mainly focused on the diagnosis of needs and implementa-tion of projects.

the formulation of a new CAS in Peru. The Peruvian government consented to this process but declined to participate. Consultation workshops were decentralized and involved NGOs, indigenous organizations, peasant organizations, the Association of Municipalities of Peru, and other urban social associations dedicated to the distribution of food to the poor.

However, publication of the CAS continues to depend on the political decisions of the national government, and the contents of the final document were never released. It is therefore not possible to verify the extent to which the concerns of civil society were taken into account (Campodónico 1999).

In Colombia, also in 1996, the World Bank promoted civil society participation in the design of the CAS for the first time. During this process the CAS went through three reviews (within the Bank, by the Colombian government, and by civil society). Of the 140 people invited to attend the civil society workshop, 60 attended, including representatives from NGOs, academia, the private sector, and the church, but not from trade unions. Even though the contribution of civil society was valued, and the document was later published and translated into Spanish, it was clear that the World Bank and the government would continue to be the most important actors in the formulation of the document (Ahumada 1999).

In Argentina for example, an ex post debate was conducted on the country assistance strategy approved for the 1997–1999 period, so amendments were foreclosed. Moreover, only the parts of the document (containing references to social assistance funding) were made available for debate.

In adjustment programs the pattern is the same: Policies and reforms are oriented to improve the efficiency of services, reduce the role of the state, and decentralize provision, but they rarely involve active participation by stakeholders. Consultation with civil society organizations is limited to surveys of client preferences and satisfaction with services. As several cases in Latin America have shown (especially Argentina, Brazil, Colombia, and Mexico), civil society groups whose interests are endangered by the reforms are usually excluded.[5] In cases such as health sector reform, workers' organizations and trade unions constitute the civil society groups most affected. Though not invited to participate, many of these organizations have successfully mobilized resources and influence to force governments to modify the content of the reforms.

By contrast, compensatory programs usually include civil society participation. These projects are essentially social assistance loans directed at alleviating the most pressing needs of vulnerable groups. Both the IDB and the World Bank have directed an increasing volume of their portfolios to social assistance programs. For example, Programa Materno Infantil (in Argentina) combines policy-based lending and social assistance, but civil society involvement takes place only in the compensatory portion of the loans. Other social assistance loans such as the Fondo Participativo de Inversión Social (in Argentina), Social Development Fund (FOCONDES, in Peru), and the Facilidad de Financiamiento para Pequeños Proyectos para Grupos Marginados (in Mexico) also illustrate the effective and systematic application of participatory mechanisms, though the degree and intensity of participation may differ from one to another. Even in compensatory loans, participation is present only in certain phases of the project cycle. Diagnosis and identification usually involve major consultation with primary stakeholders and NGOs. The design of the project, however, is usually left in the hands of the MDBs and governments who decide and negotiate the details of the loan.

These experiences show that participatory mechanisms are not implemented in key aspects of MDB portfolios. The disparity in implementing participatory mechanisms is strongly related to the political context of loans. The World Bank fosters the involvement and participation of citizens and NGOs when it considers it appropriate and likely to be approved by government (World Bank 1991). Given that new areas of intervention by the MDBs are increasingly linked to the reform programs of governments, participation is not usually welcome. Reforms are generally approved by the executive branch of government through decrees, to avoid resistance in congresses and opposition by civil society. MDBs rarely object to these procedures, given that most negotiations between MDBs and governments have traditionally been settled directly with the respective executive branches, affording a degree of discretion valued by both sides.

The commitments of the MDBs to participation and transparency are constrained not only by the character and cycle of the loan concerned but also by the pivotal role that macroeconomic priorities occupy in their portfolios. Participation and accountability seem to wane when economic crises emerge. Both the Mexican crisis of 1995 and the Brazilian monetary devaluation of 1999 proved that macroeconomic goals remain the primary concern of MDBs in the region. In many country strategies, commitments were modified without any consultation in order to prioritize support for balance of payments over social programs or governance. This was the case in Argentina, Brazil, and Peru, where commitments already undertaken were canceled or rescheduled to meet the economic urgencies unleashed by the effects of the crisis.

Another set of impediments to full implementation of participatory mechanisms lies in the fact that operational changes are mostly applied in regional and country offices, where NGO pressure on MDBs is generally weaker. Thus, the implementation of these mechanisms is very uneven and depends on factors such as staff commitment to participatory practices, and on the capabilities of local civil society organizations to lobby and influence the policies and operations of the banks. In short, several factors have contributed to the fragmented implementation of participatory practices in the region. The selective application of participatory mechanisms limits any possible spillover effects in other areas and at other levels of decision-making. This tends to create pockets of participation that are not easily replicated elsewhere.[6] However, as the MDBs become more active domestic actors in all spheres of politics, observers may see a new pattern of interaction emerging among MDBs, governments, and civil society.

MDBs, Governments, and Civil Society: New Patterns of Interaction

The involvement of MDBs in new areas of policy-based lending, as well as their increasing engagement with civil society, has created new tensions in their operations. The nature of second-generation reforms requires that those affected be involved in design and implementation in order to improve results and make the reforms more legitimate and sustainable. However, the inclusion of civil society challenges the authority traditionally exercised by the MDBs, since these groups generally resist models imposed from above and demand a greater degree of control over the management of resources and the direction of development. This tension fosters an ambiguous strategy toward participation, characterized by the discretionary application of these mechanisms and the discretionary selection of the organizations invited to participate. MDBs show a tendency to fragment the dialogue, and to take NGOs as a proxy for civil society (Nelson 2000). The World Bank handbook on NGO law, the Bank's annual reports on NGO operational collaboration, and maintenance of a joint NGO–World Bank Committee suggest the privileged standing given to these organizations (Nelson 2000). Other forms of collective action with a long-standing presence in the region—such as trade unions and public interest groups—are usually excluded. This raises questions of legitimacy and representation.

NGOs appeal to the MDBs because they are attracted by the features that characterize such organizations—the way in which this particular manner of organizing collective action replicates self-regulation, individualism, and voluntarism—all principles embedded in the free-market system. However, it is highly problematic to privilege this kind of social organization in Latin America, where for historical reasons the culture of individualism, freedom of association, and entrepeneurship has always been weak (Pearce 1998). The MDBs' interest in domestic laws that foster the formation of new NGOs can be seen as a contribution to reconfiguring state-society relations, but this model of organization is alien to the political culture of the region. The World Bank works with a notion of civil society that is more akin to the Anglo-Saxon experience than that prevailing in Latin America for centuries, a view that puts individual interest ahead of notions of the public good or collective rights. In this view, civil society is comprised of different individuals banding together with specific shared interests, often to avoid encroachment by the state. The IDB is developing a more timid but less antistate concept of civil society in which governments remain at the core of its strategies.

The different governance structures and corporate cultures of each MDB shape their pursuit of the participatory paradigm (Casaburi and Tussie 1997). Therefore, relations with civil society organizations evolve in different ways. The World Bank actively promotes the strengthening and participation of civil society, assuming that increasing civil society involvement and the demands that citizens make will, over time, improve the quality of governance. In contrast, the IDB concentrates on relationships with civil society from the government's perspective, addressing civil society involvement as part of the agenda of state modernization.[7] While the World Bank sidesteps governments by establishing a more direct relationship with civil society and building a constituency of its own, the IDB responds first and foremost to its member states. These differences flow through MDB strategies and policies, but at the project level the results are quite similar.

Civil society organizations, and particularly NGOs, have also modified their strategies in response to MDB reforms. Although widespread knowledge of new practices is confined to a small number of organizations, changes in the attitude of NGOs are widespread. One general shift in the region has been to use the reforms as a means to influence or oppose government policies. The reforms offer a platform that civil society can use to its advantage. Effectiveness and impact, however, depend on the politics of the context and the capacity of government to resist, ignore, or coopt these initiatives. Perhaps the most salient case here is Mexico, where civil society organizations have used MDB projects to claim their right to participate in politics. Together with the Mexican Congress they have used the new mandates as an instrument to force a more general opening in the policies of government (Fernández and Adelson 2000). Even though these strategies are still incipient and alliances have not yet coalesced, room for maneuver is slowly being expanded.

Another example comes from ProHuerta, a social and microfinance program in Argentina. The Centro de Estudios Legales y Sociales (CELS), an NGO active on human rights issues, has used the World Bank's Inspection Panel to partially block the Argentine government's attempt to arbitrarily dispose of funds committed to social objectives through ProHuerta.[8] CELS filed a claim through the Inspection Panel and exerted enough pressure to force the government to reverse its decision. At the same time, it also forced the World Bank to stand by its agreement and guarantee delivery of the allotted funds. This proved to be a landmark case, since the Inspection Panel had not dealt with social funds before. The claim by CELS could also set a precedent in that it widens the range of issues reviewed by the panel and provides new avenues of action for civil society demands. Originally, the Inspection Panel was created to provide greater transparency and accountability in World Bank operations as well as to protect those harmed by projects. However, through the claim process launched around PROHUERTA, CELS was able to turn passive project beneficiaries into an active social group. Furthermore, the CELS claim has turned loan contracts and conditionalities into instruments that can be used to activate demands and empower previously silent voices.

New mechanisms for civil society involvement bring significant opportunities, but the risks that go with them must also be evaluated. Indirect pressure is an expedient that may further weaken the internal structures of accountability that have long been eroded in the region as a result of long periods of dictatorship. Civil society groups must maintain a delicate balance between external and internal strategies to enforce accountability in government. The danger of focusing overmuch on MDB mechanisms to the detriment of domestic avenues for participation is real and must be addressed. Brazil may be an exception to this problem. Here, civil society networks have made strenuous efforts to combine forces, not only with trade unions and grassroots movements but also with political parties, to monitor and control the executive's dealings with the international financial institutions. A key feature of this relationship has been the active role played by the Brazilian Congress, which is absent from the scene in almost all other countries in the region. The endeavors of Brazilian groups to redirect demands to the domestic political level in order to make governments responsible for their actions offer important lessons for the future (Vianna 2000).

The slow transformation of the MDBs poses additional risks. Underpinning the new approach to civil society is the assumption within governments and MDBs that NGOs should be vehicles for channeling increasing volumes of foreign aid. This view perceives NGOs as agencies that can alleviate the effects of economic adjustment on vulnerable groups and contribute to implementing postadjustment recovery policies in order to reduce poverty, develop human resources, and protect the environment. The danger is that this conception not only reduces state responsibilities drastically but also bestows a predetermined role on NGOs in policy development. The role of NGOs as contractors to official programs has grown significantly in the last few years in Latin America, carrying real risks that NGOs might become the implementers of donor policies (Smillie 1995; Hulme and Edwards 1997). The arbitrary use of funds, especially by local governments, has produced a wave of new NGOs and in some cases has fostered new patterns of old practices of patronage (Tussie 1997). The reliance of Latin American NGOs on government agendas and resources can also be extended to Northern donors. As Pearce (1997: 261) points out, dependence on external funding often results in organizations becoming "accountable to their funders rather than beneficiaries, reflecting their funder's agenda rather than setting their own." This is especially true in Latin America where NGOs face severe funding difficulties, stringent budget cuts, and weaknesses in human resources. In situations of high financial vulnerability like this, funding can influence not only the issues addressed by NGOs but also the precedence given to local and regional priorities.

High levels of dependency do not stem solely from funding issues. The influence exercised by transnational NGO coalitions as a result of greater communication and networking resources is also important. Northern NGOs (especially those based in Washington, D.C.) have considerable influence on civil society in Latin America. Many benefits have come from this interaction—international alliances have allowed Southern NGOs to gain more resources, expertise, and information about multilateral institutions as well as greater knowledge of their operations. They have also enabled joint action and advocacy, as in the IDB-funded highway project in Belize wherein local civil society groups, working with Washington-based NGOs, were able to the remove the project from the World Bank's pipeline, gaining valuable time to renegotiate the conditions of the loan (Nelson 2000). However, NGO coalitions also tend to reproduce the hegemony of the global North. Northern NGOs often steer the direction of the coalition, partly because they control the management of resources but also because they have more influence over the definition of the campaign's goals and agenda (Vianna 2000).

As Mansbach and Vasquez (1980: 97) have pointed out, "Access to a system requires understanding the rules of the game, a willingness to follow the rules and the skills to do so—assets that can only be acquired with experience." Unfortunately, exposure to such rules is limited to a small number of civil society organizations in Latin America. History and problems of resources hinder the ability of civic groups to lobby the MDBs, but they are learning quickly, sometimes seduced by the high political and financial payoffs that may come from taking part in reforms. The limited ability of Latin American organizations to influence the MDBs stems from a range of factors:

- Local civil society is mostly unaware of new mechanisms that foster the transformation of MDB operations in borrower countries;
- Local civil society organizations rarely engage in lobbying activities toward the international financial institutions, due to the lack of ownership of MDB activities in society; and
- Civil society organizations that do engage in these activities are, in most cases, too weak in terms of leverage and economic and human resources to accomplish significant results.

The one exception to this generalization seems to be the Brazilian network, made up of NGOs, trade unions, and grassroots movements. This network has been able not only to establish a monitoring system for the activities of the MDBs in the country but also to permeate congressional circles in taking forward the results (Vianna 2000).

Participation:
Window Dressing or Window of Opportunity?

Increased participation and transparency in lending operations have undoubtedly modified the relationships among MDBs, governments, and civil society in Latin America, but the impact of these changes on democratization remains uncertain. Our analysis of the World Bank and the IDB shows that there is still a wide gap between rhetoric and operational realities. Participatory practices are implemented very irregularly in pockets of participation at the microlevel, but these are rarely replicated at significant levels of decisionmaking. Thus far, participatory mechanisms have been used to legitimize top-down policy processes rather than to innovate in key areas of decisionmaking.

Nevertheless, operational reforms in the MDBs are gradually helping to reshape the political landscape. Significant opportunities are being offered to some civil society organizations (especially NGOs) but not to others such as trade unions and economic interest groups. NGOs can contribute to enhancing transparency and accountability in government, but there are clear limits to their impact since NGOs often create vertical links with governments and the MDBs at the expense of horizontal links across civil society. In this sense, there is a danger that opportunities for participation will be little more than window dressing, making it imperative that civil society organizations adjust their strategies toward the MDBs. These groups must expand the space they have been given to open up negotiations between governments and creditors, and they must democratize decisionmaking where it matters most.

Notes

The authors gratefully acknowledge generous and insightful comments from Gabriel Casaburi and María Pia Riggirozzi.
    1. These case studies were developed under the FLACSO/Argentina coordinated project Strengthening the Role of Civil Society in Global and Local Governance: The Looming Reform Agenda of Multilateral Development Banks, directed by Diana Tussie. Case study authors are Argentina, Carlos H. Acuña and M. Fernanda Tuozzo; Brazil, Aurelio Vianna; Colombia, Consuelo Ahumada;

Mexico, Manuel Fernández Villegas and Naomi Adelson; Peru, Humberto Campodónico.

2. Two internal reviews, the Wapenhans Report (World Bank 1993) and the Tapoma Report (IDB 1993) revealed the difficulties in program implementation and high failure rates in MDB portfolios.

3. Binding mandates on participation in the World Bank are Environment (Operational Directive 400 Annex A), Indigenous Peoples (Operational Directive 4.20), and Resettlement (Operational Directive 4.15). The IDB does not have operational directives as such but it requires civil society consultation in the following instances: environment projects of high risk (category IV) and resettlement of affected communities. The normative framework that sustains the participatory policies in the IDB rests primarily on four pillars that can be found in working documents presented at the Forum on Social Reform and Poverty, 1993 (Washington, D.C.); in the IDB meeting, the Eighth Replenishment of Resources, 1993, which provided the initial framework for the agenda for modernization of the state and strengthening of civil society; and lastly in IDB, Department of Policies and Strategic Planning, *Modernization of the State and Strengthening of Civil Society* (1997).

4. The Brazilian constitutional reform in 1988 enabled Congress to approve or disapprove foreign loans and granted congresspersons the power to ask the executive for the MDBs' strategic documents (Vianna 2000). On the process of the publication of the CAS, see Vianna 1998.

5. For further information see Acuña and Tuozzo 2000; Fernández and Adelron 2000; and Ahumada 1999.

6. This draws from the conclusions of the project Strengthening the Role of Civil Society in Global and Local Governance: The Looming Reform Agenda of Multilateral Development Banks (2000).

7. For further information on the IDB's engagement with civil society through the agenda of state modernization, see "Summary Report of the Conference on Strengthening Civil Society," 12 September 1994 (Washington, D.C.).

8. The Inspection Panel was created in 1994 to provide a more independent investigation mechanism to monitor the appropriate application of the World Bank's Policies and Directives and to recommend that the executive board—if violations had been committed—give the proper compensation to those who had been damaged.

PART 3

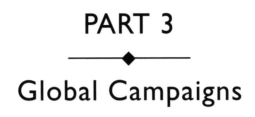

Global Campaigns

9

◆

Danger—Landmines!
NGO-Government Collaboration
in the Ottawa Process

◆

Matthew J.O. Scott

*The success of the landmines campaign was not a unique event, never to
be replicated in the world of diplomacy. ... The landmines campaign was
the harbinger of the new multilateralism: new alliances among states,
new partnerships with non-state actors, and new approaches to international governance. (Axworthy 1998a: 453)*

A Treaty with Few Precedents

The Convention on the Prohibition of the Use, Stockpiling, Production, and
Transfer of Anti-Personnel Mines and on Their Destruction is a landmark in
international humanitarian law. This convention was drafted, negotiated,
signed, and ratified wholly outside the UN Conference on Disarmament,
the traditional international arena for such agreements. By the time it was
signed by 122 states in Ottawa on December 3, 1997, the convention had
received wider assent in less time than any other UN agreement. Less than
three years passed between the first major international landmine conference in Cambodia in early 1995 and the Convention's signature. At a fol-
low-up conference to Cambodia in Ottawa in 1996, Canada's foreign minister, Lloyd Axworthy, surprised diplomats and activists alike when he
challenged all like-minded states to agree on a treaty within a year. In the
fourteen months following Axworthy's challenge, the main players of the
"new multilateralism," with Austria, Norway, South Africa, New Zealand,
and Canada prominent among them, carried the treaty through a host of
international conferences and demonstrated the efficacy of determined and
like-minded middle powers in reforming international relations. In the

same period, NGOs displayed diplomatic, analytical, and political skills that challenged the stereotype of NGOs as naïve do-gooders. One NGO representative in particular, Jody Williams, became an exemplar of an increasingly connected global civil society able to mobilize powerful public constituencies with great speed. The joint efforts of the middle-power governments and the coalition of NGOs known as the International Campaign to Ban Landmines (ICBL) mobilized a worldwide effort that culminated in 122 signatures on the first day of the Ottawa conference. Immediately following its signature, the UN Secretary-General reintroduced the treaty to the UN through the General Assembly, and it has since been ratified by ninety-four states.[1]

The Ottawa treaty is rare in successfully combining humanitarian law and disarmament practice in a single convention. Other civil society campaigns, notably the nuclear nonproliferation movement in the late 1980s, that have attempted to marry these two fields have not seen the same speedy progress as the landmines campaign. Much scholarship has already been devoted to the significance of its detour around, and re-entry into, UN processes, but that is not the focus of this chapter. The goal here is to explain how two traditionally disparate streams of civil society and government came together to exchange ideas and hold each other accountable for different outcomes.

The Ottawa process also blurred the traditional distinctions between diplomacy and humanitarian action in ways that merit further examination particularly as other NGO-government campaigns, on topics from small arms to child soldiers, are incubating. These campaigns have tried to build on the invigorating speed and energy of the landmines campaign and have studied the Ottawa process in considerable detail. Civil society around the world sees the success of the convention as a precedent, paving the way for similar campaigns to ban small arms, child soldiers, child labor, and a variety of other global problems. Does this soft-power model hold genuine promise for a future era of foreign policy cooperation between governments and NGOs, or is it the exception that proves the rule, never to be repeated?[2]

The convention's success was facilitated by a variety of factors: personal relationships, the innovative use of technology, raw perseverance, and, most importantly, the specific and finite nature of the task of banning one class of highly destructive weapons. Whether or not these factors rule out successor campaigns remains to be seen. In one sense, the fate of the Ottawa process seems to have been predestined; by their own unanimous admission, everyone involved was astonished by the speed and scope of its success. Over the course of the last years since the treaty's signature, however, internal tensions have surfaced and subsided within the coalitions that drove the campaign. Relations between civil society and government have strained and threatened the campaign's steady progress toward its goal of a total ban with no exceptions, loopholes, or reservations.

Because the campaign prominently and graphically portrayed the horrific injuries inflicted by landmines, it has been described by many as an obvious approach. Who, after all, would publicly defend a weapon that terrorizes millions of innocent civilians? Although the landmine campaign was complex and intricate, most of the campaigns being proposed as sequels to the Ottawa process focus on issues that are even more diffuse.[3] Most important, these other campaigns face far more determined, vocal, and sustained opposition, overshadowing the lack of support shown by the United States during the Ottawa process.[4] However, it is important not to be defeatist. Early in the campaign, Canadian government representatives were discouraged by their peers in their efforts to pursue the landmines ban. Mark Gwozdecky, a key Canadian diplomat during the landmine campaign, was warned early in his tenure about the prospects of a global ban: "Nobody here is interested in this file, and nobody else in the world will let it go anywhere" (Tomlin 1998).

Issues of Focus:
Reparation and Regulation

As with any successful movement, criticism of the ICBL has come from both within and outside. When it had the opportunity to expand its reach to broader issues, the campaign remained narrowly focused on achieving a ban on antipersonnel landmines only. In doing so, critics claimed that the campaign had sacrificed the opportunity to ride a rising wave of support for "global human security," passing up an important chance to highlight poverty in the developing world. Others had more practical fears that the ICBL had an excessively narrow focus. For example, mine-clearance experts working to make a Cambodian village safe will clear any and all dangers they detect—whether they be unexploded ordnance, antitank mines, or antipersonnel mines. All of these remnants of war pose great dangers to local inhabitants, but the Ottawa treaty only addresses the last of the three. Most of the operational NGOs that became involved in the campaign did so out of a desire to effect substantive change for those affected by landmines on the ground. Generally more reluctant to be seen as political, the operational NGOs were more concerned with removing mines than with fostering a paradigm shift in global governance.

Others criticized the campaign as being excessively broad in its humanitarian mandate, thus distracting from the main political goal of achieving a ban that might actually be implemented. These more activist elements within the campaign cited the lack of substantive Russian, American, Chinese, and Indian participation in the process as a sign of diluted effectiveness. They contended that real, sustained change would only result by shaming the major powers into signing the UN convention.

Such critics contended that broadening the campaign to include assistance to landmine victims and mine clearance allowed offender states such as the United States to divert attention away from the ban. By pledging millions of dollars in humanitarian assistance for these areas while openly opposing the ban, states that still deployed landmines threatened to subvert the goals of the Ottawa process. From the perspective of many activist NGOs, the most important achievement of the campaign was its contribution to the democratization of foreign policy, with a ban on landmines as an important precedent and sustained international political will to work with NGOs as a primary goal. Other factors, like attention, public support, and resources for humanitarian action, would follow later.

Although the campaign did not set out to reform the UN's disarmament apparatus or to democratize foreign policy in Northern countries, important progress was made toward these goals along the way. The ICBL had previous campaigns to draw on as models of bringing foreign policy formulation further into the public square. The democratizing tone of the ICBL was reflected in the People's Treaty that was opened for public signature by the ICBL at the Ottawa conference. By November 1997, however, public support for a landmines ban had in fact brought the Ottawa conference to fruition, and the People's Treaty was not a critical element of the strategy for a global ban. It reflected more the personal history of some of the ICBL's members in antinuclear activism as well as other civil society campaigns with an agenda of democratization. Beier and Crosby (1998) maintain that the significance of the Ottawa process resides in the fact that it aimed at more than gradual disarmament. Rather than simply instituting a treaty that applies to states within the UN system, the Ottawa process has, at its root, the intent not simply to regulate, but to *solve* the problem of antipersonnel mines. The campaign was unique in disarmament terms for remaining reparative in its outlook; it aims not only to stop new mines from being planted but to remove those already in the ground and assist those already the victims of landmine accidents. Articles 5 and 6 of the treaty (concerning the clearance of mined land and assistance to victims of landmines) form the core, not only of the treaty text itself, but also of the spirit of the Ottawa process.

This dual concern with regulation and reparation is the result of the blurring of the campaign's two streams—humanitarian praxis and disarmament law. But while intriguing, this synergy remains too poorly understood to be successfully replicated. Many have described it as a victory for NGO policy analysts and the advocates of foreign policy democratization, yet—although many academics have speculated on the question—few NGOs have asked themselves what it really means to "democratize foreign policy" (Cameron 1998). Bringing government and nongovernmental actors together like this challenges the way each goes about its business. Over the course of the campaign, activists learned to work the cocktail circuit, while diplomats began to let their hair down and become more outspoken. This has not come without some soul-searching within each camp. In the journal of the Canadian Professional Association of Foreign Service Officers, *Bout de Papier*, Kneale (1998) speculates that continuing to work with NGOs will pose major challenges to the way diplomats work. Ultimately, however, this will prove a symbiotic relationship:

> Diplomats will have to work constructively with non-traditional partners. … There is much that we need to learn about the new issues; but there are also some specialized skills and knowledge that we have that the special interest groups need. (Kneale 1998)

New Ways of Working: Campaigning in Cyberspace

One of the keys to the landmines campaign was the technological mastery shown by the ICBL. Even after a global ban had been achieved, the ICBL is still able to execute an agile strategy of countering opponents and critics and persuading would-be allies in government, the media, or other NGOs. The impressive abilities of this global network of humanitarians have been described elsewhere in almost mythological terms (Williams and Goose 1998). A highly diverse set of organizations within the ICBL were tightly connected to each other by electronic mail and fax, often enlisted at very short notice to lobby a particular government or international forum. As NGO campaigners took to the Internet in droves in the mid-1990s, many governments also experienced a simultaneous shift toward e-mail as a primary means of communication. On balance, the shift towards e-mail seems to have benefited NGOs more than governments, at least for the landmine campaign. In particular, NGOs in the South gained inexpensive access to a powerful mass communications medium in a very short period and, in the process, a direct megaphone to opinion-shapers and decisionmakers in the North.[5] As Beier and Crosby (1998) note, "The new communications technologies facilitate the identification of civil society expertise in specific issue areas, and the organization of that expertise into networks of knowledge-based relations amongst the world's peoples."

The personal tenacity and energy of Jody Williams, cofounder and former coordinator of the ICBL, was well suited to this form of network-based specialized advocacy. Under Williams's leadership, subgroups on victim assistance, mine clearance, and nonstate actors interacted electronically on a regular basis and continue to do so, long after the treaty's signature. In 1998–1999 this network of networks became the Landmine Monitor, facilitating the ongoing work of monitoring the implementation of the Ottawa treaty. The Landmine Monitor network published the first global survey of landmine infestation, activity, and legislation, which was presented at the First Meeting of States Parties in Mozambique in mid-1999. The Landmine Monitor's ongoing stability well after the treaty's signature demonstrates the potential of civil society data-gathering networks for other campaigns. Indeed, the entire landmine network still stands on the communications infrastructure that Williams and other activists pieced together, involving over one thousand different organizations across forty countries (Beier and Crosby 1998).

Action alerts sent out to this network by the ICBL executive office were crucial in using late-breaking information to urge domestic advocacy by campaign members across the globe. For example, when the U.S. delegation delayed proceedings at the Oslo treaty-text negotiations in 1997, the ICBL viewed this as an attempt to divide and rule, a tactic designed to intimidate other countries into softening the language of the proposed treaty. In a news flash posted to the conference website, the ICBL urged the following action among members in typically informal Internet style (capital letters denote shouting in Internet etiquette): "alert: U.S. of COURSE still high alert, and they are still getting support from australia, poland and japan... CAMPAIGNERS KEEP UP THE ALERT FROM YESTERDAY, spain as well, thank you spanish campaign for your fast response but PLEASE KEEP IT UP, and JAPAN get to work!!"[6]

Campaigners all over the world quickly followed these instructions and blitzed their own representatives by e-mail and fax. This electronic immediacy, and the personal relationships that had developed between activists and diplomats, also succeeded in imparting some sense of accountability in the process of negotiating the text of the treaty. The U.S. delegation's strategy did not prevail, and many middle powers stood their ground on strong wording. Throughout the campaign, some battles were won and others were lost, but the synergy and interaction facilitated by e-mail contributed to the perception of a united front by the campaigners. Even when unity did not exist among the activists, government representatives knew they would have to confront the ire of their NGO colleagues if they did not maintain their position on "no loopholes, no exceptions, no reservations."[7] The fact that this ire might be expressed over a beer in a bar near the conference center did not reduce the effect of NGO pressure.

Internet-based collaboration and campaigning benefits from high levels of flexibility and dynamism, along with very short iterative cycles. However, it has the concomitant weakness of being susceptible to paralysis, and occasionally fraudulent behavior. In the case of the ICBL landmine campaign, the ability to act quickly and multilaterally on time-sensitive information exhausted campaigners, who waded through hundreds of e-mails on the same topic from the vast network of NGO and government contacts. So far, the ICBL has largely been free of campaign espionage, but future campaigns may face more concerted opposition. Recently an aggressive gun-lobby activist posed as an "interested researcher" in order to join an e-mail discussion list on restricting trade in small arms and used the information gathered from that discussion to foment opposition to the campaign to ban small arms. The capacity of electronically based campaigns to unite activists through virtually instantaneous information exchange is considerable, but there are substantial liabilities in relying solely on electronic means of communication. Without strong personal relationships to hold these virtual networks together, the campaign would have been severely handicapped. Its success has undoubtedly paved the way for a new phase of more sophisticated electronic civil-society networking, particularly as the campaign moves toward treaty verification and monitoring.

Personalities and Relationships

"Will you marry me?" was Jody Williams's very public and good-humored proposal to then Canadian Landmine Ambassador Jill Sinclair in 1998. Sinclair had just delivered the keynote address at an NGO-government meeting hosted by Canada to commemorate the first anniversary of the treaty signing. Such relational facility among diplomats and humanitarian activists has been a hallmark of the Ottawa process and has characterized conference protocol and correspondence between the two sectors. This interpersonal chemistry, combined with the charisma of some of the campaign's more prominent personalities, gave it a life and vigor all of its own. Internationally, Princess Diana's popular appeal added unprecedented levels of public support to the campaign's efforts. After two highly publicized visits to mine-affected regions during 1997 (Angola and Bosnia), she raised the campaign's profile from that of just another group of disarmament activists haranguing the UN to a humanitarian cause célèbre. Although the Canadian arm of the campaign had enlisted celebrity spokespersons to educate Canadians on the landmines problem, Princess Diana's photogenic Angolan visit catapulted the issue onto millions of television screens and forward to international prominence. This came as a welcome gift to the international campaign, which had struggled to find an internationally recognizable spokesperson to speak compassionately on behalf of the 26,000 casualties of landmines every year. Ironically, Diana's untimely death served to raise the profile of mine victims even further, coming only days before the international meeting in Oslo at which the text of the UN Mine Ban was drafted.

On the Canadian political scene, Lloyd Axworthy, minister of foreign affairs, played a crucial role. His entry into the foreign affairs portfolio was hailed by some as a watershed event that eventually served to galvanize the governing Liberal Party's commitment to pursuing the treaty, at some cost internationally. Months earlier, Axworthy's predecessor, André Ouellette, had already raised the possibility. At a meeting with NGOs in 1995, Ouellette publicly contradicted the official government position by stating that Canada should lead the world toward a landmine ban, beginning by setting an example in the destruction of its own stockpiles. His outburst may have been prompted by even earlier developments. Fellow Liberal caucus member Jane Stewart had recently returned from a World Vision–sponsored trip to Cambodia, where she had visited hospitals, rehabilitation centers, and mine clearing sites. On her return, she spoke out on the matter—publicly, in her own caucus, and particularly with Ouellette—and presented a pro-ban petition in the House of Commons on behalf of the Canadian campaign. The collegial relationships that developed among NGO activists and diplomats were key to the campaign's success, but in the aftermath of the treaty, many activists experienced a nagging sense that the paradigm shift in NGO-government relations was more apparent than real. Was collegiality a sign of confidence or cooptation?

Paradigm Shift or Co-optation?

One of the most hotly debated issues among participants in, and analysts of, the landmines campaign remains the question of causality. A substantial change in diplomatic style took place from one set of meetings to another in preparation for the first Ottawa conference, prompting some commentators to ask "whether elements of an emergent global civil society acted as agents of that change or served as a conduit through which broader military, political, and economic forces could find new ways to realize old interests" (Beier and Crosby 1998).[8] While unprecedented levels of coordination and information sharing within and among NGOs and governments put to rest much of the skepticism about false motives on both sides, the suspicion that NGOs were being coopted by the process never entirely dissipated, despite Lloyd Axworthy's assurances (Axworthy 1998b). Some skeptics contended that the campaign simply served as another vehicle through which NGOs tried to gain international legitimacy at the negotiating table.

There were certainly examples of campaign manipulation for political purposes. In May of 1998 for example, Valerie Warmington (then chair of the Canadian campaign) was invited to Taiwan to observe the island's efforts to join the international consensus on landmines. Warmington's visit was packed with meetings with the prime minister, high-ranking generals, the diplomatic corps, and the media. Tours of abandoned stockpiles of mines and declarations of Taiwan's mine-free status were carried out to convince the world that Taiwan—in stark contrast to China—was ready to join the campaign. Given Taiwan's international political goals, however, some would be justified in seeing the visit as a thinly veiled exercise in self-interest. Similar skepticism faced the Afghan Campaign to Ban Landmines, which succeeded in gaining a landmark public statement from the fundamentalist Taliban regime in 1998. Citing verses from the Qur'an, the official declaration denounced the use of landmines as "un-Islamic" and urged other Islamic states to join the Taliban in ceasing the use and production of antipersonnel landmines on grounds of faith.[9] Although a major achievement, this was largely unreported by the international press and viewed skeptically by most countries.[10]

Some of the NGOs in the ICBL may have had just cause for feeling coopted. The 1997 Ottawa Treaty–Signing Conference coincided perfectly with Canada's intense campaign to fill one of the vacant seats on the UN Security Council. Skeptics might have viewed the entire Ottawa process as a chest-beating affair to demonstrate the value of Canada's soft power assets in the global human security arena (Axworthy 1998a). A less sinister view among campaigners regarded the two events—Canada's campaign for a Security Council seat and its leadership of the landmines ban—as complementary at best, slightly disingenuous at worst. Naturally, the government players, headed by Axworthy, are quick to rule out any notion of coopting NGOs or of government being prey to special interest groups: "Our diplomats did not compromise Canada's position through cooperation, nor did NGOs become co-opted by the state. We worked together to achieve common ends" (Axworthy 1998b). While Canadian government officials had gone to great lengths to invite NGOs to almost every major consultation and place NGO representatives on government delegations during sensitive site visits, some NGOs were still suspicious.[11] During the post-treaty announcements of Canadian government funding for humanitarian mine action (the reparative aspect of the treaty process), a generous landmine-related allocation was given to the Canadian Department of National Defence (DND). Only a few years earlier, DND had been openly opposed to a Canadian-led ban on landmines. When the defense minister announced that CDN$17 million of the mine clearance and victim assistance funds would be spent over five years for the development and marketing of Canadian mine clearance technology, many activist NGOs reacted critically.[12] The notion that humanitarian funds would be used by the military to develop potential replacements for landmines was anathema. The government's reply was that replacement technologies were necessary to entice offender states to surrender their antipersonnel mines in exchange for less harmful alternatives. Many Canadian NGOs had a strongly pacifist orientation, and to them, the DND funding merely replaced a machete with a switchblade. The purist, "no exceptions" rhetoric of the campaign was forced to confront the mundane political reality of government funding and its multiple stakeholders. Axworthy's contention that "civil society has earned a place at the table" (1998b) made some NGOs ask whether they indeed wanted to be there.

In part, the campaign may have been a victim of its own success. Governments saw the NGO contribution chiefly in terms of motivating public support for the Ottawa process, which they did very successfully. Perhaps because many of the bureaucrats and activists involved shared a history of campaigning against nuclear proliferation, there may have been a perception that building public support was the *only* NGO role, at least in Canada. But most of the large operational NGOs saw their involvement in the campaign not only in terms of public engagement or lobbying but also as an extension of their field-based work in mine clearance and victim assistance. World Vision, the Mines Advisory Group, the Red Cross, CARE, and many others joined the ICBL because they saw the chance to address the landmine issue at a systemic level, not just at the level of removing the mines and patching up the victims.

In the year following the signing of the treaty however, the Mines Advisory Group (a UK-based mine clearance agency) was forced to shut down projects and dismiss staff because of funding shortages. Instead of an anticipated increase in support from the Ottawa process, this group and others saw their budgets shrink and watched public monies for landmine work become more scarce, not less. Operational NGOs involved in humanitarian mine action attempted to reverse the public perception that the landmines problem had been solved by the treaty. Rhetoric about the ban suddenly became more complex. NGOs sent the message, Actually the ban is the first step; now we need your time and money to help victims and remove mines. But the second part of the request was lost.[13]

In a sense, the interests of operational NGOs have diverged from their activist colleagues. Many activists see the predominant achievement of the campaign in terms of the new multilateralist, soft-power model of global governance they nurtured, backed by substantial government commitment. While this is clearly a vitally important development, others fear that the new model may have come at the expense of real change for mine-affected peoples on the ground. The success of the treaty negotiations has not been translated into gains at the grassroots, forcing NGOs to ask themselves some serious questions about strategy and accountability.

Conclusions

Global civil society campaigning can learn much from the landmines example. The importance of strong government-NGO relationships, charismatic campaign personalities, and effective electronic constituency management cannot be overemphasized. Some of the other attributes that contributed to the success of the Ottawa process are less tangible, and in some ways contradictory. Clearly, as the other contributors to this volume demonstrate, citizen action is inherently complex and multicausal. But the question of causality remains important for humanitarian agencies with lofty ideals and limited budgets. Whether or not there is a clear answer, operational NGOs in particular want to know, So what worked? These NGOs have a mandate to make the donor dollar stretch further, which forces them to ponder the causality question before investing in new research, lobbying, and public constituency building. Whatever the prioritizing of its various causes, the campaign's success was fueled by the zealous idealism of activist NGOs, tempered by the cool pragmatism of the operational NGOs. This combination yielded a treaty that made few concessions but remained focused on what was realistic and achievable. Although the campaign does illustrate the possibilities of the new multilateralism, it also suggests some limitations: Activists engrossed in the short-term outcome—banning an entire class of weapons—may have lost sight of the longer-term process of ensuring that the ban is implemented.

It is important to remember that "the struggle over land mines was not a two-cornered fight between government and NGOs, but a three-ringed fight between governments, NGOs and global public opinion" (Cameron 1998). Still, however, shifts in public opinion have not materialized. The same globalizing forces that enabled the landmine campaign to function across borders have failed to reverse increasing isolationism and apathy in the industrialized world. Gruesome pictures of landmine victims helped the campaign to shock the public into rapid action toward a ban, but they did little to cement a lasting constituency for change. Will similar campaigns need to employ still more dramatic tools? If so, who will build the broad-based support to ensure that gains made on paper eventually translate into results on the ground?

Operational NGOs involved in the campaign have consistently maintained that the ban was only a beginning, and that a "world free of landmines" would require ongoing commitment. In a *Newsweek* (1999) feature outlining the Mine Convention's progress and implementation, Michael Edwards was cited as saying that NGOs should expect slow movement: "Social change is a long haul, not a sprint, and anyone who is not prepared to run the marathon is in the wrong business." Following the treaty's ratification by over forty countries in 1998, operational NGOs became keenly aware that long-term, sustained, and substantial commitments of humanitarian resources were vulnerable to the changing winds of politics. Integrated action on landmines requires the coming together of a number of different specialties—community education, explosive ordnance disposal, highly specialized medical and prosthetic interventions, and many others—

that are scattered among a wide range of organizations. Focusing and coordinating these interventions on a global scale means harnessing substantial resources to a long-term vision. While various attempts to coordinate donor funding have been made in the post–Ottawa process years, harmonizing global donor response with the landmines problem is a Herculean task, far beyond the three-year time frame of most government aid grants

In the long-term, malaria, malnutrition, and HIV/AIDS will kill far more people annually than landmines ever will. Though landmines and the havoc they wreak deserve our attention, the continuing campaign to ban landmines and repair their damage must locate itself in a broader context of poverty alleviation and disaster relief. An ancient Hebrew proverb says, "For everything there is a season." While the past century has witnessed seasons of famine, war, and poverty, perhaps the current one will see that season's death. In the meantime, civil society has the opportunity to trigger the kind of courageous multilateralism that can ban an entire class of weapons, protect children from war, and—over the very long haul—turn swords into ploughshares.

Notes

1. This was true according to Mines Action Canada as of April 10, 2000. See the Mines Action Canada website at http://www.minesactioncanada.com.
2. "Soft power is 'the art of disseminating information in such a way that desirable outcomes are achieved through persuasion rather than coercion'" (Axworthy 1998b).
3. The International Conference on War-Affected Children, convened by the Canadian government in September 2000 in Winnipeg, for instance, has broad aims to reduce the impact of armed conflict on children. It is not clear, however, what would constitute success in the case of this campaign, apart from a complete end to the involvement of children in war.
4. The U.S. National Rifle Association (NRA) and other gun lobby groups have already set their sights on opposing any international effort to control small arms. The NRA and other similar groups have secured NGO consultative status with the UN and have publicly stated their intent to expand their horizons to the international arena.
5. "The South" is used here as a blanket term for developing countries.
6. This landmine ban treaty newsflash was the second such alert to be posted on the Vietnam Veterans of America Foundation website, http://www.vvaf.org/landmine/1997/news9_3b.htm, on September 4, 1997.
7. In another example of the informal, yet coherent style of the campaign, the slogan "No exceptions, no loopholes, no reservations" had become a mantra of the ICBL at various international conferences, and a catch-phrase reflecting its determination for a pure treaty. It became the tagline on a variety of internal and external public relations materials.
8. Until the establishment of the Ottawa process, the Geneva-based Convention on Certain Conventional Weapons (CCW) had been the primary arena

of NGO advocacy against antipersonnel landmines. At best, the CCW could only accomplish weak restrictions on mine use. The convention's failure to achieve any substantial progress against mines largely motivated the Canadian-led initiative.

9. See the Taliban's statement to the Non-State Actors Working Group of the ICBC at http://www.icbl.org/wg/nsa/library/nsadeclarations.htm/.

10. Despite the Taliban regime's military rule, clearance efforts in Afghanistan have proceeded at a rapid pace, thanks to the Afghan-based Mine Clearance Planning Agency (MCPA), highly regarded within the campaign for the safety, speed, and cost-efficiency of their mine clearance.

11. Axworthy (1998b) notes that the government negotiation team at a Geneva meeting in 1996 included Valerie Warmington, chair of the Canadian campaign. The author also accompanied the Canadian government delegation to a regional meeting of interested states in Sydney, Australia, in July 1997, when Australia's stated position at the time ruled out signature of the Ottawa treaty for national security reasons.

12. The ministerial remark was later clarified—CDN$1.5 million would be allocated over five years to conduct research and computer modeling of combat without antipersonnel mines. This research is intended to convince mine-using militaries that they can continue to conduct effective warfare without antipersonnel mines, as an incentive to sign the UN mine ban convention. No new weapon systems would be developed and no lethal weapons were to be tested with these federal funds.

13. Within a month of the Ottawa treaty, World Vision Canada mailed a funding appeal for landmine awareness work to just over 80,000 Canadian donors. The response rate, below 6 percent, was among the agency's lowest response for this kind of appeal in 1998.

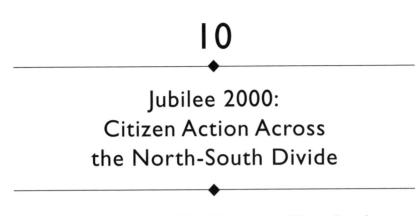

10

Jubilee 2000:
Citizen Action Across
the North-South Divide

Carole J.L. Collins, Zie Gariyo, and Tony Burdon

Strategically challenging, politically complex, relatively successful—that sums up the global advocacy movement known as Jubilee 2000, a worldwide campaign to cancel the unpayable debts of the world's most impoverished countries by the dawn of the new millennium. Jubilee 2000 is far from achieving all of its supporters' goals. Indeed, the biggest challenge has been to reach a degree of consensus on those goals within the movement; activists around the world would be the first to say that they have yet to achieve a true jubilee. Yet Jubilee 2000 has effectively pressured creditor governments to make significant moves to write off unpayable third world debt. And it has focused unprecedented global public scrutiny on official macroeconomic policies and decisionmaking processes, historically the areas least transparent or accessible to democratic debate.

Jubilee 2000 has grown dramatically since its launch in the UK in the early 1990s as a call by development-oriented NGOs, church, and labor groups for debt relief in order to free more resources to reduce global poverty. It now counts over sixty national Jubilee campaigns, including seventeen in Central and Latin America, fifteen in Africa, and ten in Asia. Jubilee 2000 petitions have been circulated in over 100 countries, and more than seventeen million signatures had been collected by June 1999 (including one million from Bangladesh and a quarter of the Irish population). In some debtor nations such as Uganda, national Jubilee 2000 campaigns have won an explicit role for civil society groups in deciding how to spend the savings from debt cancellation and in broadening national development planning. While some debtor governments have resisted calls for greater transparency and civil society participation, others have become more militant than they would otherwise have been in demanding debt relief from their creditors.

What is it about this global advocacy movement that has so captured the imagination of ordinary citizens, prominent artists, and politicians around the globe? What factors have contributed to the character, focus, and success (or failure) of national campaigns in debtor and creditor countries and the global campaign as a whole? What are the challenges that face Jubilee 2000 as a global advocacy movement, and what are the long-term prospects for success? How will Jubilee 2000 evolve as a global campaign beyond the year 2000, the self-imposed deadline for achieving its goals?

Debt As a Global Issue

Global citizen action on debt is not new. Many groups began working on this issue at the time of the first major developing country debt crisis in Mexico in 1982. As the social costs of debt mounted during the 1980s, the issue began to be popularized by political leaders including Julius Nyerere, Michael Manley, and Willie Brandt. During the mid-1980s and early 1990s, NGOs and church groups began to document and analyze the suffering generated by structural adjustment programs imposed as a quid pro quo for international loans. Churches began to raise the issue of debt in a series of economic statements and pastoral letters, while development and economic justice NGOs began to popularize it through their grassroots education and media campaigns. The transnational efforts of these groups provided the foundations from which Jubilee 2000 emerged in the mid-1990s.

As a global issue, unpayable debt presents more complex challenges than, for example, the banning of landmines. The suffering of those wounded by landmines is vividly clear, and few—bar a small number of military interests—defend their use (see Chapter 9). As a global public policy issue, debt has proved more difficult, in part because ordinary citizens are ambivalent about repayment. Most feel a moral obligation to repay their debts and expect other people and other nations to feel the same. At the same time, they are sensitive to the oppression of debt as well as the opportunities it forecloses for development. This is one reason why the biblical call for a "Jubilee," the wiping away of all debts every 50 years, resonates with so many.

Adding to the complexity of the debt problem is the diversity of its causes, which include:

- Irresponsible lending by commercial banks eager to invest OPEC "petro-dollars" in the late 1970s and early 1980s;
- Irresponsible borrowing by oft-unelected ruling elites (such as the

Mobutu regime in the former Zaire), who often squandered or stole what they borrowed;

- Loans to finance poorly designed programs and projects that failed to generate sufficient income to repay;
- Politically driven lending (especially during the Cold War), with little or no regard for the ultimate repayability of the loans;
- Responsible borrowing by countries that could not sustain their debt repayments due to falling commodity prices or increases in oil prices, as in the Gulf War (which, with reduced remittances from the Middle East, caused at least thirteen sub-Saharan African economies to lose over one per cent of their total GDP);
- Distorted policy environments in many developing countries caused by poor planning and management;
- Increased multilateral lending during structural adjustment programs that added to debt;
- Periodic rises in global interest rates, which boosted the cost of refinancing debts or repaying variable interest rate loans;
- Ethnic conflicts (such as in Rwanda or Liberia) that disrupted economies so much that repayment was impossible as well as loans for military equipment that helped to fuel such conflicts; and
- Political instability generated by social cutbacks required under structural adjustment programs.

Given these diverse causes, Jubilee 2000 has emphasized the co-responsibility of creditors (whether governments, international financial institutions, or private commercial banks) and debtor governments for creating the burden of unpayable debt. The campaign questions why ordinary people in the world's poorest countries should be forced to bear this burden through paying higher taxes or going without essential public services such as education and health care so that their governments can accrue sufficient funds to repay their foreign creditors.

Unpayable debt also reflects the fundamentally unequal nature of economic relationships between the global North and the global South. It is the creditors who, until recently, have unilaterally dictated the terms of debt renegotiation and repayment, without any neutral arbiters. The Jubilee 2000 movement has begun to challenge these unequal power relationships at the most fundamental level. It is also questioning the decisionmaking processes of both debtor and creditor governments and multilateral creditors such as the IMF and the World Bank. The campaign has pressed for debtor countries, and ordinary citizens of those countries, to have a greater say in determining the terms of debt rescheduling or cancellation. Growing input from national campaigns in the South has helped to shift the global campaign from an initial emphasis on charity ("Let's give a gift to a billion people for the new millennium") toward an attempt to change how national and international economic policies are made. In demanding more transparency and accountability from debtor and creditor governments and the international financial institutions, Jubilee 2000 is challenging long-entrenched patterns of global economic behavior.

The Campaign's Growth and Global Impact

How has Jubilee 2000 grown as a global campaign since its launch in the early to mid-1990s, and what impact has it had on the financial institutions and governments it has targeted? In 1996, the IMF and World Bank established an official debt relief program known as the Heavily Indebted Poor Country program (HIPC). In doing so these institutions conceded for the first time a key argument of Jubilee 2000 and development NGOs—that most poor country debt would never be repaid. The number of national Jubilee 2000 campaigns grew steadily from 1996 through 1998 as the idea spread and the eve of a new millennium lent greater urgency to the campaign's timetable. During this period it became clear that HIPC's rigid preconditions and lengthy decisionmaking processes would keep all but a handful of the forty-one countries defined by Bank and IMF criteria as eligible to apply for HIPC debt relief from actually receiving any benefits until after the year 2000. By the end of 1998, over sixty national campaigns had been organized, and thirty-nine convened in Rome in November to reach a new consensus on goals and strategy.

Jubilee 2000's global political visibility and impact (especially among creditors and policymakers) grew dramatically after May 1998, when 70,000 supporters formed a ten-kilometer ring around the G7 summit meeting site in Birmingham (UK). At the summit meeting, Germany, supported by the United States, Japan, and Italy, blocked British proposals for deeper debt relief, but the G7 chair (British Prime Minister Tony Blair) implicitly conceded Jubilee 2000's growing political influence when he reversed an earlier decision and met with British campaign leaders immediately after the rally. Birmingham marked a turning point in the attitude of major creditors and gave the campaign new strength in stepping up its critique of HIPC and proposing alternative solutions.

After Birmingham, the campaign made rapid progress:

- In August and October 1998, the heads of the IMF and World Bank attended two major debt conferences organized by the Anglican and Catholic churches, both of which were major supporters of Jubilee 2000 globally as well as in national campaigns.

- In September the head of Jubilee 2000/UK participated in a World Bank seminar during the Bank's 1998 annual meetings.
- In March 1999, officials of the IMF, World Bank, Paris Club, and G7 finance ministries attended an all-day meeting in London with representatives of ten Jubilee 2000 national campaigns to discuss their critique of current debt relief and a rough cost of alternative proposals for debt cancellation.
- By April 1999, every G7 government had announced its own proposals for debt relief, and Canada had committed itself to canceling 100 percent of bilateral debt. On the eve of the spring meeting of the IMF and the World Bank, the IMF also issued a sixty-five-page review of critiques of the current HIPC initiative, extensively quoting analyses by Jubilee 2000 national campaigns and other debt relief proponents.
- During the G7 summit in Germany in June 1999, 50,000 Jubilee 2000 supporters lined the roads, bridges, and banks of the River Rhine in Cologne and Stuttgart to demand that G7 leaders adopt deeper cuts than they had accepted in the Cologne Debt Initiative announced the day before. A Jubilee 2000 delegation—including campaign representatives from each continent, Irish rock star Bono, and Archbishop Oscar Rodríguez from Honduras—also met the G7 chair, German Chancellor Gerhard Schroeder, to underscore their demands.
- During July and August, Jubilee 2000 representatives critiqued official debt relief measures at several major international conferences, including a day-long forum at IMF headquarters organized by the U.S. Treasury with presentations by Southern Jubilee 2000 campaigns, a seminar in Addis Ababa hosted by the UN Economic Commission for Africa and the World Bank, and another in London organized by the commonwealth secretariat.
- At the IMF-World Bank annual meetings in September, and days after a Jubilee 2000 delegation had met with the pope, U.S. President Bill Clinton broke a key psychological barrier in announcing that the United States would cancel 100 percent of bilateral debt (Britain followed suit in December). The IMF and the World Bank also invited Jubilee 2000 representatives to respond to a summary of post-Cologne reforms of the HIPC initiative (now dubbed HIPC II) adopted earlier that month.
- In December 1999, about 30,000 Jubilee 2000 supporters, including several major U.S. labor unions, braved pouring rain to ring the World Trade Organization conference center in Seattle on the eve of its opening reception. Thousands also joined protests against the

IMF and the World Bank in Washington, D.C., in April 2000, in which the call for debt cancellation was highlighted.

This steady increase in public pressure pushed creditors to offer successively greater cancellation, from less than U.S.$55 billion prior to the Cologne G7 Summit to over U.S.$100 billion afterward and (by the end of 1999) a further U.S.$11 billion in U.S. and UK commitments to cancel 100 percent of their bilateral debt. This has benefited, for example, Bolivia, Cameroon, Burkina Faso, Uganda, and Tanzania, all of which have reached the HIPC "decision point" (qualifying them for cancellation of 100 percent of debt service). In addition, the IMF and the World Bank agreed late in 1998 to defer debt service payments for at least a year for the four Central American countries affected by Hurricane Mitch, and they offered Mozambique the same terms early in 2000.

Perhaps the greatest testament to the campaign's impact was the fact that G7 leaders borrowed from Jubilee 2000's language in their June 1999 Cologne Debt Initiative and in all subsequent official statements—the battle over basic messages had been won. Government pronouncements were full of references to "faster, deeper, and broader debt relief," "the threshold of a new millennium," and the need for "poverty reduction plans for the effective targeting of savings derived from debt relief," developed through "consultation with civil society."

The G7 also announced at Cologne that IMF and World Bank programs would henceforth be placed within a government-led framework for poverty reduction with transparent budget processes, to be developed in collaboration with civil society groups—the so-called Poverty Reduction Strategy Program, or PRSP. If fully implemented, these improvements in the process of economic policymaking might prove more important than the campaign's achievements in winning increased levels of debt cancellation. Although focused on the need to cancel unpayable debts, the global Jubilee 2000 movement has also stimulated a much broader debate among the members of the public, policymakers, and journalists on other debt-related issues, including:

- The development of a more neutral international debt arbitration mechanism that would place debtors on a more equal footing with creditors;
- The recapturing of stolen public wealth, including the proceeds from international loans;
- The moral right to repudiate odious debts accrued by unelected and repressive regimes;
- The implementation of debt relief within a financial and policy

framework that explicitly aims to reduce poverty and environmental destruction; and

- Assurance that future borrowing and lending is conducted using a more democratic and inclusive decisionmaking process in both debtor and creditor countries as well as in multilateral financial institutions.

Defining Common Goals: The South Asserts Its Voice

Much of the global campaign's efforts have focused on the G7, because G7 governments are both major creditors in their own right and majority shareholders in the IMF and the World Bank. They are in a position to pledge new funding for debt relief, secure changes in Bank and IMF policies to achieve deeper debt relief for more countries under less onerous conditions, and insist that civil society organizations be accorded a greater role in setting the conditions for debt relief and future loans. However, the focus on Northern targets does not reflect the dynamic and often dramatic successes of national campaigns in the South: These groups have built credibility for their critiques of existing debt policies, mobilized public support for Jubilee 2000 goals, and engaged national political leaders and finance ministries in adopting policies that empower civil society to play a role in debate and decisionmaking.

Indeed, a major facet of Jubilee 2000 has been the growing participation and importance of Southern campaigns in the global effort and their growing role in redefining goals and strategies. Examples include Uganda (detailed later in this chapter) and Tanzania, where Jubilee 2000 collaborated with the late Julius Nyerere on a high-profile public campaign and participated in the development of the Poverty Reduction Strategy for Tanzania, including the provision of assistance to ensure that grassroots views were heard at the district level. Meanwhile, Jubilee 2000 groups and other NGOs in Nicaragua (such as Grupo Positivo de Cabildeo) and in Honduras (such as ASONOG/INTERFOROS) managed to make immediate links between debt relief and reconstruction in the aftermath of Hurricane Mitch. Creditors were forced to agree to stop collecting debt service from both countries for a period of three years.

Speaking to global policymakers with a united voice obviously carries greater political weight than speaking with many, but defining common goals and objectives has been a challenging process for Jubilee 2000, given the different historical and regional realities within and between the global North and South. Since its first international gathering in Rome in November 1998, Jubilee 2000 has worked hard to achieve as much consensus as possible on aims and strategy and to ensure that tactics in one national context do not inadvertently undercut efforts in others. This unification is still a work in progress; improved and more frequent communications are proving critical. While national and regional campaigns agree on the global movement's overall goal of debt cancellation, many disagree on which and how many countries should be eligible (and on the basis of what criteria), the extent of debt cancellation, and whether to require any conditions and if so who should set them. Some of these differences stem from contrasting definitions of unpayable or immoral debt. Others are rooted in disagreements over how best to negotiate with policymakers in various national contexts. Particularly strong tensions arise between those seeking to reform existing debt relief programs, processes, and institutions and others who feel they need to be replaced.

For example, many members of the U.S. campaign initially focused their efforts on achieving debt cancellation for the poorest countries under the existing HIPC initiative, since they saw this as most likely to win support in a Republican-controlled Congress. However, most Southern campaigns reject the HIPC categorization of countries, since many middle-income countries have major debt overhangs and pressing problems of poverty that should also be addressed by the international community. Southern campaigns have cautioned that actions in creditor countries, while understandably adapting their strategies to suit political realities at home, must be careful to respect—and not inadvertently undermine—negotiating strategies in the South.

Despite such differences, the global campaign has provided a platform for Southern activists to project their views and proposals to policymakers in world capitals. In the Accra declaration, signed in April 1998, fifteen African Jubilee 2000 campaigns called for total and unconditional debt cancellation of all African countries' external debts, arguing that they are rooted in a history of slavery and colonialism, an unjust system of international trade and investment, and a legacy of unaccountable government. The Declaration of Tegucigalpa, signed by sixteen Latin American and Caribbean campaigns in January 1999, urged limiting external debt service obligations to no more than 3 percent of a nation's annual budget, citing as precedents Peru's debt renegotiation in 1946 and Germany's in 1953. Coalescing as Jubilee South, many of these campaigns adopted a common slogan: "Don't owe, won't pay!" reflecting their conviction that most developing country debt is odious debt, lent to repressive regimes such as ex-President Marcos in the Philippines, the former apartheid government of South Africa, and Latin American military juntas during the 1970s and 1980s to help preserve their power base and enrich elites. They rejected the Cologne Debt Initiative as a hoax that largely repackaged debt bondage in a more palatable form. While most Northern campaigns have focused primarily on debt cancellation, Southern activists have emphasized other debt-related issues, including the need to recapture stolen public wealth.

At the first international Jubilee 2000 gathering in Rome in late 1998, Southern campaigns decided to meet separately during part of the conference in a South-South exchange in order to share their experiences and try to achieve a greater consensus on a strategic vision. During South-South meetings organized on the eve of the June 1999 Cologne summit, Southern campaigns emphasized the importance of strengthening local and national efforts on the ground as well as of South-South exchanges and the need for the South to assume more leadership of the global campaign. These points were reaffirmed at the subsequent Jubilee South-South summit convened in Gauteng, South Africa, in November 1999.[1] The summit demanded "restitution and reparations by creditors for the human, social, environmental damage caused by their debt policies"; rejected the G7 Cologne Debt Initiative as inadequate; and supported the formation of a debtors' alliance to collectively repudiate "odious, onerous, criminal, fraudulent and illegitimate" external debt.

More broadly, campaigns in both the North and the South have decried the disempowering effect of Northern campaigners' disproportionate share of the global movement's resources. Northern campaigns have significantly greater access to funding, equipment, technical skills, global policymakers, and international meetings, realities which mirror the historic inequalities between North and South. Indeed, some Northern activists have had greater contact with Southern campaigns than activists in the South themselves.

Building a More Equal Partnership: The Experience of the Uganda Debt Network

Much of Jubilee 2000's global impetus has been generated by collaborative relationships among civil society groups including churches, trade unions, student organizations, research groups, and development NGOs in the North and South, many of which predate the campaign. The experience of the Uganda Debt Network (UDN), which leads Uganda's Jubilee 2000 campaign, illustrates many of the complexities and opportunities of this emerging global movement.

The UDN was founded in 1996 as an ad hoc coalition of local and international NGOs to mobilize Ugandan civil society to engage in the national debate on Uganda's debt problems. UDN is one of a number of debt advocacy networks in the South, including counterparts in Tanzania, Mozambique, Nicaragua, and Honduras. Many have been supported from their inception not only by a local NGO membership but also by international NGOs such as Oxfam, ActionAid, ACORD, World Vision, and

Eurodad (the European NGO debt network). These larger groups have provided not only funding, but also support for capacity building, information, and assistance in accessing international policymakers. Also, as national networks have grown stronger, their relationships with NGOs in the North have become more reciprocal, with Southern campaigns providing policy analysis and views, information, and access to local policymakers. As a result, Northern NGOs have begun to pay more attention to issues they had previously ignored. Oxfam, for example, focused initially on Northern creditors and the poverty priorities of the Ugandan government. The UDN brought in other issues, such as future lending priorities, budget transparency, and the role of parliamentarians, which helped to broaden Oxfam's program.

When UDN was launched, few Ugandans focused on the issue of external debt. Most regarded it as largely a government problem that was too complex for ordinary citizens to understand. Yet twelve years of structural adjustment programs since 1987 had left their mark on Ugandan society, large parts of which had become progressively poorer as Uganda's debt burden grew from under U.S.\$1 billion in 1986 to over U.S.\$3.6 billion in 1998. Oxfam had worked on debt since 1992, and on Uganda in particular. The initial absence of strong local groups active on this issue made Oxfam keen to support a strong local network like UDN when it emerged.

As the network evolved it developed a close synergy with other Northern partners as well. Eurodad provided UDN with its first comprehensive information on HIPC as well as with detailed analyses of Uganda's debt burden. Oxfam's position papers also provided information used extensively by the local media and in UDN's public education programs. Other Northern groups (such as the Bretton Woods Project, Bread for the World, the Africa Faith and Justice Network in the United States, and Jubilee 2000–UK in London) also provided useful information. Access to e-mail proved crucial in increasing the national campaign's dynamism and effectiveness, making it possible for UDN to develop greater visibility and close working relationships at the international level so that it became a prominent voice in the global campaign.

These international connections gave UDN timely access to key information and analyses, boosting the network's capacity to undertake effective national advocacy and its credibility as a key voice in national debates. In turn, this pushed the Ugandan government to be more active and forthcoming on debt issues. For the first time, the government developed and made publicly available a comprehensive debt strategy, and officials began attending civil society meetings to discuss the causes and effects of Uganda's external debt burden. Government reports became freely available to the public, and UDN used some of them to prepare its own updates. The government's new willingness to discuss its debt policies provided a forum for dialogue between policymakers and ordinary citizens. UDN also reached out to parliamentarians who had challenged the government's decision to repay external debt ahead of what it owed to domestic banks.

Over time, the Ugandan government began to seek partnerships with civil society groups, seeing them as allies in their efforts to pressure creditors to accelerate debt relief. Officials shared a 1997 government letter to the IMF and World Bank that UDN in turn shared with the local media, increasing pressure on the Bank to speed up Uganda's completion point for qualifying for significant debt cancellation and forcing the local Bank representative to engage in dialogue with civil society groups. UDN also mobilized locally to bolster the international effort, coordinating the collection of signatures on the Jubilee 2000 petition, cultivating media contacts, and sharing local intelligence with international NGO colleagues. The network's presentation at an IMF seminar on poverty reduction in Washington, D.C., in 1998 highlighted to IMF officials that HIPC debt relief was still inadequate, even for those few countries like Uganda that had received HIPC assistance. In addition, UDN helped to persuade the Ugandan government to set up a Poverty Action Fund (PAF) through which NGOs now work jointly with government officials to decide how savings from debt relief will be spent. Furthermore, growing NGO pressure at quarterly meetings with the IMF helped to persuade the government to initiate an open audit of the national budget. Proceeds from Uganda's debt remissions have partly gone to fund the Universal Primary Education Program, which dramatically improved access to primary education from 1998 to 2000, doubling school enrollment during that time to almost six million children. Similar funds proposed by national Jubilee 2000 campaigns in Zambia and Tanzania have since won government support.

UDN's real challenges have been to create a pro-poor political environment in Uganda and to empower grassroots constituencies to participate in the national policy dialogue on debt. Both have been difficult, and the debate on debt still engages mostly urban and academically oriented groups. Many grassroots groups, especially in rural areas, have little or no access to newspapers, television, or even radio. The fact that most information on debt is written in English has also curtailed grassroots participation, though UDN has made recent efforts to translate their analyses into, and conduct educational workshops in, local languages.

These problems undermine the legitimacy and effectiveness of the campaign. For example, during 1996–1997, the Uganda Poverty Eradication Action Plan was developed with significant input from civil society groups, but little feedback came directly from the poor. As a result, the government was keen to carry out a series of "participatory poverty assessments" (PPAs) in nine districts in order to understand the changing profile of poverty in Uganda. These PPAs were also designed to provide a voice for the poor in national planning as well as to build national and district capacity to undertake participatory action-research and improve local planning. The PPAs have since begun to influence areas of government policy, for example in winning a larger budget for Uganda's water department after a majority of groups identified water supply as a key gap in government strategies to address rural poverty. They have also been a key component in the development of Uganda's Poverty Reduction Strategy Program (PRSP), with the UDN playing a coordinating role in incorporating civil society analyses into the PRSP process.

As can be seen from UDN's experience, Southern NGOs are developing greater expertise, access to the Internet, capacity to popularize and demystify complex terminology, and sophistication in taking advantage of political openings at the national and global levels. These advances have been key to the growing success of the overall Jubilee 2000 campaign. However, national efforts still suffer from a lack of resources and information, difficult relations with often undemocratic governments, and the challenge posed by the diversity of local languages, especially in Africa.

The Lessons of Experience

Central to Jubilee 2000's success as a global movement has been its effectiveness in marrying strong public action to high-quality analysis and well-defined policy alternatives. Other key factors include:

- The rising expertise and sophistication of NGO critiques and policy alternatives, which have generated more confidence among the public and the media;
- The growing use of the Internet and computer-based technologies, which have facilitated inexpensive, wider, and more timely dissemination of information and interventions in the policy process;
- The effective popularizing of a complex issue, framed in moral terms: Most of this debt was contracted by nonelected governing elites who misspent the funds, making it immoral to require that debts be repaid at the expense of cutbacks in education and health care;
- The campaign's adroit use of the psychological effects of the millennium, placing greater public pressure on policymakers to act with a sense of urgency;
- The failure of creditors' own policies and programs to reduce debt and poverty, which increased the acceptability of proposals for reform: As a bipartisan commission established by the U.S. Congress noted in its report of March 2000, "The World Bank's

evaluation of its own performance in Africa found a 73 percent failure rate. Only one in four programs, on average, achieved satisfactory, sustainable results";

- Successful mobilizing of media attention and the use of prominent personalities in support of debt relief;
- Flexibility: By refusing to back specific formulations for debt relief (arguing this might undercut the demands of Southern colleagues), Jubilee 2000 has been able to use each new commitment from creditors as a basis for demanding that they go even further.

The greatest challenge for Jubilee 2000 as a movement is that it continues to reflect the same North-South imbalances that it criticizes in international economic policy, in terms of access to resources, information, and global decisionmaking. A key measure of its success, therefore, will be how effectively it can address these internal contradictions and forge a qualitatively different partnership among civil society groups in the North and the South. Additionally, whether in the South or the North, the key actors in Jubilee 2000 are still a small number of largely capital city–based NGOs and religious groups, some of whom lack strong links with grassroots constituencies.

Jubilee 2000 supporters come from diverse backgrounds, with contrasting decisionmaking styles and political orientations. The challenge—managed more effectively by some national coalitions than others—has been to keep these constituencies mobilized under the same umbrella as the campaign moves forward. Another challenge has been the need to shift, sometimes quite rapidly, between different levels and styles of advocacy work, from popular education to high-level policy analysis for instance. Though difficult to maintain, the combination of levels and styles of advocacy has helped to make Jubilee 2000 a powerful global force. Radicals and reformists have worked together, and the movement has held back from trying to force a common position across the global coalition. The movement has worked to use this diversity creatively, without compromising its goals.

Conclusions

Jubilee 2000 has achieved levels of debt cancellation far beyond what its supporters initially thought possible. It has forced creditors and financial institutions to focus on poverty reduction and opened up a much broader debate on fundamental reforms in economic policymaking. It has also challenged many NGOs to deepen and broaden their contacts in civil society and to involve poor people more directly in their efforts.

Civil society demonstrations at the World Trade Organization meeting in Seattle in December 1999 created a new political environment and momentum for global citizen action on economic justice. During the millennium year, Jubilee 2000 groups began to discuss how to advance the campaign into the future, and how to strengthen links with other related campaigns on trade, investment, labor standards, migration, and the growing movement for economic and social rights. Debt has contributed significantly to rising levels of poverty and inequality, but for many, debt reduction provides a mere starting point for raising broader issues of globalization and global governance. Some campaigners feel that linking debt to trade issues is now critical, given that trade barriers in the North cost developing countries around U.S.$700 billion in lost income. Others feel that the simplicity of the campaign's current focus is what has made it so effective, and thus should be preserved. Many Jubilee 2000 supporters joined in large-scale demonstrations against the IMF and the World Bank at their spring meetings in April 2000. For them, and for the campaign as a whole, the challenge is how to involve the grassroots in a genuine global movement and make globalization work for poor people around the world.

Notes

1. See Jubilee South, *Towards a Debt-Free Millennium,* South-South Summit Declaration (meeting of Jubilee South, Gauteng, South Africa, November 21, 1999). Available online at http://www.jubileesouth.net.

11

Crossborder Organizing Around Alternatives to Free Trade: Lessons from the NAFTA/FTAA Experience

John Cavanagh, Sarah Anderson, and Karen Hansen-Kuhn

The massive outpouring of public resistance to free trade in the streets of Seattle in December 1999 was the culmination of years of organizing and educational work in many parts of the world. Although the target of the demonstrators in Seattle was the World Trade Organization (WTO), many arrived at their critique of the free trade model through their involvement in related issues. These include sweatshops, debt relief, and perhaps most importantly, the North American Free Trade Agreement (NAFTA). For many Americans, it was the NAFTA debate that first exposed them to the social issues related to trade and investment liberalization. Dozens of unions, religious groups, and others organized delegations to the U.S.-Mexico border and other educational activities related to NAFTA. For the first time, a debate over an international economic issue became a matter of intense public interest. Thus, when the WTO announced it would hold its ministerial in Seattle, there existed a solid base of activists, many of them veterans of the NAFTA fight, who were eager to use the summit as an opportunity to voice their criticism of the WTO and free trade in general.

In this chapter we examine one strain of the organizing work around NAFTA that helped set the stage for the Battle in Seattle. This is the process of crossborder, cross-sectoral citizen dialogue to develop consensus around an alternative to the free trade model. The process began among Canadian, U.S., and Mexican activists and scholars in the context of the NAFTA debate. However, since the announcement of plans for a "Free Trade Area of the Americas" (FTAA) in 1994, this work has expanded to include activists and scholars from across the hemisphere. As participants from one country in this citizen dialogue, our views are necessarily limited, but we attempt to share insights offered by our colleagues from other countries.

The Evolution of an Alternative Vision

"A Just and Sustainable Trade and Development Initiative for North America"

Beginning in 1991, the U.S.-based Alliance for Responsible Trade (ART) joined with a counterpart coalition in Mexico, the Mexican Action Network on Free Trade (RMALC) as well as a handful of Canadian groups to begin the negotiation of an alternative to NAFTA. Since the beginning of the NAFTA debate, these groups worked together to develop national and trinational critiques of official proposals and to offer alternative approaches. Our institutions, the Institute for Policy Studies and the Development Group for Alternative Policies (GAP), were involved in the process through ART, which, like RMALC, is a coalition representing a broad range of organizations, including union, family farm, human rights, religious, environmental, and consumer groups. In later years, a similar Canadian coalition, Common Frontiers, also took on a lead role in this process.

The decision to devote energy to this initiative has been controversial among some other groups who fear that it could highlight divisions within the anti–free trade lobby, thus weakening their chances of defeating NAFTA and other trade pacts in the U.S. Congress. Yet another group of NAFTA critics oppose efforts to develop alternative international rules related to trade and investment because they believe that any international institution is likely to be unaccountable to the world's citizens. Instead, they say, the focus of progressive activists should be on pursuing social change through local and national governments.

However, proponents of the initiative for alternatives argued that it was necessary for three reasons:

1. NAFTA did not create the massive social and environmental problems of North American economic integration; it simply accelerated them. Even if NAFTA were defeated, those problems would remain and there would still be an urgent need to create a new set of rules to reshape the integration process in the direction of the majorities in each country.
2. It is easier to fight something with something else. NAFTA proponents attempted to brand those opposed to the plan as old-line protectionists. With an alternative, we could say, We are not against

trade and investment; we are for a new set of rules and a new framework to guide trade and investment.

3. Ultimately, the greatest challenge facing civil society across the hemisphere is to articulate a clear, reasonable, attractive alternative to the dominant neoliberal model.

At citizens meetings held parallel to the official NAFTA negotiations, time was set aside to meet within and across sectors on the issue of "alternatives to NAFTA." Members of ART and RMALC created the working document, "A Just and Sustainable Trade and Development Initiative for North America." The introduction spelled out how our process differed from the official NAFTA process: We were dedicated (1) to different policies; (2) to a different process for arriving at integration agreements (a more democratic and inclusive process); and (3) to a different politics (more participatory and less corrupt). In the main text, we documented the points of consensus that had evolved out of the trinational dialogues. In areas where there seemed to be disagreement, we put the text in brackets and noted the differences.

The ten-page "Just and Sustainable Trade and Development Initiative" was released with nineteen endorsing organizations in mid-1993. Gaining media coverage of the document was difficult in each of the three countries, as the mainstream media preferred to characterize the debate on trade as one with only two sides: free traders versus protectionists. However, the development of the document helped strengthen our crossborder alliances, and participants felt that the process should continue, despite the fact that NAFTA passed the U.S. Congress and went into effect on January 1, 1994.

The "Alternatives for the Americas" Document

The "Just and Sustainable" paper remained the most detailed articulation of a jointly developed alternative vision until a new initiative was undertaken in preparation for the Peoples' Summit of the Americas, held in Santiago, Chile, in April 1998, parallel to the official Summit of the Americas attended by thirty-four heads of state. RMALC led an effort to draft a more in-depth discussion document on alternatives to the FTAA that included contributions from more than thirty people, primarily from RMALC, ART, and Common Frontiers but also from other countries in the hemisphere. The document proposes an alternative set of rules to regulate the global and hemispheric economies, based on the conviction that trade and investment should not be ends in themselves but rather the instruments for achieving just and sustainable development. Citizens must have the right to participate in the formulation, implementation, and evaluation of hemispheric social and economic policies, and the central goals of these policies should be to promote social welfare and reduced inequality at all levels. At the Peoples' summit, these coalitions joined with broad-based alliances from Chile and Brazil to host a forum that engaged trade unionists, environmentalists, family farmers, and others from across the hemisphere in a productive discussion of the draft document. For several months after the Santiago meeting, these and additional comments were incorporated and a new draft, titled "Alternatives for the Americas: Building a Peoples' Hemispheric Agreement," was released in the fall of 1998.

This paper, at fifty pages, is more detailed than the "Just and Sustainable" document. It addresses the major topics on the official agenda of the FTAA negotiators (investment, finance, intellectual property rights, agriculture, market access, and dispute resolution) as well as topics that are of extreme social importance but which governments have ignored (human rights, environment, labor, immigration, the role of the state, and energy). An additional chapter on gender issues was developed in 1999 and will be included in the next version of the document. The document is available in four languages (English, Spanish, French, and Portuguese) and has been distributed widely in several countries. For example, in Brazil, the Central Workers Union (CUT) labor federation published 5,000 copies for their members. (See the summary in the appendix.)

Commonalities, Differences, and Ongoing Discussions

The process of developing the "Just and Sustainable" document, and of debating it widely, helped to clarify a number of areas of commonality and differences across the borders. Commonalities include the following points:

Corporations Versus the Rest of Us

The sharing of analysis reinforced what became the central thesis of most of our critiques of free trade, namely that the acceleration of corporate-led integration benefited the few (mainly large corporations) at the expense of workers, the environment, small farmers, women, and indigenous people in all three countries. A subset of this general point that gained wide acceptance in our circles was that it is not Mexican workers who take jobs from U.S. workers but instead U.S. companies that play U.S. workers against Mexican workers. Similarly, American and Mexican participants learned about the enormous job losses in Canada that resulted from corporations moving south to the United States to avoid unions and generous social benefits. Dialogues among U.S. workers around NAFTA abounded with stories of how, in bargaining sessions, management would often use the threat of moving production to Mexico or elsewhere to bargain down wages and working conditions in the United States. A survey by Cornell University professor Kate Bronfenbrenner (1996) confirmed the pervasiveness of this whipsawing phenomenon.

Shared Principles

There is a common perception that U.S. fair trade activists want to impose U.S. labor, environmental, and other standards on all other countries. To the contrary, the citizens' dialogue around alternatives to NAFTA and the FTAA focused on upholding the standards embodied in international agreements, such as the core labor standards of the International Labour Organization, the UN Declaration of Human Rights, and UN declarations on sustainable development, among others. A major thrust of the work on the alternatives has been to demand that these international agreements take precedence over rules embodied in NAFTA, the WTO, the FTAA, or any other trade agreements.

Rejection of the Casino Economy

The economic crises that erupted in Mexico in 1994 and Asia in 1997 demonstrated how a crisis in one country can spread like wildfire across borders and even oceans. Virtually no country was completely immune to the contagion. These experiences resulted in broad consensus among most countries in the Western Hemisphere that international trade needs a financial system radically different from the free market approach promoted through NAFTA and in the talks around the FTAA. As a result, two chapters of "Alternatives for the Americas" provide detailed recommendations on foreign direct investment and capital flows designed to insure that foreign investment supports dignified jobs and sustainable development.

There were also differences among network participants on which significant progress was made over time. An early area of contention in the citizen dialogue had to do with the use of trade sanctions to deter violations of basic labor and environmental rights and standards. U.S. groups offered the model of the U.S. Generalized System of Preferences, amended in the 1980s to state that countries found violating core labor rights would lose trade benefits.

This generated a heated debate among Mexican groups. Some felt that the North American governments could use these sanctions to pressure each other to improve labor and environmental law enforcement. Others were deeply skeptical of the wisdom of ceding such power to a supranational body that would likely be dominated by the United States, a country that has more often than not used trade sanctions to send a political message to particular countries or to protect certain industries.

As a compromise, dissenters suggested a process that would target the offending firms. If Ford Motor violated the rights of its workers in Mexico, the workers (and others) should have the opportunity to bring Ford before a trinational enforcement mechanism that included some kind of civil society participation and, if found guilty, Ford would pay damages (not the Mexican government).

A second component of the progress in this area was offered by Mexican scholars Jorge Casteñeda and Carlos Heredia. They proposed the notion of a "grand bargain" for any agreement between developed and developing countries that would address issues central to developed countries (for example, new rules to protect existing labor and environmental rights and standards) at the same level as issues central to developing countries (for instance, debt reduction and other compensation mechanisms to close the North-South gap). This proposed grand bargain transformed what could be differences into a common agenda.

In Seattle, the International Confederation of Free Trade Unions (ICFTU), which represents unions in about 150 countries, issued a proposal for WTO reform that is similar to the grand bargain in that it supports the linkage of internationally recognized core labor standards to trade rules as part of a longer list of demands to support development in poor countries. Unfortunately, this proposal received little media attention, as most journalists portrayed the debate over a trade-labor connection as one that broke down neatly along North-South lines. Thus, instead of quoting ICFTU delegates from South Africa or Brazil who are strong advocates for worker rights in trade agreements, the media focused on developing country officials and some NGOs who fear that the United States and other high-wage nations would take advantage of labor provisions in the WTO to shield their workers from international competition. The sharp divisions on this issue in Seattle underscore the need to explore whether the grand bargain pursued in the NAFTA and FTAA dialogues could gain broader support.

Issues of Continuing Discussion

Understanding Sovereignty

U.S. NAFTA opponents Ralph Nader, the well-known consumer advocate, and Pat Buchanan (1999), the frequent presidential candidate, centered their critique on the point that NAFTA would undermine U.S. sovereignty. U.S. laws, often the result of hard-fought citizen struggles, would be open to challenge in new international, sometimes secretive, institutions. Citizens' groups from outside the United States had a different perspective on the sovereignty issue, stressing that their nations' sovereignty has been repeatedly undermined by U.S. power. As part of the discussions on "A Just and Sustainable Trade and Development Initiative," David Brooks, a Mexican journalist who has coordinated a series of U.S.-Mexican dialogues, and others attempted to shift the discussion by replacing the term *national sovereignty* with *popular sovereignty.* They argued that corporate-led integration undermined the popular sovereignty of the majority in all three countries and that this is what the NAFTA alternative should fight.

These semantic differences are significant because they affect the model for dispute resolution, not to mention the mechanism for enforcement, in trade agreements. The emphasis of some U.S. activists on the value of sovereignty raises serious questions about whether they, much less the U.S. government, would be willing to accept a supranational body that may at times rule against the United States. With these questions hanging in the air, activists from less powerful countries are hesitant to advocate the creation of one more international institution in which the United States would likely call the shots. Thus, while much progress has been made in identifying alternative rules to govern the economic integration process, the task of developing the mechanisms to enforce and resolve disputes related to these rules has been more difficult. A chapter on this issue is included in the "Alternatives for the Americas" document, but it is designed as a starting point for a discussion and is in the process of being revised.

Immigration

The dialogue has deepened the conviction among all that the abuse of immigrants in the United States is an abomination and that the rules governing the integration of our continent should promote stronger enforcement of immigrant rights. There is also widespread agreement on the need to address the causes of immigration, namely economic stress, through international support for specific development programs in areas that are major net exporters of labor.

However, there remains a high level of disagreement on the issue of lifting barriers to immigration flows. On the one side are those, such as Institute for Policy Studies Fellow Saul Landau, who have argued that if capital and goods are free to move across borders, then there will be enormous pressures for labor to move across borders. In a world of free trade, Landau argues, borders should be opened to people as well. Many developing-country organizations agree with this analysis. Alternatively, Maria Jimenez of the American Friends Service Committee, argues not for open borders but for "equality of mobility," so that everyone would be treated equally under immigration law, no matter their professional status or country of origin.[1] In contrast to both Landau and Jimenez, many U.S. groups support maintaining strict controls on the numbers of immigrants who can work in the United States, including some who argue that these controls are necessary to prevent the erosion of wages for low-skill U.S. workers.

Technology Transfer

In the dialogue around alternatives to the dominant international investment model, it has become clear that there is a conflict on the issue of technology transfer. U.S. unions, the AFL-CIO in particular, have opposed a position held by many in the developing world in support of the government right to require corporations to transfer appropriate technology as a condition of foreign investment. (NAFTA abolished this right, along with a number of other performance requirements on foreign investors.) The U.S. union position is based on the fear that jobs often follow technology. For example, they point to the loss of U.S. jobs related to China's demands that U.S. aerospace firms transfer technology in order to invest in that country. Developing country activists, on the other hand, see the lack of access to high technology as an impediment to economic development.

Lessons Learned

We want to share six insights from our experiences in working on these two documents:

1. The negotiation of alternative approaches has led to deeper understanding of the commonalities and differences among groups across borders. A common understanding of the issues discussed in the previous section developed only as groups from across the borders began to attempt to work together. When the NAFTA process began, few U.S. citizen groups knew much about Mexico or Canada. Likewise in Mexico, one RMALC member commented that before the trinational work on NAFTA, he saw Canadians as simply "gringos in overcoats."

In this context, the anti-NAFTA work in general and the alternatives work in particular offered an enormous educational opportunity. Through numerous hours of discussion, the process of developing an alternative vision deepened participants' understanding of each country's culture and economy, trade-offs and priorities. The mainstream media coverage of the NAFTA debate tended to magnify and oversimplify differences, reinforcing the then popular notion that low-wage Mexican workers were stealing U.S. jobs. Crossborder dialogue helped to identify the true winners and losers under a specific set of policies. Participants and observers alike realized that workers in all three countries shared common problems, though admittedly the problems vary in intensity.

2. There is growing public support in the United States for an alternative vision. The alternatives work has been conditioned by the political reality that there does not currently exist a political coalition in any of the three countries with a majority to pass the vision posited in "Alternatives for the Americas." Hence, it becomes easy for the press and politicians to dismiss this vision as utopian.

At the same time, public opinion polls, in the United States at least, show that the majority support some notion of fair trade. A December 1999 poll by the Business School of the University of Maryland (2000) indicates that an astounding 93 percent of U.S. citizens support the inclusion of labor and environmental standards in trade agreements. This public perception, which the alternatives document and debate helped foster, was a key ingredient in the Clinton administration's failure in 1997 and again in 1998 to obtain fast-track authority from the U.S. Congress to negotiate new free trade agreements. It could also be argued that the alternatives work helped block progress by the WTO in Seattle and defeat, at least for the time being, the Multilateral Agreement on Investment. In this sense, a portion of the alternatives debate became popularized and played a role in the most important victories of the forces allied against corporate-led globalization in recent years.

3. The development of alternative approaches should coincide with the development of representative structures. A central, often unasked, question about the negotiation of an alternative vision is, Who should be at the table and what do they represent? Trade unions have constructed representative structures at the local, regional, national, and hemispheric levels. Other organizations involved in the trinational process have large memberships but varying practices on how to involve members in the positions taken by their organizations. Another set of organizations, such as research institutes, have small or nonexistent memberships and varying degrees of connections to popular movements. Yet all tend to sit around the table as "equal" participants in discussions over common positions taken by coalitions. In the United States, we worked to consult with people from each sector who had a good sense of where others in their sector would stand on any given issue. During the NAFTA debate, we were impressed by the efforts of our counterparts in Canada and Mexico to go beyond this to solicit more broadly the views of people outside of capital cities. Still, we see no ideal models for participation in any of the countries that took part in the alternatives process.

Hence, the question of integrity arises: What is the value of a document pieced together from employees and representatives of this diverse group of organizations? This is a question worth a great deal of reflection. We have stressed that the alternatives document is an organic one that will continue to evolve with the contributions of participants from sectors and regions not previously involved in this effort, but we need to continue to develop better mechanisms for a more democratic and inclusive process.

4. More resources are needed to develop the infrastructure of effective crossborder work. To negotiate NAFTA, the three governments devoted millions of dollars to infrastructure. They had top-level translators and interpreters. They had hundreds of people freed from other duties for the process. As citizen groups, we are still in the beginning stages of developing such an infrastructure. Unions have a relatively strong infrastructure for this work; some other organizations have also built effective structures. Yet overall, across sectors, we lack effective, well-staffed, and resourced entities. This is not to belittle the extraordinary work that members of RMALC, Common Frontiers, and ART did and do in crossborder linking. It is simply to say that the lack of financial resources made the work much more difficult, particularly with regard to document translation, professional interpretation at meetings, and the capacity to consistently reach groups outside of Washington, D.C., with trinational or multinational communications

5. Public support can and must be mobilized for an alternative vision. It is a challenge for our work in the future to present the alternative vision in a way that is more interesting and understandable to the general public. In Mexico and Canada, citizens groups have proved that it is possible through creativity and grassroots mobilization to disseminate alternative ideas more broadly. In Mexico, RMALC was involved in the Liberty Referendum, in which 500,000 citizens endorsed a ten-point agenda for an alternative economic policy. In Canada, Common Frontiers has been involved in the Alternative Federal Budget process, which engages thousands of Canadians in education and dialogue around the country's economic priorities. Both of these efforts featured short, accessible pamphlets based on more detailed documents that were instrumental in reaching a broader audience. The next phase of work on "Alternatives for the Americas" will be to draw on the diverse talents and expertise of many people involved in this dialogue to disseminate this vision more broadly and continue to develop consensus around an alternative.

6. Our work must extend beyond simply reacting to the official agenda. The work described in this paper resulted from outrage over a corporate and government proposal to further reduce barriers to trade and investment among our nations. We organized nationally, sectorally, cross-sectorally, and across borders to counter the corporate government agenda. We met at the time of their meetings. When they expanded the official talks from North America to the rest of the hemisphere, we expanded our organizing accordingly. In other words, our work has been reactive to their agenda. This raises the question, if governments were to abandon the further spread of free trade agreements, would our crossborder work stop as well?

The problem is a simple one. It is easier to organize against a very bad proposal of those in power than it is to organize for something among those with less power. Yet here, the defeat of fast-track trading authority and the paralysis of the WTO in Seattle offer a new moment. The forces attempting to slow and reshape the globalization agenda have scored major victories, yet our collective power has been strengthened. In this new period, we should consider ways to balance the creation of our own dynamic with our work reacting to the official agenda.

Conclusions

The debate over the global economy has reached a turning point. The WTO debacle in Seattle, the defeat of fast-track authority in the U.S. Congress and of the Multilateral Agreement on Investment (MAI), and the increased criticism of the global financial system in the wake of the Asian financial crisis have all contributed to a breakdown in the official consensus around free trade and investment. For the citizens' movement, the challenge for the future will be to push alternative agendas through this crack in the consensus. Over the past decade, we have begun to articulate the principles, policies, and politics of fair trade that place the goals of equality, democracy, good jobs, and a clean environment above the goal of increased corporate profits. Now is the time for the citizens' backlash to overcome its many challenges and become the "frontlash" for a new global economy that steers the benefits of economic activity to the majority and ensures that our planet will be preserved in the twenty-first century.

Appendix—Alternatives for the Americas: Building a People's Hemispheric Agreement

This document reflects an ongoing, collaborative process to establish concrete and viable alternatives, based on the interests of the peoples of our hemisphere, to the Free Trade Area of the Americas. The full document is available on the following website: http://www.web.net/comfront or by writing to: Common Frontiers, 15 Gervais Drive, Suite 305, Don Mills,

Ontario, M3C1Y8, Canada. Comments are welcome, as the document will continue to be revised.

General principles. Trade and investment should not be ends in themselves, but rather the instruments for achieving just and sustainable development. Citizens must have the right to participate in the formulation, implementation, and evaluation of hemispheric social and economic policies. Central goals of these policies should be to promote economic sovereignty, social welfare, and reduced inequality at all levels.

Human rights. Countries of the Americas should build a common human rights agenda to be included in every hemispheric agreement, along with mechanisms and institutions to ensure full implementation and enforcement. This agenda should promote the broadest definition of human rights, covering civil, political, economic, social, cultural, and environmental rights; gender equity; and rights relating to indigenous peoples and communities.

Environment. Hemispheric agreements should allow governments to channel investment towards environmentally sustainable economic activities, while establishing plans for the gradual "internalization" (taking into account) of the social and environmental costs of unsustainable production and consumption.

Labor. Hemispheric agreements should include provisions that guarantee the basic rights of working men and women, ensure proper assistance for adjustment as markets are opened up, and promote the improvement of working and living standards of workers and their families.

Immigration. Economic and financial agreements should include agreements regarding migrant workers. These agreements should recognize the diversity in immigration-related situations in different countries by allowing for variation in immigration policies but also facilitating funding for programs designed to improve employment opportunities in areas that are major net exporters of labor. At the same time, governments should ensure uniform application of their national labor rights for all workers—regardless of immigration status—and severely penalize employers that violate these rights.

Role of the state. Hemispheric agreements should not undermine the ability of the nation-state to meet its citizens' social and economic needs. At the same time, the goal of national economic regulations should not be traditional protectionism, but ensuring that private sector economic activities promote fair and sustainable development. Likewise, agreements should allow nation-states to maintain public sector corporations and procurement policies that support national development goals while fighting government corruption.

Investment. Hemispheric rules should encourage foreign investment that generates high-quality jobs, sustainable production, and economic stability, while allowing governments to screen out investments that make no net contribution to development, especially speculative capital flows. Citizens groups and all levels of government should have the right to sue investors that violate investment rules.

Finance. To promote economic stability, agreements should establish a tax on foreign exchange transactions that would also generate development funds, while allowing governments to institute taxes on speculative profits, require that portfolio investments remain in the country for a specified period, and provide incentives for direct and productive investments. To help level the playing field, low-income nations should be allowed to renegotiate foreign debts to reduce principal owed, lower interest rates, and lengthen repayment terms.

Intellectual property. Agreements should protect the rights and livelihoods of farmers, fishing folk, and communities that act as guardians of biodiversity and not allow corporate interests to undermine these rights. Rules should exclude all life forms from patentability and protect the collective intellectual property of local communities and peoples, especially with regard to medicinal plants. Rules should also ensure that copyright laws protect artists, musicians, and other cultural workers, and not just the publishing and entertainment industries.

Sustainable energy development. A hemispheric agreement should allow members to file complaints against countries that try to achieve commercial advantage at the expense of sustainability. International agencies should cooperate to create regulatory incentives for energy efficiency and renewable energy and promote related technologies, while eliminating policies that subsidize or encourage fossil fuel sales, consumption, and use.

Agriculture. To ensure food security, countries should have the right to protect or exclude staple foods from trade agreements. Hemispheric measures should also support upward harmonization of financial assistance for agriculture (as a percentage of GDP), strengthened protections for agricultural laborers, and traditional rights of indigenous peoples to live off ancestral lands.

Market access. Access for foreign products and investments should be evaluated and defined within the framework of national development plans. Timetables for tariff reduction should be accompanied by programs to ensure that domestic industries become competitive during the transition. With regard to nontariff barriers, measures are necessary to ensure that they reflect legitimate social interests rather than protections for specific companies.

Enforcement and dispute resolution. If the proposed rules and standards are to be meaningful, they must be accompanied by strong mechanisms for dispute resolution and enforcement that are focused on reducing inequalities and based on fair and democratic processes. Agreements may also include special safeguards for countries suffering as the result of surges in imports.

Notes

1. Landau's and Jimenez's statements were made during the "Lessons from U.S.-Mexico Binational Civil Society Coalitions" conference, University of California–Santa Cruz, July 9–11, 1998.

12

National Coalitions and Global Campaigns: The International Children's Rights Movement

Tom Lent and Roy Trivedy

In 1989, the United Nations Convention on the Rights of the Child (CRC) passed into international law, subsequently to be ratified by 160 governments around the world. This makes the CRC the most widely supported international legal instrument in existence. In the decade since its adoption, the convention has helped to unite a wide variety of organizations working with and for children in a coordinated effort to promote children's rights. The children's rights movement shows how a very broad legal framework can help disparate agendas to come together, find room to maneuver between universal human rights and the diverse ways of interpreting and realizing those rights in practice, and enable mutually reinforcing actions at different levels of the global system. NGOs and other groups in civil society embrace radically different ideologies and approaches to the needs and rights of children, but they have been able to work together synergistically under the broad umbrella of the convention. Perhaps most important of all, the two cases reviewed in this chapter show how national and international NGOs can support each other in developing campaigns from the bottom up, so that policy positions and new legislation are solidly rooted in a domestic constituency, including at the grassroots. In this sense, these efforts represent a new generation of NGO advocacy that seeks to break free from the asymmetries and inequalities of previous global campaigns.

Franklin and Franklin (1996: 96–98) identify three phases in the recent history of the child rights movement. The first phase, in the 1970s, was characterized by organizations that claimed the right of participation for children, especially in education. The second phase, they note, recalls the child-saving efforts of the first half of the century, culminating in the International Year of the Child in 1979 and its emphasis on children's welfare and protection. Phase three commenced with the signing of the CRC in 1989, signaling a shift to a more holistic understanding of children's rights and explicit recognition of the right to participation. As Franklin and Franklin explain, the CRC has four "baskets," or categories, that advance different dimensions of children's rights: child survival, integrated protection, development, and children's participation. While the first three of these baskets are significant, the fourth breaks new ground in recognizing that children have a right to be heard on issues that affect them. The CRC also calls for coresponsibility between state and civil society in making children's rights a reality.

This shift continued in the major UN conferences of the 1990s, especially the Social Summit in Copenhagen in 1995, and in the form of increasing worldwide concern over child labor, child soldiers, and street children. Work on these issues has established children as social actors in themselves and has broadened commitment to children's rights to development and participation in a range of settings beyond the family and welfare arenas.

The child rights movement is ideologically diverse and includes groups from different political persuasions, contexts, value-bases, and tactics: rural as well as urban, activists as well as welfare groups. Although much of the impetus for the CRC came from international NGOs such as members of the Save the Children Alliance and from multilateral agencies such as UNICEF, the movement has developed strong roots in many countries of the South, especially around the child labor issue. These capacities and connections have helped to make the movement somewhat more democratic than other, issue-based campaigns. In this chapter we review the experience of building such multilayered coalitions in two countries, Guatemala and Mozambique.

The Social Movement for Children in Guatemala

Over 50 percent of Guatemala's population are aged eighteen or under, with estimates of the number of working children as high as two million in a country of only eleven million people (LaRue et al. 1998). Fewer than half of all school-age children are in school. In addition, children continue to suffer the consequences of a thirty-six-year civil war that left over one million people displaced and over 250,000 dead or missing (Arzobispado de Guatemala 1998; CEH 1998). Violence, together with a political culture of authoritarianism, exclusion, intolerance, discrimination, and inequity, are reflected in social and institutional relationships that include the school and the family. Child discipline often takes the form of verbal and physical abuse in the home and school. However, rural Guatemala also has a strong tradition of community organization and self-help as well as pride in Mayan heritage. Peasant organizations, the women's and environmental movements, and bottom-up democracy via civic committees are all gaining momentum.

In May 1990, Guatemala became the fifth country in the world to adopt the UN Convention on the Rights of the Child. The convention obliges signatories to enact legislation that puts its provisions into national laws and practice. Over the next few years, NGOs and government agencies working with children formed an umbrella organization called the Committee for the Defense of the Rights of the Child (PRODEN), along with similar networks for children's rights groups and for child-focused international NGOs and donor agencies. Early financial support and experience came from UNICEF, Save the Children, the German Foreign Aid Agency (GTZ), and the European Union, but it was Guatemalan organizations that took the lead in developing the new Legal Code for Children and Young People, which was approved unanimously by the Guatemalan Congress on September 27, 1996. Because the new code required the setting up of new juridical processes for children and new institutions to promote, defend, and protect children's rights, Congress determined that a year was needed to make the necessary preparations and resource allocations for the new law to go into effect as planned. PRODEN and the other umbrella bodies began to prepare for implementation of the code by forming a national institute on children, state-level CRC committees, municipal "children and youth councils," a central technical support unit, and translations into the major Mayan languages. Although the Guatemalan Peace Accords of December 1996 provided a political framework for these changes through their support for civic participation and institutional reform, they also intensified feelings of xenophobia as a conservative reaction to foreign influence and what some saw as unwarranted international interference in domestic affairs.

As the date of enactment approached, opposition to the code began to grow in influential parts of the media, government, and Congress, culminating in postponement of the code for a further six months. Opposition came from economic interests (concerned at measures against child labor and stricter controls on adoptions by foreign nationals), religious interests (alarmed at measures perceived as antifamily and as threats to parental authority), and political parties who used the debate to further factional interests. In the face of this opposition, and seeing the likelihood of another postponement, PRODEN and its allies called a meeting to discuss future strategy. Participants realized that the code had not come from consultation with parents, families, and children themselves. Nor had they been sufficiently sophisticated in their lobbying efforts. The code was more than a set of laws—it was a redefinition of social relationships and commitments within and across society, but the reforms lacked the necessary social base to support them. As a result, PRODEN and the other networks increased their work with the mass media, including procode spots on radio and television and articles in major newspapers. The message was also taken to the highest levels of government by building targeted support in Congress and working to find allies in the executive branch. A detailed mapping exercise identified key actors and their positions on the code, and strategies were elaborated to work in different ways with those who supported reform, those who opposed it, and those still undecided.

While progress was being made in taking the case to the media and to other power brokers, a large gap still existed in social mobilization—in stimulating a broadly based movement for children's rights. Following centuries of racial and class discrimination and three decades of political repression, children's rights—still less a legal code for children—were not issues that were easily understood or accepted by the majority of the public. Children's rights groups had not built enough bridges with other social movements, including women's and Mayan organizations, universities, labor unions, peasant associations, and progressive mayors. Rather than marketing the code to a skeptical and suspicious public, PRODEN formed and trained a group of facilitators to reach out to different sectors of society in a succession of meetings and workshops. The aim was to help ordinary people see, feel, and promote children's rights as their own as well as to define how to apply them in their own context. The task was to build a social movement to defend children's rights across the country.

As the movement evolved, tensions emerged around membership, leadership, and strategy—principally, how much time and resources to devote to media campaigns, lobbying Congress and the executive branch, and social mobilization. The social mobilization group focused on preparing for the Summit for Children, to be held immediately prior to the code's enactment as a display of mass support. At the first "multisectoral encounter," held to prepare for the summit, eighty-nine organizations attended, including national and international NGOs, PRODEN and other apex bodies, mayors and municipal authorities, and representatives from government. Other representatives came from teachers' associations, youth organizations, the national network of parents and organizations that work with disabled children, Mayan organizations, human rights organizations, and the women's movement. The Summit for Children was held on March 24, 1997 (three days before the deadline for enactment), with over sixty-five organizations in attendance and two thousand people (including 600 children) marching to the National Palace. A second summit was held in Quezaltenango (the country's second largest city) and a third in a key rural department that surpassed even these numbers. A sense of identity and momentum in the movement was developing.

During the weeks leading up to March 27, the debate intensified in the media and in Congress. President Alvaro Arzu encouraged Plan Avanzado Nacional (PAN) Party leaders in Congress to hold a series of open forums with all the relevant parties, aimed at securing a consensus around the most contentious parts of the legal code. Support came from all sides except the political opposition (fundamentalist religious groups and conservative economic forces), who walked out of these sessions when they saw that they were losing their argument in order to delay enactment. Three days later, the government decided to postpone enactment for another six months. Predictably, when that deadline arrived, the code was postponed yet again, this time for eighteen months until March 27, 2000 (after the national elections in November 1999). With municipal elections on the horizon, the government had decided that they could not risk alienating the opposition by acceding to the code. Indeed, it was the opposition party that won the November national election, led by a former general who had become an outspoken member of a fundamentalist religious group. Within weeks of coming to office, the new government had shelved the code.

Lessons Learned

Despite these setbacks, the movement for children's rights in Guatemala made significant advances in the years between 1996 and 2000. Official support from the Catholic Church was secured, and efforts were made to build bridges with the Alliance of Evangelical Churches, an influential source of opposition. This resulted in a temporary agreement with the leadership of the alliance.

The Social Movement for Children and Youth Rights created a secretariat, a strategic plan, and an evaluation of lessons learned. Other groups now refer to the group publicly by name and invite it to participate in their forums. Congress, for example, recently requested a progress report from the movement on children's issues, and movement representatives have been asked to appear in Congress in key meetings related to children.

However, a number of important questions emerge from these lessons. First, how does one create a national movement that represents a diverse population and offers participants a genuine sense of belonging and ownership? That means working much more deliberately and creatively at the grassroots level in rural and urban areas as well as with local government. The UN convention and the proposed legal code are valuable legal instruments, but they are essentially top-down in nature. What is lacking is the process of understanding and internalizing children's rights to create a public culture of respect and enforcement.

Second, the movement needs to facilitate closer relationships with parts of civil society that are not directly engaged with children's issues but can identify with the general principles of social justice, civic participation, and equity and that might eventually assume coresponsibility for acting in children's best interests.

Third, the movement recognizes that in order to become a viable alternative, it needs to build a new kind of leadership that is multicentered and shared. A different paradigm of internal organization, structure, and coordination is required to reflect core values of equity and democratic participation.

Fourth, the movement needs to define clear criteria for choosing the issues it wants to pursue—for example, progressive abolition of the worst forms of child labor, educational reform, and peace-building. And in order to secure its legitimacy with the public at large, it must create a stronger identity that conveys credibility, expertise, representation, openness, transparency, and effectiveness.

On a practical level, the movement for children's rights in Guatemala now has an administrative structure, a governing body, a work plan to address the key strategic questions, and a long-term vision. But it still needs to build stronger links within civil society and increase its capacity to influence the state at different levels (these two things being closely related). Forging a true social movement, rather than just a network of NGOs and their allies, requires a high degree of commitment, vision, and capacity among members.

The debate over children's rights and the legal code, though not formally part of the Guatemalan Peace Accords, should be seen within this broader context with its intention to build new relationships within and between civil society and government. The peace process provided a positive atmosphere for change and reform, and the children's rights movement took advantage of the political openings this atmosphere created. On the other hand, both the peace process and the children's rights movement were seen by conservative elements in Guatemalan society as driven by foreign agendas. The legal code became an especially easy target for these critics because it lacked the national and international backing given to the broader peace process. The future of the movement will be determined by the quality of the links it develops with children's rights organizations at both the international level and at the grassroots. Until now, however, these international links (especially with UNICEF and the International Save the Children Alliance) have been stronger than the movement's local base. So although international support and advice have fostered the early growth of the Guatemalan children's rights movement, these connections have not been enough to force change. Nevertheless, the movement may have laid the foundations essential for future success. As national and international forces and pressures continue to converge, it will be easier to transform the status quo at both levels because of a strong social base and an engaged public constituency. This may herald a new era in the global movement for children's rights.

The Agenda for Action for Children in Mozambique

In February 1998, the three Save the Children Alliance organizations active in Mozambique plus UNICEF organized a retreat for senior staff to identify possible areas for collaboration in capacity building and commitment to children's rights. The group agreed that priority would go to developing the Agenda for Action for Mozambican Children, founded on a broadly based understanding of the situation of children in the country and a national consensus on the way ahead. The Agenda for Action was regarded as a critical initiative because it was seen as a way of addressing the situation of children in the country in an integrated fashion (children being the majority of people regarded as poor). As a result, the Save the Children Alliance and UNICEF provided financial and technical support for the Government of Mozambique's *Report to the UN Committee on the Rights of the Child* and helped to develop a national strategy for child rights training and an advocacy and communications strategy for the Agenda for Action.

This common agenda was formulated in a series of workshops organized by the Save the Children Alliance, UNICEF, and the *Fundacao Para O Desenvolvimento da Communidade*. The workshops involved representatives from government (the Ministries of Social Action, Finance and Planning, and Education and Health), civil society, and international organizations. For most participants, these workshops represented a first attempt to forge a broad alliance in defense of children's rights in Mozambique. Young people also participated in the drafting process—this was the first time that many of the adults had been involved in a meeting with young people. For many adults, working alongside children who were articulating their own rights was a new experience, at times uncomfortable, but several organizations later used this approach in their own work. Workshop participants agreed that the Agenda for Action would serve as a common framework to guide the efforts of all those working to promote the needs and rights of Mozambican children—a compact between government, civil society, and international organizations. It was also agreed that the agenda would be used to guide the advocacy, social mobilization, and programming efforts of all organizations toward a common set of objectives over the period 2000–2020.

Four key principles underlie the development of the agenda:

- The need to analyze clearly the existing situation of children in Mozambique (approximately 55 percent of the population of the country is under the age of eighteen);
- The importance of developing a communications strategy to promote understanding of children's rights as well as society's obligations;
- The importance of developing, among adults and children, a vision

of rights for Mozambican children, along with the identification of goals and strategies to achieve this vision;

• The need to facilitate a process in which participants can integrate learning, discussion, and planning in order to develop a concrete plan of action.

Since the Agenda for Action sought to mobilize a broad alliance of organizations and the general public, its preparation had to be inclusive, tied into a strategy to promote awareness and commitment at the grassroots. That meant it had to be easily accessible, user-friendly, and short. The agenda has mirrored the structure of the UN Convention on the Rights of the Child, but it ties the realization of these rights explicitly to the Mozambican context: first, by beginning with a detailed review of the policy environment and the extent to which current policies and actions respond to children's needs; and second, by crafting a vision for (and by) Mozambican children for the future, including how young people themselves will be involved in shaping this vision on the ground. Clear goals and strategies are being identified for each priority area, along with the resources required to meet them, methods for monitoring progress, and clear institutional arrangements that define how different organizations intend to work together.

This process will be guided by a preparatory commission comprising representatives from government, NGOs, international organizations, and a technical working group located in the Ministry of Women and Social Action to support and facilitate the commission's work. District and regional consultations are being held to generate popular support for the agenda, with the aim of developing a social pact—a genuine movement in defense of children's rights. The first stages of this process were completed by the end of the year 2000.

Outcomes and Lessons Learned

Although it is too early to judge the extent to which this process will result in genuine improvements in the lives of children and young people in Mozambique, the initial phase of the work has resulted in some positive signs. First, the willingness of government, NGOs, and other civic leaders to participate in shaping the agenda has been very high. Within months of the launch of the process in 1998, over one hundred organizations committed themselves to work for the agenda and its implementation. Since 1999, the alliance has seen continued interest and active involvement from a wide group of agencies and individuals.

Second, Mozambican organizations show growing ownership of the process; collaboration among groups continues to increase, along with greater motivation and commitment among their staff. This has been supported by the launch of the National Child Rights Resource Center, which has created the sense of an active movement in society.

Third, the development of the agenda is stimulating innovation around the tools and techniques required in advocacy and public communications, including a Portuguese version of the Training Pack for Journalists on Interviewing Children; printing and dissemination of the Ministry of Women and Social Action's policies related to children and of the Child Rights Convention; and a training manual in Portuguese on child rights, field tested in Mozambique. Many organizations have commented that these tools have increased their capacity to plan and implement child rights work.

Fourth, a variety of innovative methods were used to compile a situation analysis for children, highlighting the diversity of children's lives and visions of childhood in the country, the aspirations of children and young people for the future, key areas for additional research about children's lives, and the implications of public policies relating to children (for example, work on the implications of government expenditure patterns).[1] The government's *Report to the UN Committee on the Rights of the Child* has also been completed. The report documents the existing situation of children in the country (in key sectors—health, education, and so forth—and geographically) and outlines the measures that are currently supported by government, civil society, and others to address the gap in rights. The report also provides details of some of the most innovative and exciting plans for working with and for children in Mozambique from 2000 to 2010.

Fifth, children and young people are beginning to be viewed as social actors in their own right in Mozambique, rather than as passive recipients of foreign aid. Organizations that have always worked with children as beneficiaries have begun to consult and involve them in decisionmaking, and to help them to think more critically about their activities. This has also been evident among key organizations in the emergency operations following the recent Mozambican floods.

Sixth, there is some evidence that work on the agenda has enhanced capacity in Mozambican society for the fulfillment of children's rights—for example, in the Ministry of Women and Social Action, which is responsible for coordinating the preparation of the government's report for the child rights committee—and is the lead ministry for the development of the Agenda for Action. There is also some evidence to suggest that work on the Agenda for Action has strengthened the capacity of some NGOs. By strengthening relations among individuals, communities, and organizations across society, the process also has great potential to enhance social capital in Mozambique. A key element in the success of the process thus far has been that each organization has respected and valued the contributions of the others. This has not removed disagreements along the way, but thus far it has been possible to resolve or manage these tensions successfully. Mutual respect, a strong sense of reciprocal accountability, and a common commitment to a process that has been inclusive and participatory have been important factors here.

Seventh, the International Save the Children Alliance and UNICEF have sought to strengthen the agenda-setting process by constantly looking for ways of linking the national process with the international movement for children's rights. Examples include connections with other human rights networks; work on HIV/AIDS elsewhere in Africa; work on the Children's Budget in South Africa; and work on child-centered participatory research that builds on experiences from West and Eastern Africa, South Asia, and Latin America. These international links are crucial, but they are complementary to, not a substitute for, a genuine national process—not just something restricted to the capital Maputo, but one built on regional and other subnational consultations. The challenge for development organizations is to find ways of working more effectively together across boundaries of geography and sector in order to promote common goals. In this way, the international movement for children's rights will grow from strong local foundations, and international pressure will reinforce local activism and experience.

Although the Agenda for Mozambican Children has generated positive early gains, critical areas remain to be addressed, including the need to

- develop mechanisms to ensure that children and young people are genuinely involved in the process, girls as well as boys;
- find better ways of mobilizing organizations in civil society (community based organizations as well as NGOs, adults as well as children);
- ensure that all government ministries that have a bearing on children's lives genuinely participate in this movement and that participation is not just confined to the Ministry of Women and Social Action;
- involve the media and the private sector in promoting the agenda much more forcefully;
- ensure that the agenda becomes a national priority, not something confined to the work of specific organizations working in certain parts of the country;
- develop networks and links with the global children's rights movement that can both support and be supported by work at local and national levels.

There is clearly much still to do and learn. One of the key lessons so far has been the importance of actively seeking to involve grassroots constituencies (especially children themselves) at every stage in the process. Another key lesson is that every opportunity must be used by participants to reinforce and strengthen social movements during the early stages of their formation—without such efforts it is difficult to maintain momentum. The Agenda for Action aims to sustain a process that will result in real improvements in the lives of Mozambican children, both current and future generations, and that will contribute to the global movement for children's rights as it continues to exert its influence around the world.

Conclusion

The 1990s witnessed significant progress in the movement for children's rights at every level. Children and young people began to be acknowledged and respected as capable citizens, development actors in their own right and not merely appendages to the adult world of democracy and decision-making. They are "key political actors seeking to establish their rights to protection, but also their rights to participate in a range of settings which extend beyond the social and welfare arenas" (Franklin and Franklin 1996: 111). It is important to note that these gains have not been driven by any central authority but by a unifying belief that children do have rights and that economic and political decisions must always be taken "in the best interests of the child." The movement has protected space for diverse and sometimes contradictory ways of interpreting these beliefs and of realizing children's rights in different contexts. This has been a major source of strength and coherence.

The two cases reviewed in brief in this chapter show that—though enormously time-consuming, difficult, and subject to constant reverses of fortune—it is possible for national and international NGOs, governments, and other actors to work together in forging a national consensus for progressive policy change and new legislation. The development of a domestic constituency for reform, and of strong links to grassroots support, should make it more difficult to overturn short-term gains and more likely that progress will be sustained by local ownership and pressure into the future. At the same time, progress on the ground in Mozambique and Guatemala would not have been possible without resources from, and alliances with, international agencies. In neither case was the combination of national and international forces sufficient to guarantee success, yet both show the importance of international pressure in generating a sustainable national movement. This has important implications for future NGO campaigns, which need consciously to plan for slow, long-term work in movement building. However, the careful groundwork laid in Mozambique, Guatemala, and elsewhere could help to drive the international children's rights movement to another level, with a stronger social base committed to internal democracy. This would be a major achievement for global citizen action and for the universal rights of children.

Notes

Roy Trivedy is grateful to Mark Stirling, Anita Menete, Joao Jussar, Etelvina da Cunha, Armando Freschaut and many others who have provided valuable advice and comments on this paper. Any errors that remain are my sole responsibility.
    1. See, for example, S. Robinson and L. Biersteker (1997).

13

Handing Over the Stick: The Global Spread of Participatory Approaches to Development

Kamal Singh

How to strengthen the participation of ordinary people in their own development has long been an important issue in international development circles. From early community participation concepts in the 1950s, to the international declarations about popular participation of the 1970s, to participatory action research in the 1980s, different generations of development activists and professionals have come together around the world to debate what participation is and how it can best be realized. The past decade in particular has witnessed its own wave of interest in the discussion of participatory methods and concepts on an international scale. The term *participation* is now used almost universally, by a wide range of adherents and proponents ranging from local development workers to the president of the World Bank.

One factor influencing the way that the ideas and values of participation became so widely embraced during the 1990s is that participatory development practitioners, academics, and people living in poor communities around the world developed exciting new practical approaches to put their concepts into action. One such approach that emerged predominantely during the 1990s is known as participatory rural appraisal (PRA), "a family of methods and approaches aimed at involving local people in the definition and analysis of local conditions as a basis for their action" (IDS 1996:1).[1] Since the first village-level experimentation in the late 1980s in Kenya and India with what is now called PRA, it has grown to become a global phenomenon. Today PRA is reported to be used in over 100 countries. There are scores of PRA-related networks throughout the world. NGOs and other development agencies have adopted its approaches in the field, while international and national development organizations are also drafting key policy papers using insights derived from its practice. In under a decade, a new cadre of participatory development practitioners has emerged worldwide, across a broad spectrum of development activities, with similar definitions of what they are attempting to do, and with the ability to maintain contact with each other in order to share experience. The spread of a value-based approach to development across institutional, ideological, linguistic, cultural, and political divides is a fascinating case of citizen action to promote new ideas and innovations in an integrated world.

The wide currency that PRA has gained is in some ways surprising. Embedded in the way PRA has been explained and promoted through writing, training, and advocacy are calls for paradigmatic shifts in development professionals' attitudes and behavior; concepts of professionalism, and thus the power relations between development workers and those they are supposed to serve; the way development workers value different kinds of knowledge; institutional processes and procedures; and generally the way we understand different social actors' roles and responsibilities in development processes. Some may argue that despite the quietly revolutionary rhetoric about PRA, it is increasingly used as a quick and dirty technology for information extraction, such that it doesn't challenge the way development business is done. But despite the risk of co-optation, the ideals of PRA continue to survive in the minds of many practitioners, and in the way they insist on practicing and promoting it. We must ask, Why has something as apparently inconvenient and potentially challenging as PRA gained such a high degree of acceptance and currency throughout the development community?

One answer lies in the way that PRA has served as a rallying point to bring together diverse combinations of trainers, government staff, researchers, policymakers, and donors at local, regional, and international levels through a variety of networking mechanisms. In the course of sharing their experiences, many have also discovered that underlying their interest in PRA are similar values and commitments, and they have built new networks and relationships among themselves as a result. In this chapter I will explore some of the ways in which these networking processes happened as well as their contribution to strengthening a global constituency in support of participation in development.

What Is PRA?

Since the 1970s development has involved the use of differing participatory approaches to research, learning, and action.[2] One of these strands, growing primarily from the area of agricultural and rural development in the late 1970s and early 1980s was initially called rapid rural appraisal (RRA).

Arising from dissatisfactions over the antipoverty biases inherent in the way outsiders interacted with the rural poor, such as the tendency to visit only villages that were close to main roads and at certain seasons, and a recognition of the shortcomings of questionnaire-led research, RRA was an attempt at effective and more timely methods of learning. Though it provided an efficient and useful range of methods and raised the status of local knowledge in the estimation of outsiders, the approach fell short of handing over processes of analysis to local people. Researchers collected information, with the cooperation of local people, and took it away in their notebooks for later analysis and use in external decisionmaking.

Development professionals first experimented with making this process more participatory, for example by handing over the creation of maps, models, and other representations of village information to local people, in Kenya and India in the late 1980s. These experiments revealed incredible potential for villagers to enter their own complex processes of analysis by using visual representations. What had previously been the preserve of researchers, sketched only in their notebooks, quickly became a powerful tool in the hands of local people, who publicly created diagrams on the ground using local materials. A plethora of methods emerged in a period of intense trials, mainly in parts of India. The resulting products confirmed the value of freeing up the process for local people to invent and innovate new forms of analysis and representation. This important step was the basis for the shift beyond RRA, to participatory rural appraisal, later simply known as participatory learning and action (PLA).[3]

Early innovators quickly learned that making this new PRA approach work also required shifts in the attitude and behaviors of outsiders.[4] These shifts start with recognizing that the previous posturing of outsiders as experts crowded out possibilities for learning from and with local people. The analysis of knowledge by local people, it was thought, could best be facilitated by development workers with

- a commitment to learning (in a reversed or inverted and shared manner);
- a commitment to handing over control of analytical processes;
- an acceptance of error, as valuable learning moments;
- trust in the ability of local people;
- a self-critical awareness of their own role, behavior, and attitudes.

The results of work undertaken by those attempting to introduce these elements proved convincing enough to inspire more and more practitioners to make similar attempts. In addition to the key aspects of methods, not to mention personal behavior and attitudes, from the early stages, innovators also placed emphasis on the notion of sharing. Initially this was taken to mean sharing in the field (of village tasks and food) as well as during PRA training (of learning and insights). Increasingly, however, the emphasis on sharing and learning from one another led to a growing movement for sharing across countries, sectors, and approaches.

The Global Spread of PRA

With an emphasis on sharing, learning, and innovation, the use of PRA spread in the course of only a decade from a few rural villages in India and Kenya to an approach familiar to development professionals around the world, used at the local as well as the policy level. The story of how this happened is an important one, with potential lessons for other efforts by civil society actors who aim to have a global impact founded on and strengthened by local work.

From the earliest days, some key individuals have played an important role in the development and spread of PRA. One notable champion of this approach, Robert Chambers of the Institute of Development Studies (IDS) at the University of Sussex, played a crucial role in actively encouraging early adopters. Chambers's training, networking, writing, and travels catalyzed PRA activities in valuable ways. He was also responsible for the early publications that informed this work widely across the English speaking world. Additionally, he has played a key role in sensitizing government officials, donor agencies, academics, and others to the ideas of PRA, and in many instances has played the roles of convenient outsider and wise foreigner.

While the role of an energetic ambassador has been important, Chambers is the first to point out that others played an equally critical role. In a short space of time, a whole cadre of experienced trainers and facilitators began to conduct PRA workshops at a furious pace around the world. Indian trainers were particularly active from the early days. For example, in 1991, Robert Chambers took part in training exercises in Botswana, Kenya, Tanzania, Sweden, UK, and Zimbabwe. Also in 1991, Neela Mukerjee, of the National Academy of Administration, India, went to Zimbabwe and Botswana to train agricultural scientists there. James Mascarenhas, of MYRADA, India, trained NGO staff in the Philippines and Zimbabwe.[5] Parmesh Shah, from the Aga Khan Rural Support Program (AKRSP), India, spent three weeks training in Vietnam, and soon Sheelu Francis and Meera Shah were also conducting many training programs. In the same year, Selina Adjebeng-Asem of Nigeria trained in Ethiopia. Jules Pretty, Irene Guijt, Ian Scoones, and John Thompson, from the International Institute of Environment and Development (IIED), UK, started to conduct pioneering PRA training in Africa, Asia, and Latin America.

These workshops were designed to reflect the core values of the PRA approach. They were relatively long, as one criticism of previous work at the local level was that it rushed at the convenience of outsiders. Workshops were conducted on site, or with intense periods of field interaction. The training style was participatory, to the extent that some early facilitators prided themselves on having no predetermined agenda for the sessions. Trainers strove to be flexible in order to accommodate participant expectations, and they used an informal style.

Most trainers, early practitioners, and hosts of training events were connected with NGOs, and, with a few notable exceptions, most were from the Southern hemisphere. It was strikingly contrary that research tools were being derived from the interactions happening at a grassroots level, involving very few academics.[6] It was significant that the seeds of a global phenomena, which would eventually reach the dizzy heights of international policy influence, were mostly sown by local development workers.

The work of traveling champions often resulted in ongoing engagement with institutions and processes in their various ports of call (for example, James Mascarenhas in Southern Africa, Kamal Kar in Southeast Asia and Bangladesh, and Parmesh Shah in Zambia). These trainers were working across the globe and within countries in a diversity of geographic locations, cultures, political configurations, sectors, and social environments. Graphic representations of these experiences, that is, slides, PRA publications, and workshop handouts, enhanced possibilities for crossfertilization but also held the dangers of the wholesale importation of inappropriate ways of working and standardization of methods. Traveling champions were often used as the wise foreigner to leverage space with governments, particularly to legitimize the use of PRA methods.

Early training initiatives, supported by IDS and IIED, quickly created a second generation of practitioners and trainers in many countries. The initial training conducted by traveling champions often involved local facilitators with little or no PRA experience. Endowed with the confidence of experience in training, however, local participants were quick to take on responsibilities as educators. In many instances, local trainers discarded previous responsibilities within their institutions, sometimes leaving their institutions altogether, to concentrate on PRA training. Some appropriated the role of traveling champion within their own regions. Their proximity, insights on local ways of working, linguistic skills, and cultural awareness were crucial additions to the manner in which PRA methodologies were being developed at the local level. Furthermore, local practitioners often assumed responsibility for engagements with longer horizons than mere training activity and probably contributed more significantly than traveling champions to processes that required more than training input, such as program design and institutionalization.

The participatory styles used in early workshops, with an emphasis on peer learning, mutual support, and sharing, led to many attempts to use the training programs themselves to lay the foundation for ongoing, postworkshop learning and sharing. These processes were often conceived of as informal networks, with regular sharing events. In South Africa, for instance, nine training events held in 1992–1993 in different parts of the country yielded nine potential networking processes. Several informal processes in turn became institutionalized as PRA networks, some with funding, staff, and offices (as in Nepal, Kenya, Tanzania, and South Africa). These served as recognized and largely accessible points of contact, where published information resources could be pooled, information on training and trainers could be made available, and activities could be coordinated. Networking activities provided unique opportunities for people working in diverse institutional, sectoral, and geographic areas to meet and share perspectives. In many cases, PRA training and networking activities provided the opportunities for NGOs and government staff to meet with each other in a peer-to-peer situation. (For example, in 1996 the Sri Lankan PRA network reported having a membership complement of 35 percent from government, 36 percent from local NGOs, 21 percent from international NGOs, and the remainder from training institutes.) Local and national networks began to play invaluable roles in sustaining interest, crossfertilizing across sectors and institutions, lobbying and advocacy, and mobilizing appropriate resources (information and skilled persons) in short periods of time.

Through the late 1990s, after the period of initial dissemination, the number of networks grew rapidly. In 1995 a list of international PRA focal points was published by the IDS. Titled "Sources and Contacts," this list pointed to institutions and individuals who had agreed to serve as a point of first reference in different countries. Some of these were already on the path to becoming fully fledged networks and resource centers. In 1995, the number of entries on the list was twelve in five countries. In January 1999 the same listing comprised eighty-eight entries from fifty-nine countries (including twenty-nine countries in Africa, three in the Middle East, thirteen in Asia, eight in the Americas, two in Australasia, and four in Europe).

The mobility of traveling champions meant that in a short space of time, individuals and institutions interested in and using PRA were identified in various parts of the world. Opportunities were created for these to network with each other, initially, through South-South exchange workshops. Exchanges have been held in India (several involving people from Asia, Africa, Latin America, and Europe), Nepal (for networkers from twelve countries), Philippines (for mainly Asian participants), Zimbabwe (for Southern African practitioners and trainers), Kenya (for African resource center managers), Guinea Bissau (for colleagues from Portuguese-speaking countries), Bolivia (for information workers from Latin America, Africa, Asia, and UK), Argentina (for colleagues from eight Latin American countries), Jordan (for participants from the Middle East and North Africa), and most recently in Senegal (for participants from French-speaking countries).

Almost all of the South-South exchanges have followed the format of PRA trainings to the extent that facilitators used a participatory structure, emphasized peer learning, and asked participants to apply PRA methods in field situations. The opportunity of spending two to three weeks with colleagues, in a retreat situation, offered participants the time to share experiences, identify emerging concerns and challenges, and celebrate new innovations. These interactions also fostered a sense of solidarity within a global project. With experienced minds from across the globe available to reflect on unique challenges and opportunities, participants were able to access a wide range of creative possibilities for their work back home. In later years, after South-South participants had become more experienced with activities in their own countries, they provided feedback and reports through their networks to a broader audience. Many participants also became trainers, involved with capacity building for participatory work, and also passed on what they learned in subsequent workshops. The intimate and involved nature of these experiences laid the basis for PRA practitioners from distant parts of the globe to remain in contact with each other.

In addition to the direct exchanges, field information from early PRA work became available internationally through publications such as *RRA/PLA Notes* (IIED) *and IDS Topic Packs*. The informal nature of these publications allowed for swift and accessible dissemination. With an initial focus on methods, these materials reflected the increasing specialization and sophistication of PRA practice, with a shift toward theme- or sector-specific topics. The availability of these publications at no cost was a crucial factor in giving grassroots institutions the world over access to emerging innovation, trends, and perspectives. The availability of information led in some instances to the establishment of local and national resource centers, often associated with the networks.

Meanwhile, the Internet has introduced a more interactive and immediate way to share experience. In a short time, the majority of PRA related networks and institutions have gained access to email. Although no empirical evidence exists yet, there are signs that South-South interactions increasingly take place using electronic means. Colleagues can now easily access each other outside of South-South workshops and in addition to reading each other's published works.

The results of the early application of PRA must have been convincing to governmental and multilateral institutions, as they were very quick to support (and often demand) PRA-related work. Large multilateral programs integrated PRA content, creating a demand for input from PRA trainers and networks. Governments began large-scale PRA projects at the national level as well. For example, as early as 1995, the Kenyan Ministry of Agriculture proposed PRA for 809 catchments covering 177,000 hectares and serving 93,000 farm families in the 1995–1996 financial year alone. Also in 1995 in India, the National Program for Watershed Management, intended for 30,000 villages in 300 districts covering 15 million hectares, incorporated PRA approaches and methods. This nearly immediate demand for PRA from well-endowed institutions contributed significantly to the spread of the approach, particularly through the training of large numbers of government and NGO staff.

While the South-South dissemination of PRA was critical, also important was the support of Northern groups such as IIED and IDS, which provided training, small-scale funding, networks among people and institutions across the globe, publishing, and key workshops. IDS and IIED also lobbied bilateral donors and international organizations. This South-North link enabled the flow of ideas from microinteractions in Southern field situations to the board rooms, conference halls, and workshops of the powerful Northern development actors. The IDS was able, quite early on, to secure funding for Southern education and networking, something that continues to prove quite difficult for Southern practitioners to do on their own given donor procedures and attitudes. While Northern NGOs and research centers played prominent roles in the initial phases of PRA development, these groups focused their efforts on the South. And, in recent years, Southern actors have taken on increased responsibilities for international events, networking, training, and advocacy.

The existing networks among PRA practitioners around the world have enabled coordinated responses to global-level processes. The project Consultations with the Poor provides a recent example. Initiated by the World Bank as a rapid consultation with poor people in twenty-three countries, this effort aimed to gather perspectives to inform the *World Development Report 2000–2001*. In a short time, colleagues from Nepal, Bolivia, Tanzania, Ghana, Sri Lanka, and India were able to study an initial draft of the World Bank's proposal and offer comments. Through various PRA networks, it was also possible to pilot appropriate methodologies in several countries in a short period of time, improving the approach later applied to the international study. Meera Shah, one of the early PRA trainers, was employed by the Bank to help train other national teams in the largely PRA-based approaches involved. National and international NGOs, as well as a number of PRA networks, mobilized to use their experience not only to influence the global consultation process but, by doing so, also to affect national poverty policy. By 2000 the World Bank and other international agencies were virtually requiring participatory methods first tried in isolated rural villages of India and Africa scarcely a decade before for consultation with poor people in program design.[7]

Factors in the Spread of PRA

What lessons can be drawn from the global spread of PRA to foster other innovations and movements? The previous section identifies a number of important ingredients to the crossfertilization of ideas and techniques. A few additional factors contributed to the worldwide effectiveness of PRA:

Personal excitement and learning generated by the use of PRA. Development professionals are commonly enthused by the depth and quality of insights and knowledge of local people, the apparent empowerment of local people who drive the analytical process, and the chance to work in a novel manner. Several training evaluations report a personal experience of transformation after engaging with villagers in participatory exercises. These trainees then sought unexplored areas of application and techniques with renewed zeal.

Indeed, some incredulous stories have found their way through what I call the bush telegraph. I have heard claims that the national census of Nepal used PRA, PRA transformed completely the entire Indian bureaucracy, and that the planning of a hospital in Scandanavia used PRA. Every contact with a fellow PRA practitioner reveals new stories. Practitioners emerge from field interactions charged with energies that threaten to change the world. The lesson is that the enabling of personal experiences, which generate enthusiasm and personal change, is critical for the spread of a new idea.

An energetic and ardent cadre of first generation champions who contributed to a second generation of champions and trainers. Again, the excitement of early pioneers quickly translated into dissemination. Early champions gave the sense that PRA was a significant breakthrough. They were also quick to support a second generation of champions, and to open the way for them to bring new innovations and energy. Subsequently, the ability of second generation trainers to carry deeper and longer-term perspectives on PRA into early South-South exchanges probably helped to broaden discussions beyond microinteractions (which held most of the early attention) to larger-scale issues related to policy.

The space for continuing innovation. In contrast to earlier mandated, blueprint approaches to development, early PRA champions emphasized innovation and local adaptation, opening possibilities for situation-specific reinvention of methods. This space for trainees to pioneer in their own right probably contributed to the swift emergence of local champions. It also encouraged practitioners to move forward with PRA, rather than clinging to practices that proved insufficient for local circumstances.

The interlocking effect of national and international networking, together with the compilation and wide dissemination of information. There was increasing synergy among these mechanisms over time that no one strategy could have had without the others. For example, national networks identified representatives to attend South-South exchanges who could present a broad perspective to others from around the world. These representatives would then send what they learned to their home network. Interactions would encourage practitioners to share their experiences in written form through *PLA Notes*, or to start corresponding electronically with newly discovered allies in other countries. The emphasis on rapid documentation and sharing— often a task not given priority by practitioners and activists—helped to promote PRA with development practitioners elsewhere. In turn, local and national networks could access a global family of networks. In effect, grassroots practitioners of PRA, operating in isolated regions of their countries, were able to draw on a web of individuals, institutions, practice, and knowledge, worldwide. This capacity, while enhancing the quality of local work, also created opportunities for global collegiality and action.

Open-ended, relatively flexible support from powerful global actors. Connections between grassroots institutions and those at the international level, such as the IDS and IIED, have contributed to the success of PRA. IDS was answerable to donors for funding tagged for capacity building for networks. However, this approach was interpreted, even in a logical framework submitted to donors, simply as "catalyzing sharing and learning." Despite this pressure to be a capacity builder, the IDS was able to play a facilitation role that attempted to interfere very little with the impulses of those wanting to undertake networking initiatives. No institutional models were suggested, nor was any formula for networking processes or best practice put forth. Instead IDS facilitation focused on developing links between colleagues in different parts of the world attempting to do similar things. IDS also encouraged local adaptation and reinvention. This open-ended approach allowed flexibility in the relationships that developed between the IDS and colleagues globally and was probably most useful in helping to develop relationships of trust and good faith. A balance between facilitation of others and active promotion is difficult to achieve. For example, while the commitment to dissemination of materials by the Northern centers (IDS and IIED) is widely credited with a crucial role in the globalization of PRA practice, in some instances it had the unanticipated drawback of crowding out local materials, often in local languages.

The loose, decentralized nature of global-level networking. In many instances of advocacy campaigns, global networking initiatives happen with a pronounced global agenda, often with a defined program and a Northern lead institution. However, despite the important role played by IDS and IIED, the PRA global phenomena has been characterized by a scattering of local networking processes, allowing groups to share with each other as the need arises. Unlike most other global networks, there is no global institutional form, no apex institution, and little standardization. Neither IDS nor IIED has fallen into this role.

The absence of a tightly defined global program has allowed significant space for diversity, adaptation to local conditions, a wide range of actors, and a locally defined agenda. The element of choice exists for all PRA-related networks to engage and participate globally (to the extent that is appropriate) according to local capacity and interest. Most have retained an emphasis on issues at a local level while contributing at different times to global efforts.

The Challenges of Rapid Growth and Dissemination

An indicator of the power of the combination of the factors described above has been the rapid acceptance of participatory methodologies (particularly in the form of PRA) by international NGOs, governmental, bi- and multi-lateral agencies in a very short time, often as a result of increased advocacy for participation by civil society actors, including PRA champions. While linear cause and effect analyses are always difficult, there can be little doubt that a synergetic effect of the various spreading mechanisms discussed above was a swift adaptation of participatory approaches from grassroots to global levels. In turn, the acceptance and promotion by large-scale institutions of participatory approaches reinforced their rapid spread.

At the same time, one of the key challenges for the future of PRA is paradoxically a result of its success. At the beginning of the chapter, I argued that PRA is a value-based approach, which has spread surprisingly quickly and widely considering the challenging implications of its adoption. The more popular PRA is with large institutions, the larger the risks of compromising the core values embedded in PRA since its early days.

Many of these concerns result from the speed at which participatory processes seem to be demanded and the increasing amounts of money that have characterized PRA-related work in recent times. While for a long time, it was assumed that more was better, the rapid scaling up and institutionalization of PRA practice has heightened concerns over quality as well as ethics and purpose.

For instance, as large, well-resourced organizations hurriedly adopted PRA through the 1990s, the resulting availability of lucrative training engagements has fostered a culture of consultancy. This commercialization of PRA work, while helping to spread the approach, holds serious dangers for networking processes. Competition for fat consultancies creates strong disincentives for learning and sharing. The rapid commercialization of PRA service provision seriously threatens notions of learning and sharing, and it legitimizes the notion that participatory work can be undertaken easily by people who carry limited responsibility for the outcome of their work.

If networks and their members are to engage in commercial service provision, the danger exists that less energy will be expended on learning and sharing activities at a local level. The danger at other levels is that regional and global outreach, contact, and exchange, which hold little pecuniary value, will be devalued and displaced. This would be a great loss, particularly in light of the value these have added to the spread and adaptation of PRA activities.

The challenge for networks and practitioners to develop and articulate clear perspectives on the quality and nature of participatory practice through honest reflection is a crucial one.[8] In an international retreat for fifty PRA practitioners and champions hosted by IDS in April 2000, there was open and heated discussion about the disillusionment many people feel in the face of these large challenges. However, as large as these challenges of misuse and abuse may loom, people talked more than ever of the need to return to their shared personal and political values and keep them in sight as the global landscape for participation shifts. For many PRA practitioners, the basic values of the approach continue, and will continue, to endure.

Notes

Thanks to Garett Pratt for his comments and contributions to this article and to John Gaventa for his invaluable guidance and encouragement.

1. For extensive resources on PRA, please see the IDS Participation Group website at http://www.ids.ac.uk/ids/particip.

2. Though I recognize the importance of a number of participatory traditions I focus in this chapter on my personal experience with PRA.

3. For many, the term *PRA* is now problematic as the approaches are used in urban and rural areas and beyond appraisal purposes. However, many practitioners still use the term to refer generally to participatory approaches.

4. Early innovators included Meera Kaul, Parmesh Shah, John Devavaram, Sheelu Francis, Ravi Jayakaran, Sam Joseph, James Mascarenhas, Neela Mukerjee, P. D. Premkumar, Jenny McCracken, Robert Chambers, Jules Pretty, and Ian Scoones.

5. James Mascarenhas is now with OUTREACH in Bangalore, India.

6. Despite the consistent protestations of Robert Chambers, he is still wrongly credited with the invention of PRA, rather than his key role in spreading it.

7. Information on the World Bank's Consultation with the Poor exercise and the *Poverty Reduction Strategy Paper,* including recommendations on participatory methods, are available online at http://www.worldbank.org/poverty.

8. The IDS Participation Group, together with colleagues in different parts of the world, has initiated the Pathways to Participation project to promote critical reflection on PRA in order to strengthen the quality and impact of participatory work. Further information is available at the Participation Group website, http://www.ids.ac.uk/ids/particip.

14

Campaigning for Corporate Change: Global Citizen Action on the Environment

Peter Newell

This chapter examines an emerging trend within the environmental movement to direct campaigns at the corporate sector. I relate this change to the globalization of economic activity and the power shifts between key global actors produced as a result. I draw on examples from a range of strategies adopted against transnational companies in order to explore the possibilities and limits of this form of citizen action on the environment.

Globalization: Opportunities and Challenges for Global Citizen Action

The growth in cooperative and confrontational forms of interaction and engagement among NGOs and transnational corporations (TNCs) coincides with a period of heightened globalization. It is arguably as a result of the renegotiation of the relationship between state and market that defines globalization that environmental NGOs (ENGOs) are increasingly targeting multinational companies. The intensification of competitive pressures and the mobility of capital conspire to make governments more unwilling or unable to regulate the conduct of TNCs. Shareholder activism, consumer boycotts, and a range of other confrontations between ENGOs and TNCs indicate a new politics in which NGOs seek to check the growth in the power of TNCs associated with globalization. Where traditional forms of state regulation have been reduced, NGOs are actively working to develop international behavioral norms that companies find increasingly difficult to escape.

The strategic turn of some NGOs, from conventional lobbying pursued through state and international organizations to lobbying companies direct-ly can be understood as a reaction to the failure of governments to regulate the activities of TNCs at the international level. The issue of TNC regula-tion was conveniently dropped from the UNCED agenda at the insistence of the United States and others (see Chatterjee and Finger 1994). Similarly, while Agenda 21, the plan of action that emerged from the Rio Conference on Environment and Development, includes recommendations that affect TNCs, it does not take the form of a code of conduct. The subject of an international code of conduct to regulate the activities of TNCs has been on the international agenda since the 1970s. The UN Center on Transnational Corporations (UNCTC) was set up in 1973, but after two decades of failed negotiation in 1993, the center was closed and replaced by the Division on Transnational Corporations and Investment, located within the United Nations Conference on Trade and Development (UNCTAD). In place of binding commitments at the international level, there has been a growth in voluntary agreements, self-monitoring, and the proliferation of sustainabili-ty audits of corporations by external consultants (Picciotto and Mayne 1999). The best known voluntary guidelines on the environment are those endorsed by the ICC (International Chamber of Commerce) known as the *Business Charter for Sustainable Development*, a document of sixteen prin-ciples produced prior to UNCED (Schmidheiny 1992).

Among the principal reasons for this lack of progress in regulating the environmental impact of corporate activity are the constraints under which states operate in a context of globalization. The globalization process makes it harder for states to adopt unilateral environmental actions, for fear of capital flight (a fear that industries have exploited to great effect) and the relocation of industry to areas where standards are lower. Unilateral or even regional environmental standards become less desirable in a context in which the state is competing with rival states and firms for a share of the world market. The entitlements of investors have also been enshrined in international and regional agreements on intellectual property rights, investment, and trade. These patterns imply a growth in the power of TNCs and a reduction in restraints on the terms of their investment (Muchlinski 1999: 47–60). It is the incongruence of the gap between the rights and responsibilities of TNCs that concerns social activists. As Vidal argues, "Corporations have never been more powerful, yet less regulated; never more pampered by government, yet never less questioned; never more needed to take social responsibility yet never more secretive. ... To whom will these fabulously self-motivated, self-interested supranational bodies be accountable?" (1997: 263).

The failure to regulate TNCs also coincides with a changed context of NGO-TNC relations informed by organizational and perceptional changes within both the business and NGO communities. The space for more cooperative relations has been created by a more solutions-oriented approach adopted by many NGOs, resulting from a perceived need to move beyond awareness-raising functions to promoting solutions, sometimes by collaborating with TNCs (SustainAbility 1996; Murphy and Bendell 1997). The growth in the size of many ENGOs (particularly during the mid- to late-1980s) also means that they cannot afford the risk of litigation undertaken by companies against their direct actions. Many now have sizeable assets that would be threatened by successful court action against them. Hence despite the ongoing role of Brent Spar–style confrontations, more cooperative approaches have become important for some groups in order to develop credibility among those able to generate reform and avoid financial loss. Some businesses have also become more proactive in the debate, rather than resisting government-led controls. More generally, the renewed emphasis in the 1990s on corporate social responsibility has forced companies to at least acknowledge their responsibilities to the communities in which they operate.

It is at this juncture, where the roles of NGOs and business appear to be in transition and more responsive to global forces, that global citizen action on the environment takes place. Though the complex processes of globalization have undoubtedly helped to produce these current forms of citizen action (cf. Newell 2000), citizen action also plays an important part in configuring new patterns of global politics. Not only do groups mobilize around issues of globalization out of a deep-seated concern about the absence of formal institutional checks and balances on increasingly powerful corporate players, their actions also affect the boundaries of corporations' rights and responsibilities.

Environmentalism in an Age of Globalization

The challenge for successful global citizen environmental action is to monitor the global activities of TNCs, made more difficult by the increasing distance between the source and the site of consumption created by internationalized patterns of production and supply. As Sachs argues, "the emergence of a globe as an economic arena where capital, goods and services can move with little consideration for local and national communities has delivered the most serious blow to the idea of a polity which is built on reciprocal rights and duties among citizens. ... Through transnationalization, capital escapes any links of loyalty to a particular society" (1997: 10). Re-embedding transnational corporate activity within frameworks of social and environmental obligation is a difficult task for NGOs to perform and gives rise to the sort of international coalition building described below.

It should be noted that many of the strategies employed by environmental NGOs in recent years targeted toward TNCs are not new. Indeed, there is a long history of the use of consumer boycotts for example (Smith 1990), and exposure of corporate misconduct and noncompliance also has a relatively long history. Shareholder activism, counteradvertising, and the emergence of stewardship councils, as they are applied in the environmental area, do seem to be a largely new phenomena, however. The point though is that all these strategies, whether new or not, appear to be applied more frequently than was the case even ten years ago. Some are more reactive in nature and others more proactive, some confrontational and others collaborative. They should not be considered as stand-alone discrete responses. They are often employed alongside one another and are intended to supplement the strengths and build on the limits of other strategies.

Cooperative Strategies

There has been a growth since the late-1980s in collaboration between NGOs and TNCs that seeks to work within the current economic system, to improve the way in which it functions, and to offset its worst environmental impacts. These efforts share the aim of rewarding good business practice with financial endorsement (as in the case of ethical consumerism) or with a symbol of responsible environmental practice (as in the case of the codes of conduct and stewardship regimes). The examples below reflect the diversity of strategies under this heading.

Eco-consumerism. Green consumerism exploded in the 1980s in the United States. In promoting eco-consumerism groups such as Greenpeace have tried to provide companies with carrots in the form of financial incentives to pursue particular markets by showing that markets exist for environmentally sound products. Greenpeace's promotion of the "greenfreeze fridge" is a prominent example. The scheme is a direct threat to TNCs' own products given that the pressure group is competing in the same market and hence serves to force the agenda and draw (in this case chemical) companies into dialogue about how their own products are produced. Ethical consumerism, while not new in itself, took on a different form in the late 1980s, responding to different impulses and addressing a broader set of issues. The magazine *Ethical Consumer* captures its contemporary form:

> It is becoming widely accepted that the global economic system should be able to pursue ethical as well as financial goals. In a world where people feel politically disempowered and where governments are becoming less powerful than corporations, citizens are beginning to realise that their economic vote may have as much influence as their political vote. This is true both for individuals and institutional purchasers. (*Ethical Consumer* 1997–1998: 3)

The key to the success of this strategy is the harnessing of consumer power to the goal of corporate reform. Its popularity centers on the fact that it offers individuals the sense that they can make a difference by exercising one of the few levers they have over global corporations. Positive consumer action has clearly been an important driver in creating and sustaining the market for ethical goods and services.

Project collaboration. There has been a substantial growth in recent years in environmental partnerships between businesses and environmental groups. One of the most famous examples of NGO-TNC cooperation is the project undertaken between the Environmental Defense Fund (EDF) and McDonald's Corporation, often held up as model of NGO-TNC collaboration. The focus of concern was the company's clamshell-shaped polystyrene container for hamburgers. Murphy and Bendell explain the background to the story: "Most targets for recycling and solid waste reduction have tended to be fairly loose with little in the way of teeth on the enforcement side. Public pressure has had a far greater influence on company policy" (1997: 193). This pressure brought representatives of McDonald's and the Environmental Defense Fund together in August 1990 to sign an agreement to establish a joint task force to address the company's solid waste issues. The agreement retained provision for EDF to criticize the company, and if parties disagreed on research findings in the final report on the project, separate statements from EDF and McDonald's could be produced. McDonald's also required EDF task force members to work in one of its restaurants for at least one day each.

It is important to recognize that the EDF project probably had a greater impact because it rode on the back of a number of local campaigns in the United States organized by groups such as the Citizens' Clearing House for Hazardous Waste, which pioneered the McToxic and McWaste campaigns in the late 1980s. These activities helped to politicize the waste problem in the first place, creating an opportunity for a collaborative project. As Dubash and Oppenheimer note, "The combination of grassroots action, bad publicity, and sound analysis and specific proposals by an outside actor (EDF) with access to top management provided the company with both the motivation to change packaging and a reasonable set of alternatives (1992: 271).

The partnership between McDonald's and EDF created tensions among NGOs working to reform the company's behavior, however. Many of the groups outside the project accused the EDF of selling out by working with McDonald's, of lending legitimacy to their business and trading their good name for minimal concessions on the part of the company. The inside-outside strategy that resulted was uncoordinated and unintentional. The effect, nevertheless, was to support change within the company. The two campaigns operating simultaneously created incentives for change through external pressure as well as by providing a mechanism for responding to that pressure.

Codes of conduct. In 1989 a coalition of environmental, investor, and church interests known as the Coalition for Environmentally Responsible Economies (CERES) met in New York to introduce a ten-point environmental code of conduct for corporations. One month later CERES, along with the Green Alliance, launched a similar effort in the UK. The aim was to provide criteria for auditing the environmental performance of large domestic and multinational industries. The code called on companies to minimize the release of pollutants, conserve nonrenewable resources, use sustainable energy sources, and use environmental commitment as a factor in appointing members to the board of directors. The principles are known as the Valdez Principles (named after the Exxon *Valdez* disaster in 1989) and have been used by groups such as Friends of the Earth to enlist corporations to pledge compliance. Companies endorsing the CERES principles are required to report annually on their implementation of the principles. Clearly the approach is one of self-regulation as companies have the option of nonendorsement, though public and NGO pressure supply incentives to join.

The principles have been used to foster shareholder pressure on companies to improve their environmental performance, to help investors decide on socially responsible investments, to justify praise or criticism for corporate behavior, and to encourage graduates to be aware of the environmental credentials of companies with whom they seek employment (Wapner 1995). The principles open up new channels of reform and avenues of pressure with regard to company conduct. They enable companies to legitimize their activities by signing principles codrafted with environmentalists and therefore to represent their activities as environmentally responsible. Though they provide a useful lobbying tool that environmental groups can use to pressure companies to remain faithful to their promises, companies have been able to use them as a way of avoiding government regulation (Humphreys 1997).

Stewardship regimes. Stewardship regimes, or private certification schemes, provide a further channel of collaboration among private and NGO actors. They bring together environmental groups, companies, and other interested parties to formulate accreditation procedures to identify good corporate conduct. These are more formalized and institutionalized than codes of conduct. They provide an ongoing arena in which dialogue and review take place. The Forestry Stewardship Council (FSC) provides an interesting example.

The background to the council's creation was decision of the World

Wildlife Fund (WWF) of the UK to pursue an alternative strategy in a campaign for sustainable forestry, a direct response to the "lack of commitment and progress being observed at the international policy level" (Murphy and Bendell 1997: 105). It was decided to pursue a campaign aimed at ensuring that all tropical wood and wood products traded in the UK would come from well-managed forests by the end of 1995. Directors of targeted companies concerned about public relations and commercial implications of protests decided that signing up to the target offered a way of retrieving some lost ground in the debate. To join the 1995 club, companies had to agree to phase out by the target date the sale and use of all wood and wood products not acquired from well-managed forests.

Manufacturers' misuse of claims about forestry management led to pressure to establish a standard-setting body with a system for verifying product claims. The result was the Forestry Stewardship Council, established in 1993. The founding group consisted of environmental NGOs, forest industry representatives, community forest groups, and forest product certification organizations. The FSC set up an independent forest accreditation program to alleviate consumer confusion about environmentally friendly wood products. Members of the FSC also agreed to nine principles of forestry management. An FSC logo denotes that the product was sourced from an independently certified forest according to FSC principles. Other such schemes exist elsewhere, with NGOs initiating buyer groups and FSC working groups. In each case, "a lack of effective government action was a significant factor in making environmental groups turn to the industry itself" (Murphy and Bendell 1997: 130).

NGOs working on forest issues outside the scheme have asked whether the FSC responds more to the concerns of Northern consumers about tropical deforestation than to the socioeconomic needs of the South (Murphy and Bendell 1997: 112). There also remains a possible conflict between the degree of confidentiality necessary for the FSC process and the need for NGOs to be accountable to their membership. Yet despite criticisms from the Timber Traders Federation about disproportionate NGO representation within the FSC, its lack of accountability to governments, and the potential conflicts that exist with principles of free competition, enthusiasm for the group remains and new companies continue to join (Murphy and Bendell 2000).

Confrontational Strategies

In contrast, alongside the proliferation of NGO initiatives aimed at engaging with corporations in order to strengthen their environmental programs or encourage more efficient and responsible use of natural resources, more traditional practices of civil resistance have developed to combat the environmentally degrading practices of TNCs. Examples include the growth in consumer boycotts and in campaigns specifically targeted *against* TNCs and the proliferation of groups whose principal aim is to document and expose corporate malpractice.

Consumer boycotts. Though consumer boycotts have been used to affect change across a range of issues, they often follow a similar path. They are often a reaction in the first instance to the unwillingness of states to interfere in an allegation of corporate misconduct. An attempt is made to publicize the issue, to expose misconduct, and to form the basis for public involvement. Demonstrations, media campaigns, and leaflets can direct attention and social pressure toward the corporation. Efforts are then geared toward ensuring that individuals and institutions (for example, churches and universities) boycott goods from the firm in question (Rodman 1998). The boycotts are often used as part of a wider portfolio of campaigning, including shareholder activism. The response of TNCs is often to deny the charges, to launch a public relations campaign, or to hope either that the poor publicity passes or that the boycott does not really take off and only then consider disbanding an operation. Even then, the company would consider disinvestment only after making every attempt to give the appearance that the concerns expressed are not justified.

The case of Shell's involvement in Nigeria provides an example of NGOs taking it upon themselves to launch a boycott in the absence of government-led pressure. There was no official boycott of Nigerian oil, and many Western car companies were anxious about the effect of a state-led boycott on fuel prices and the availability of petrol. Environmental and other groups called on their governments to impose an oil embargo and mandate disinvestment. At the same time, local grassroots NGOs tapped into international activist networks to bring pressure on Shell at all levels and successfully involved another corporation, the Body Shop, which released documents obtained from the company demonstrating that Shell was in fact responsible for the environmental damage to the Ogoni people's land.

Although boycotts of Shell did not succeed in bringing about the withdrawal of the company, Shell did retreat from its initial position that its operations were not responsible for the environmental damage. In 1996 it hired Integrity Works, a business ethics consulting firm, to use the media in defending the company's presence in Nigeria on moral and commercial grounds. The company also accepted some financial responsibility to repair the damage it had caused, committing itself to a cleanup that would cost U.S.$100 million per year for five years as well as community investments in Ogoniland (Rodman 1998). In addition, the company was forced to settle a number of lawsuits brought by communities demanding compensation for loss of income as a result of the oil spills (Frynas 1999). Finally, the company agreed to consult more with NGOs in the future. The *Financial Times* referred to these concessions as a "belated recognition of the influence on multinationals of international public opinion" (quoted in Rodman 1997: 33).

Public relations wars. Advertising of consumer products is clearly a key component of the ability of TNCs to project themselves globally. To do this successfully, to build a transnational base of loyal customers who associate a company's product with quality, requires good public relations. Acknowledgment of the importance of this aspect of corporate power has led some environmental NGOs to engage in public relations wars with companies. This strategy centers on attacking a company on the basis of the claims it makes about itself and encouraging customers to boycott its products. Such campaigns are intended to expose perceived corporate misconduct and force the company to defend its reputation in public.

The most recent and prominent example of such a campaign was the "McLibel" case involving the McDonald's Corporation and London Greenpeace (not to be confused with the larger NGO by the same name). The accusations against McDonald's, orchestrated initially by London Greenpeace and articulated in a leaflet under the title "What's Wrong with McDonald's?" were that the company exploited its workforce, treated animals cruelly, and engaged in practices destructive of the environment (including excessive packaging, litter, and the clearing of tropical forests for use as ranchland). The leaflet led to the indictment and conviction of the McLibel Two, the two activists pinpointed for their involvement in the authorship of the leaflet alleged to be libellous by the corporation, and the longest libel trial in British history. The different assets brought to the conflict by the two defendants are revealing of the new politics involved in NGO-TNC relations. McDonald's had enormous financial muscle, good political contacts, and access to the best libel lawyer in the country. The defense, on the other hand, portrayed the McLibel Two as victims of corporate suppression of their freedom of expression, successfully manipulating parallels with David and Goliath.

The attempt by the company to silence its critics provoked a strong backlash against what many consider to be suppression of dissent and an act of corporate bullying. The McLibel case underscores the importance to TNCs of their reputations, to the extent that they are prepared to take legal action against their critics. The publication of the leaflet served to engage McDonald's in a critical dialogue in which it was forced to respond to critics and defend its actions. The other key lesson from the McLibel case is the importance of the Internet as a campaign tool. A website titled The McSpotlight has served as a clearing house for information about the case, providing evidence to support the claims made against the company. It has also enabled NGOs and community groups to coordinate international "days of action" against McDonald's and to share creative ideas about campaign tactics, public relations stunts, and media strategies.

TNC monitors. Another trend within the environmental movement has been the growth in organizations solely devoted to the surveillance of TNCs. These organizations are at the front line of action against TNCs by exposing acts of environmental degradation and disseminating this knowledge to the broader community of activists. Examples of groups that fit into this category are CorporateWatch in the UK, Multinationals Resource Center in the United States, The Transnational Information Exchange in the Netherlands, and the People's Action Network to Monitor Japanese Transnationals in Japan. There are also sector-specific monitors such as OilWatch, which has offices in a number of developing countries in which oil companies operate. Based on the premise that what companies say about their own activities is not to be trusted and that government surveillance of operations is limited, TNC monitors threaten companies with exposure and the activation of NGO campaigns in order to deter them from violating their legal and perceived social obligations. Such criticism and exposure helps to pave the way for confrontational campaigning including demonstrations and company boycotts. They act as much-needed resource centers for other NGOs wanting information on particular companies.

Shareholder activism. In recent years, particularly in the United States and UK, there has been a growth in shareholder activism, whereby environmental and other groups buy a small number of shares in a company and encourage their supporters to do the same as a way of obtaining access to the annual general meeting (AGM) and to a forum therefore in which they can influence company decisionmaking. Oil, arms, and road-building companies have been principal targets of this strategy. The sponsorship of resolutions at company meetings is aimed at overturning management decisions or at the adoption of a social responsibility measure. Shareholder activists play on the hassle factor, forcing corporations to devote a disproportionate share of their resources to defend a small part of their global operations (Rodman 1997, 1998).

Shell Transport and Trading, the UK arm of Shell International, had an embarrassing confrontation with institutional shareholders in April–May 1997 over its environmental (and human rights) record. A group holding just 1 percent of the shares called on the company to improve accountability by establishing new procedures for dealing with environmental and human rights issues (Lewis 1997). The resolution, supported by groups such as WWF and Amnesty International, called for a named member of Shell's committee of managing directors to take charge of environmental and corporate responsibility policies and for an external audit of those poli-cies. It further called on Shell to publish, before the end of the year, a report on its controversial activities in Nigeria (see previous discussion in this chapter). In an attempt to preempt the shareholder motion, Shell revamped its Statement of General Business Principles to include human rights and sustainable development and published its first report on worldwide health, safety, and environmental activities in an attempt to "ward off further trou-ble" (Caulkin 1997). The failure of the AGM to pass the resolution does not detract from what its supporters regarded as a moral victory and a mile-stone in bringing about a recognition among shareholders that environmen-tal and human rights issues are a legitimate investor concern.

Possibilities and Limitations of Global Citizen Action

The extent to which these strategies will play a central part in future cam-paigning efforts will depend on the ability of the movement to address a spectrum of concerns. In invoking the public interest, NGOs will have to respond directly to the concerns of a broad base within society. Currently, even mass membership organizations represent only a fragment of the broader population, who may not share NGO concerns about TNCs and may in fact perceive themselves to benefit from TNC activities, even where they impose environmental costs. There is a danger of paternalism where elite NGOs assume an understanding of what is in the public interest. Some strategies depend on large-scale popular support in order to make an impact. Boycotts in particular must be undertaken by a significant number of people in different markets if TNCs are to take them seriously. Private collaborations between NGOs and companies are less open to wider partici-pation and scrutiny, however, and may fuel concerns about whose interests are represented by NGOs.

At the moment, these strategies tend also to be ad hoc and limited in geographical scope, as well as focused on particular TNCs. To be effective, boycotts have to be adopted in those markets of greatest importance to the TNC. Fortunately for the environmental movement, many of the TNCs that have been the target of consumer action have depended for their profit mar-gins on success in Western markets, where consumer power is currently strongest. But though there are often fewer checks and balances on corpo-rate misconduct in the developing world; if pressures for reform come from Western NGOs outside the host country, they may be regarded as illegiti-mate political interference. It can be expected, however, that as TNCs invest further in the South, groups will mobilize their own responses to cor-porate misconduct. Many forms of resistance are clearly already apparent (Guha and Martinez-Alier 1997: 109–127; Gorelick 1997), and there is evidence of more cooperative NGO-business partnerships beginning to develop (cf. Plante 1998).

The challenge for future transnational action will be to find areas of agreement around which a broad spectrum of organizations can coalesce while maintaining scope for groups to express their own concerns within an orchestrated campaign. Not only is it inevitable and desirable that campaigns reflect a particular socioeconomic reality, it is important to their success and reputation that they are not seen as subsumed by the agenda of more powerful NGO partners.

The problem for advancing citizen action of this nature remains, however, that many TNCs are relatively insulated from NGO campaigns. This is especially the case for companies whose activities have the largest environmental impact. Rodman shows in his discussion of NGO pressure on TNCs investing in Burma that the oil companies there have been "the most impervious to non-governmental pressures" (Rodman 1997: 29). The conflict over Shell's operation in Nigeria demonstrated the failure of activists to exact a price high enough to elicit compliance with their demands (Rodman 1997: 36). Where companies' access to technology, expertise, and distribution networks cannot easily be replicated by other companies, host nations will often provide inducements to encourage the company to stay. Campaigns likely to be most successful are those targeted against particular projects of negligible value to the overall operations of the company, so that the potential for reduced profits and damaged reputation in other, more important, markets makes the targeted operation a liability. Only those TNCs vulnerable to NGO pressure and where consumer preference really matters are affected by these strategies.

A major challenge for future citizen action against the corporate sector will be to change the practice of companies less vulnerable to consumer pressure, suppliers further down the supply chain and more insulated from NGO influence. From an environmental perspective this is where much of the most damaging extractive activity takes place. Pressuring commercial buyers to take responsibility for monitoring sourcing and production strategies along the supply chain is useful, but targeting individual parts of the chain through coordinated NGO monitoring, exchange of information, and pressure will also be needed.

Conclusions

The challenge for global citizen action in light of the rising power of TNCs is to re-embed the market within a framework of norms and expectations regarding corporate responsibility to the environment. There may be a tension here between conflicting norms and expectations about what counts as environmentally acceptable behavior that differ across regions and social groupings. Companies may find themselves having to address multiple issues of concern simultaneously. This makes it more difficult for companies to anticipate expectations in a way that will constructively shape their investment practices. It also explains why some companies are in favor of nonbinding international standards of environmental protection; benchmarks that indicate a certain level of environmental performance. Developing countries remain concerned that such standards, developed within the International Standards Organizations (ISO) and other bodies, will come to constitute a nontariff barrier to trade that will exclude their products from Western markets. Given the right degree of transparency and flexibility, however, international standards can provide useful benchmarks against which to assess business performance in given sectoral and socio-economic settings, while also creating a lobbying tool to ensure that the globalization of production is not at the expense of the resource security of the world's poorest communities. NGOs should not fail to recognize their own contribution, through the campaigns and strategies described above, in determining which forms of international regulation are desirable and necessary. This should be the impetus for future global citizen action on the environment.

Notes

Parts of this chapter are drawn from other work by the author, including "Environmental NGOs, TNCs, and the Question of Governance," in Stevis and Assetto (2001); and "Environmental NGOs and Globalization," in Cohen and Rai (2000).

15

From the Corridors of Power to the Global Negotiating Table: The NGO Steering Committee of the Commission on Sustainable Development

Felix Dodds

A large number of books are now being produced on global governance and the role of NGOs, but much of this literature is written at second- or third-hand by observers removed from the actual meetings and negotiations that are forming this new agenda. By contrast, with this chapter I attempt to capture the evolution of key examples of NGO participation as someone who has been actively involved in both the Rio Earth Summit and its aftermath.

The Earth Summit in Rio de Janeiro in 1992, the UN Conference on Environment and Development, offered a powerful focus for NGOs to work together internationally on issues of environment and development. Although environmental groups had already started working together successfully around single issues well before Rio, the agenda of the earth summit required a considerably more integrated approach. The challenge for these organizations was to weave together a diverse range of environmental, social, and economic positions into a cohesive series of documents and to bridge the gaps that existed among large and small NGOs, as well as those from the North and the South, to produce a coalition capable of influencing the negotiations.

Initially, the lead in this process was taken by the Centre for Our Common Future. The center had originally been set up to promote the outcomes from the UN Commission on Environment and Development, which produced the "Brundtland Report" under the former secretary to the commission, Warren "Chip" Lindner. In June 1990, the center called a meeting of representatives from what would later be called "major groups" to set up an international facilitating committee (IFC) to work on preparations for the Rio summit.[1] The IFC had representatives from trade unions, industry,

NGOs, the scientific and academic community, youth, and women's organizations. It was set up to act as a facilitating group, not to work on policy development itself.

Some NGOs were unhappy that the IFC was limited to facilitation and was therefore unable to agree on joint policy statements (McCully 1993). Others disliked the involvement of industry. One of the key NGO networks, the Environment Liaison Centre International (ELCI), helped set up an international steering committee (ISC) for NGOs that held a major preparatory conference in Paris in December 1991, with financial support from the French government (Princen and Finger 1994). Although the conference was initially described as dreadful by many, attendees did agree on a paper called "Roots of Our Future." The conference also set up a successor to the ISC, the International Non-Governmental Organizations Forum (INGOF). INGOF worked with NGOs in developing what would become the alternative treaties that shaped NGO positions at the earth summit. As Bigg and Dodds explain, "The treaties were an attempt to negotiate common positions to enable NGOs to cooperate more closely at the international level. They were not intended for consideration by governments preparing for the negotiations in Rio but constituted a parallel alternative process" (1997: 4).

At the Rio summit, NGO activity coalesced around the Global NGO Forum, with meetings taking place in a series of tents, sometimes packed with people and sometimes in the heat in the middle of Flamenco Park (the beach-site park that became a virtual world's fair for sustainable development and an alternative movement of NGOs who drafted a series of comprehensive alternative treaties). It is estimated that over four thousand individuals took part in this process, drafting thirty-nine treaties over the ten days of the summit (Padbury 1997). The second phase of the treaty development process consisted of a series of regional meetings, since "participants wanted to avoid a centralisation of power and specifically wanted sub regional forums as caretakers of the process" (Padbury 1997). These treaties were intended as a tool to facilitate coordinated work by NGOs around the world.

From Rio to New York: The Formalization of the NGO Steering Committee (1993–1995)

The Rio Earth Summit produced two concrete outcomes: the Agenda 21 Action Plan and the United Nations Commission on Sustainable Development (UNCSD, or CSD) to oversee its implementation, based in New York. At the first meeting of the CSD in June 1993, the United Nations Environment and Development UK (UNED-UK) produced a questionnaire asking all the NGOs in attendance a series of questions about the sort of organizational backup they needed to be effective participants (Howell 1999).[2] The results were clear: NGOs wanted information between meetings, the ability to prepare position papers prior to each CSD meeting, training for new NGOs coming to the meetings, preparation for the morning strategy sessions and the evening government NGO dialogue sessions, and an ongoing relationship with the CSD secretariat and government missions in New York.

On the evening of the penultimate day of that first CSD meeting, NGOs agreed to the need for a coordinating mechanism. Time did not allow for the establishment of such a mechanism before the end of the meeting, but with the help of the UN Non-Governmental Liaison Service (UNNGLS, or NGLS), a series of regional telephone conferences were held in the autumn of 1993. They resulted in the establishment of an ad hoc committee that met in Copenhagen in December 1993 at an NGO conference entitled Down to Earth—Between the Summits. This conference tried to bring those NGOs that had been involved in Rio together with those involved with the World Summit for Social Development and the Fourth World Conference on Women in Beijing. At Down to Earth, the ad hoc committee met and agreed to establish an umbrella coordinating committee to provide a basic structure, and to employ Michael McCoy from the U.S. Citizens Network to draw up a fundraising proposal for an office to coordinate NGO preparations for the CSD. A small grant was subsequently provided by the Canadian Council for International Cooperation (CCIC).

At the second meeting of the CSD in May 1994, NGOs and other major groups met after each daily session to discuss the setting up of an NGO steering committee (Mucke 1997).[3] Some of the residual mistrust between NGOs from the North and the South that had not been resolved at or after Rio prevented an agreement to have a single office for all NGOs. By the end of the second week of the meeting, however, an agreement had been forged to set up three "NGO clearinghouses" under the steering committee, one each for the North, the South, and small island developing states, though the latter was never established. The CSD NGO Steering Committee Guidelines agreed on by the NGO community as a whole at the meeting had a built-in majority of NGOs from the South as well as an intentional gender balance.

These guidelines included a code of conduct to govern NGO participation, the result of two incidents that led NGOs to realize the need for guidelines on how to deal with internal matters. The first was an issue of personal behavior that created significant conflict within the NGO community. Subsequently, the steering committee agreed that it could remove a representative after the person concerned had been informed by the cochairs in writing and had failed to rectify the matter even after formal attempts at resolution. The second incident occurred when the cofacilitators of an NGO caucus put out a position paper listing organizations that had supposedly signed up, without showing it to the organizations concerned. This caused serious problems for some of the NGOs involved. For example, the Canadian Environmental Network (CEN) was summoned by the Canadian ambassador to ask why they had signed a document that was inaccurate and not representative of the Canadian position. As a result, the caucus was closed and reestablished under new coordinators. The pressure for caucuses to act professionally resulted in a further addition to the guidelines, as follows: "A person sitting on the Steering Committee shall be removed automatically if the caucus or body from which they come no longer recognizes their representatives or the body that they represented ceases to exist or is no longer representative of NGOs in that major group doing work related to the Commission on Sustainable Development" (NGO Steering Committee 1998: 3).

The CSD NGO Steering Committee is unique among coordinating mechanisms in UN processes because it is a multistakeholder body, including industry and trade unions as well as NGOs. It performs two basic tasks: first, ensuring that all major groups have the best information possible to use the space provided by CSD sessions; and second, facilitating NGO caucuses on specific issues. Each year, the NGO community at the CSD holds elections for caucuses by issue, region, and major groups. Over eighty organizations were elected to the steering committee in 1999, with 36 percent from North America and Western Europe, and 64 percent from developing countries, Eastern Europe, and what the committee calls the Southern diaspora.

In 1997, NGOs were polled to find out their views on the steering committee and its work. The results produced a package of reforms that addressed the need for:

- Norms and standards for steering committee and management committee meetings;
- Guidelines for caucus membership and representation;
- A finance subcommittee;
- Open and inclusive communication by the steering committee and caucuses;
- Procedures for ensuring fairness, effectiveness, and maximum utility in the management of travel funds;
- Northern and Southern caucus membership and election processes.

The management committee consists of eight representatives elected from the steering committee (four from the North and four from the South, plus the two cochairs). Its role is to oversee the work of NGOs in preparing for each CSD between meetings of the steering committee. Strict rules were adopted as part of the reform package to deal with election procedures for the caucuses, including by-elections to formalize the composition of the management committee. Clear rules now exist on how elections must be advertized, and elections that do not adhere to these rules are declared invalid. The Northern caucus has introduced term limits for its representatives (a maximum of three consecutive terms), but the Southern caucus has not followed suit, causing disquiet among some Southern NGO members.

One of the key reasons for setting up the steering committee was the need to manage a space in which thousands of NGOs wanted to be active. Adopting no structure at all would have meant that the larger, predominantly Northern, NGOs would be able to dominate this space, resulting in major distortions in access to the debate. It is important to remember that the committee is not a policymaking body: "The activity of this committee would in no sense be one of political nor policy representativeness for the NGO community. No such mandate would be delegated to the committee and political representatives or interventions will remain the domain of the entire NGO and Major Groups community" (NGO Steering Committee 1998: 1). The main policymaking body is the morning strategy session of all NGOs. Nevertheless, as the number of NGOs attending the CSD grew (to over 1,000 by 1997), the process suffered by trying to ensure that everyone was involved in all decisions on every issue. This slowed down the committee's ability to prepare for and respond to debates. The reform package recognized the difficulty of trying to develop common policy positions by bringing everyone together the Sunday before the CSD, but this failed on a number of accounts: It was too late to influence initial government positions, and at times, decisions were taken by people who had little knowledge of the issues under discussion.

Therefore, the steering committee moved to implement a caucus-led approach to policy development. To recognize a caucus, the steering committee requires that the group "consist of at least ten non-governmental organizations accredited to UN Economic and Social Council. Each issue caucus will present a one-paragraph statement of purpose reflecting the issues to be covered and not positions to be taken" (NGO Steering Committee 1998: 6).

The development of a steering committee website and individual listservs for each NGO caucus has produced a highly transparent process. The website contains the minutes of all steering committee and management committee meetings, and details of issue-based, regional, and major groups coordinators. It has also facilitated outreach since coordinators now know who the members of their caucus are. Most of the caucuses have between 100 and 200 members. The steering committee recognizes that not everyone has access to email and has a section in its guidelines titled Open and Inclusive Communication to deal with this problem.

One of the problems facing the caucuses was arriving at a consensus

position, so the reform package included a provision that "minority positions if any must be represented in the document" (NGO Steering
Committee 1998: 9). This allowed different positions to be reflected, recognizing and celebrating the diversity that characterizes the NGO world.

UNGASS and Habitat II (1996–1997)

In preparation for the 1997 United Nations General Assembly Special
Session (UNGASS) to review Agenda 21 (also known as Earth Summit II),
the CSD NGO Steering Committee coordinated the drafting of a global
NGO position paper, "Towards Earth Summit II." This paper had active
involvement from over 2,000 NGOs from around the world and was tabled
at the first preparatory meeting for the special session in February.
"Towards Earth Summit II" was significant in that it became the central
lobbying document of nearly all NGOs involved—the first time that NGOs
had achieved such an active agreement prior to the official negotiations.
Four of the ten issues prioritized by NGOs in the document were successful
in affecting the substance of the text agreed by governments at UNGASS,
including the campaign against a global forest convention and the agreement to replenish the Global Environmental Facility. Perhaps as significant
was a push by predominately environmental NGOs for increased development finance.

Earth Summit II was also significant in expanding the involvement of
major groups in the negotiating process. Accreditation of NGOs and major
groups to the Economic and Social Council (ECOSOC) of the UN had
always allowed them to contribute to formal sessions of subsidiary bodies
of ECOSOC, which include the CSD. This enabled limited access and participation in UN commissions, but usually in a very formalistic manner. At
Rio, an NGO could only attend the informal negotiations if it was included
as the NGO representative on a government delegation. From 1993 to
1997, NGOs and other major groups involved in the CSD advanced their
ability to participate enormously, mostly using informal procedures. By
1997, NGOs and other major groups were attending all the negotiations
(formal and informal). Today, NGOs at the CSD are able to meet with governments and circulate their position papers freely. And in nearly all cases
they are invited to contribute their consolidated viewpoints from the floor
during the negotiations.

For the UNGASS process, these gains were uncontroversial during the
preparatory meetings, which were converted meetings of the Commission
on Sustainable Development. However, the final meeting was a General
Assembly meeting, where NGOs and major groups have no rights of participation. Nevertheless, ten representatives of the major groups were allowed

to address the General Assembly, the first time that the role of nonstate actors had been recognized at the highest level. Some governments (including India, Cuba, and Iran) were unhappy at this development lest it be seen as a precedent, but the president of the General Assembly at the time (Ambassador Razali from Malaysia, who had been the first chair of the CSD), successfully pushed it through. Since the General Assembly session was at the heads of state level, this raised the interesting question of whether the representatives of the major groups were equivalent to heads of state. UNGASS set a second important precedent for nonstate involvement, in that the Committee of the Whole of the General Assembly, where the negotiations took place, adopted the practice of the CSD with regard to the involvement of major groups. Unfortunately, this precedent has not been extended to other UN conferences since 1997.

While the CSD continued to advance involvement by NGOs and other major groups, other UN conferences were also building on the approach developed after Rio. Perhaps the most advanced was the Habitat II Conference, the second UN Conference on Housing and Development, held in Istanbul in 1996. At the second preparatory committee for Habitat II held in Nairobi in May 1995, NGOs and other major groups adopted a revised structure for their coalition similar to the CSD NGO Steering Committee, called the International Facilitating Group (IFC). The IFC tried to learn from some of the mistakes that the CSD Steering Committee had made previously. Instead of two cochairs, it chose two from the North and two from the South, with a gender balance from each region. Wally N'Dow, the secretary-general of Habitat II, also pushed strongly for the involvement of all stakeholders in the conference process. Habitat II produced four key breakthroughs.

First, governments were unhappy with the text being negotiated at the second preparatory committee and agreed to two informal drafting meetings before reconvening. During these negotiations, NGOs and local authorities were given seats at the table to suggest amendments to the texts. If a government agreed with the suggestion put forward, the text was open for negotiation. Second, during these informal meetings, NGOs were allowed to chair informal groups. In some cases, joint NGO-government texts were even entered into the negotiations. Third, the UN brought out the "NGO Composite Text" amendments as an official UN document at Habitat II. Fourth, Committee Two at Habitat II provided an opportunity for different stakeholders to say what they wanted out of the conference. Unfortunately, these statements were being presented at the same time that the official negotiations were going on in Committee One, and therefore could not influence the negotiations.

Throughout this process, Ambassador Kakakhel of Pakistan played a key role in ensuring that NGOs and local authorities retained their seats during the negotiations. Most of the breakthroughs achieved at Habitat II came as a result of trust built among stakeholder groups and governments, supported by key individuals and precedents from previous negotiations. Sadly, these breakthroughs did not translate from the conference to the operations of the UN Commission on Human Settlements (UNCHS). UNCHS did try to give nonvoting seats on its board to NGOs, local authorities, and business, but this was defeated at the commission meeting in 1997.

Deepening the Dialogue (1998–2000)

Although the Habitat II Committee Two process had not been completely successful, it did offer an interesting model that could be developed for use in the Earth Summit II process that followed. In 1996, UNED-UK suggested to the CSD NGO Steering Committee that a set of dialogues might be developed for the Earth Summit II processes in the following year. A letter was sent by the steering committee to Undersecretary-General Nitin Desai, asking that such dialogues be held at the CSD in April 1997. The suggestion was that each major group have half a day to examine what they had done, what they wanted to see Earth Summit II deliver, and what they would contribute to the future. This approach was supported by governments at the UN General Assembly discussions in October 1996. Another suggestion (made by the International NGO Task Group on Legal and Institutional Matters) was that a subcommission of the CSD be established to act as the body for major group and government dialogues (Pace and Maria 1997). This idea took root since for many governments, the model was already familiar from the human rights subcommission.

Unfortunately there turned out to be little dialogue in the 1997 Commission on Sustainable Development. As in Istanbul, the formal and informal sessions were held at the same time. Although some government delegates attended the informal (Committee Two) sessions, they tended to come from industrialized countries with large delegations and were rarely the key members. Nevertheless, the idea of structured stakeholder dialogues was written into the program of work for the CSD for the next five years. The first dialogue session was to be on the subject of industry in 1998. To prepare for this meeting, the director of the UN Division on Sustainable Development brought together the key major group representatives in Geneva, including the CSD NGO Steering Committee, the World Business Council on Sustainable Development (WBCSD), the International Chamber of Commerce (ICC), and the International Confederation of Free Trade Unions (ICFTU). These groups helped to frame the approach used in the dialogue sessions, and each was asked to consult with its members and produce position papers to be given to the UN by mid-January 1998 on responsible entrepreneurship, corporate management tools, technology cooperation, and industry and freshwater.

Significantly, each group was asked to produce a paper that had been peer reviewed by its stakeholder group. This was important since it moved the dialogue away from papers that merely expressed opinions toward positions that had been properly researched and referenced. In addition, industry representatives (the ICC) sat as members of the CSD NGO Steering Committee and so were fully aware of NGO positions. Combined with the close relationships built among individual NGO and industry representatives, this developed a level of trust that countered opposition from the more extreme members of each sector.

At the CSD meeting in 1998 there were two additional developments. The first was the opportunity to have peer group review of position papers between different stakeholders. The second was that governments were given the opportunity to challenge the ideas put forward by NGOs and major groups. Normal UN procedure is for major groups to make isolated presentations and for these to be noted, rather than discussed. To ensure that governments took the dialogues seriously, they were moderated by that year's chair of the CSD, Cielito Habito (minister for the environment in the Philippines). This persuaded governments to provide high-level representation. Positions were questioned by the chair or by governments, and this resulted in one of the key outcomes of the dialogue—a multistakeholder working group set up to review voluntary initiatives by industry. NGOs had been campaigning for such a mechanism for some years without success.

The dialogue process for 1999 focused on tourism. The four issues covered in the tourism dialogue were industry initiatives for sustainable tourism; consumer behavior and how to influence it; broad-based sustainable development through tourism; and the coastal impact of tourism. The new CSD Bureau under Simon Upton (environment minister for New Zealand), decided that there would be four major groups involved: NGOs (coordinated by the CSD NGO Steering Committee), business and industry (by the World Travel and Tourism Council and the International Hotel and Restaurant Association), trade unions (by the International Confederation of Free Trade Unions), and local authorities (by the International Council for Local Environmental Initiatives). The subject of tourism presented problems for NGOs since it is not a chapter of Agenda 21. Therefore, the CSD NGO Steering Committee embarked on a large-scale program of outreach to tourism-related NGOs. Over 300 NGOs were sent information on the CSD and its NGO steering committee as well as a questionnaire on their work on tourism.

The result was the establishment of a new NGO caucus on tourism under the cochairs of the steering committee. Building on lessons learned from the 1998 dialogue sessions, the steering committee recommended that papers produced by the major groups should be no longer than four sides, structured around four key issues: the problems to be addressed, possible solutions, institutional responsibilities, and possible partnerships. In addition to bringing in a whole new set of NGOs who had never participated at the CSD before, two of the major group coordinating bodies were also new to the dialogue process (local authorities and industry representatives). The steering committee provided advice and training to these groups, further cementing the trust that is critical to successful dialogue. These relationships were also nurtured during a gathering of the coordinators of the stakeholder groups involved in the tourism dialogue prior to the actual meeting. This gathering focused on finding common ground among stakeholders in terms of positive outcomes.

As in the first dialogue session there were significant breakthroughs. The outcomes of the 1999 dialogues were placed in front of the government negotiators by the chair of the CSD as they started negotiating on tourism, along with the outcomes from the high-level ministerial segment of the meeting. The second important outcome was the setting up of another multistakeholder working group under the World Tourism Organization to look at issues such as financial leakage, that is, the amount of money leaking out of the destination country. This group would also discuss how to encourage the involvement of local communities in the tourism industry as well as how to maximize benefits for these communities. The working group was also charged with improving information availability, building the capacity of NGOs and others to participate, and addressing other matters relevant to the international program on sustainable tourism.

Conclusion

As this chapter shows, the momentum for involving nonstate actors in UN negotiating processes that began with the Earth Summit gained considerable strength in the years that followed. The changes pioneered by the CSD NGO Steering Committee are now being examined for adaptation to other, similar processes. For example, the UN Environment Program's governing body has discussed a paper that would incorporate the dialogue process into its own deliberations for 2001. The final meeting of the Intergovernmental Forum on Forests (in February 2000) discussed a recommendation to establish a new permanent structure on forests with built-in multistakeholder participation. And the structure of the CSD NGO Steering Committee has been copied in other forums including the preparatory process for Earth Summit 2002, though not, as yet, for the Commissions on Social Development and the Status of Women. At a time when NGOs are being criticized for failing to put their house in order in the global arena, the NGO steering committee represents a valuable, concrete demonstration that it is possible to agree on formal standards for transparency, accountability, representation, and professionalism—a form of self-governance and self-regulation that avoids the dangers of heavy-handed intervention from above.

Since many of the major groups serve as the delivery system for implementing Agenda 21 and the other global agreements, they must be more involved in debates and discussions; otherwise governments lack the reality checks that NGOs can bring to the table and the commitment they can bring to implementation. NGOs are not asking for a seat at the table to vote on agreements; what they want is the opportunity to present their ideas and expertise. Governments—as in most cases the elected representatives of the population—should make the final decisions on global regimes. However, those decisions will be more informed, more rooted in reality, and more likely to be implemented if all relevant stakeholders have been involved in the discussions. If Earth Summit 2002 is to be a success, then approaches such as the dialogues described in this chapter should be integrated into all decisionmaking processes. The work of NGOs around the UN Commission on Sustainable Development over the last decade has become a beacon of hope for changing the intergovernmental negotiating process from a talking-shop approach to a democratic space for global problemsolving. This augurs well for the future of global governance.

Notes

1. Major groups are defined in Agenda 21 (the action plan that emerged from the Rio conference) as local authorities, NGOs, women, youth and children, academics and scientists, trade unions and workers, farmers, and indigenous people. Each has a chapter in Agenda 21 that defines their responsibilities.

2. UNED-UK is the National Committee for UNEP in the UK and the focal point for UNDP. It was set up in 1993 as a major groups forum in the UK.

3. Attending the discussions on behalf of the community were the International Confederation of Free Trade Unions (for trade unions), the International Network of Environment Managers (for industry), Women's Environment and Development Organization (for women), a group of NGOs including UNED-UK, the German Forum on Environment and Development, International Network for Small Island Developing States NGOs, and Pan African Movement.

PART 4

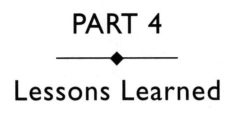

Lessons Learned

16

International Networking for Women's Human Rights

Charlotte Bunch
with Peggy Antrobus, Samantha Frost, and Niamh Reilly

In the last half of the twentieth century, women's activism reached a critical mass that was both reflected in and enhanced by the United Nations Decade for Women from 1976 to 1985 and four world conferences on women culminating in Beijing in 1995. Central to women's organizing in the 1990s has been a global movement for women's human rights. In asserting that "women's rights are human rights," it seeks to demonstrate both how traditionally accepted human rights abuses are specifically affected by gender and how many other violations against women have remained invisible. This international movement has many manifestations and reflects women's collaborative efforts across diverse contexts. This chapter examines one aspect of that development—the Global Campaign for Women's Human Rights and other global networks such as the Development Alternatives with Women for a New Era (DAWN).

The Global Campaign for Women's Human Rights is a loose coalition of groups and individuals worldwide, formed in preparation for the UN Conference on Human Rights held in Vienna in 1993.[1] Since the initial call for the conference did not mention women or recognize any gender-specific aspects of human rights in its proposed agenda, this became a natural vehicle for women's activities. One of the early actions of the campaign was a petition launched in 1991 that called on the Vienna conference to "comprehensively address women's human rights at every level of its proceedings" and to recognize "gender violence, a universal phenomenon which takes many forms across culture, race, and class ... as a violation of human rights requiring immediate action." The petition, distributed by the Center for Women's Global Leadership and the International Women's Tribune Center, was circulated through dozens of women's networks and taken up by women at all levels to further their organizing efforts. The petition was reissued after Vienna and directed to the Fourth World Conference on Women in Beijing two years later. By the time of the Beijing conference, the petition had gathered well over one million signatures from 148 countries in 26 languages, and had garnered over 1,000 sponsoring organizations.

This petition had been launched at the first annual campaign of Sixteen Days of Activism Against Gender Violence, which provides a global umbrella for local activities that promote public awareness about gender-based violence as a human rights concern. Groups participating in the campaign select their own objectives and determine their own local activities, within a larger global effort with some common themes. The campaign grew steadily during the 1990s, involving groups in over 100 countries in events including hearings, demonstrations, media campaigns, cultural festivals, and candlelight vigils. Many of its activities also mobilized women to participate in the UN world conferences, and since 1995, some have been directed at implementing the promises made to women in the various conference documents as well as in UN treaties such as the Convention on the Elimination of All Forms of Discrimination Against Women. The success of the global campaign was rooted in the activities of national and regional women's groups who defined the issues important in their countries as they focused attention on the world conferences. For example, at the UN regional preparatory meetings for the Vienna conference held in Tunis, San José, and Bangkok, women demanded that the human rights of women and gender-based violence be discussed. Women in Latin America organized a parallel women's human rights conference called La Nuestra, wherein they prepared a nineteen-point agenda to present to the regional meeting in San José (FIRE 1992). Women in Law and Development in Africa (WiLDAF) organized a series of subregional meetings in which women defined their human rights concerns and drew up a regional women's paper that was presented at the preparatory meetings (Butegwa 1993b).

As part of this process, the Center for Women's Global Leadership held a strategic planning institute to coordinate plans for Vienna with women from around the world who had been active regionally. This meeting worked on lobbying strategies for the conference, including further development of recommendations on women's human rights that built on regional proposals and served as the focus for the final international preparatory meeting in Geneva in April of 1993. Institute attendees also began preparations for a Global Tribunal on Violations of Women's Human Rights that would give vivid personal expression to the consequences of such violations. Participants would provide graphic demonstration of how being female can be life threatening, discussing such abuses as torture, terrorism, and slavery. Thirty-three women from all regions of the world testified in the tribunal about violations in five interconnected areas: human rights abuse in the family, war crimes against women, violations of women's bodily integrity, socioeconomic violations, and political persecution and discrimination (Bunch and Reilly 1994).

The UN World Conferences

At the UN Conference on Human Rights in Vienna, the message that "violence against women violates human rights" came through loud and clear. It advanced the introduction of new human rights instruments, including the adoption of the UN *Declaration on the Elimination of Violence Against Women* and the appointment of a UN special rapporteur on violence against women (United Nations 1994). Women effectively challenged the public-private divide in the global human rights arena and exposed violence against women as a human rights violation whether perpetrated by a male relative in the home or by a soldier in a war zone. The Vienna conference declaration devotes several pages to equal status and human rights of women as a priority for governments and the United Nations (United Nations 1994).

This progress was the product of women's organizing and networking nationally, regionally, and globally both before and during the conference. Daily women's caucuses formed at the final preparatory committee meeting in Geneva and during the Vienna conference proceedings constituted a critical part of this process. These caucuses crossed lines of North and South as well as NGOs and government in a concerted effort to make gender visible. The women's caucuses lobbied governments, but they also provided a space where women could learn about the process and debate what they wanted to achieve. The experience at Vienna provided the emerging women's human rights movement with a place to formulate an identity, which in turn facilitated the networking that has continued to take place among activists at other world conferences, as well as at other UN sessions and in various regional and international settings.

Much of the focus of the global campaign during 1993–1995 continued to be directed toward the various UN world conferences. In order to move beyond the initial focus on violence against women, the campaign sought to underscore the indivisibility of women's human rights and to emphasize the interconnectedness of the civil, political, social, economic, and cultural dimensions of all human rights in its activities. These included workshops, strategic planning meetings, human rights caucuses, and hearings on women's human rights at the UN World Conference on Population and Development (ICPD) in Cairo (Dutt 1995), the World Summit for Social

Development (WSSD) in Copenhagen, and at the Fourth World Conference on Women in Beijing.

At Copenhagen, the Hearing on Economic Justice and Women's Human Rights was coconvened in 1995 by the Center for Women's Global Leadership and DAWN. It highlighted the U.S. complicity in perpetrating human rights abuses at home and internationally, with women from around the world testifying about violations resulting from structural adjustment programs, budget cuts against social welfare, trade polices, and economic sanctions indifferent to women's human rights, forced prostitution, and the abuse of female migrant workers (Dutt et al. 1995). While women did not transform the social summit's final program of action, there were positive advances toward a gender-aware understanding of human rights as indivisible and toward greater accountability on the part of international financial institutions (World Summit on Social Development 1995). These advances included an affirmation of the importance of core human rights standards as well as a recognition of the increased burden on women created by poverty and a call for the valuation of women's unremunerated work.

The culmination of this series of hearings was the Global Tribunal on Accountability for Women's Human Rights, which took place at the NGO forum in the city of Huariou, outside of Beijing where the United Nations Fourth World Conference on Women was convened. The key issue for Beijing was accountability for implementing the promises that had been made at previous UN conferences. The tribunal therefore sought to move the women's human rights agenda from visibility to accountability, and from awareness of violations to active implementation of women's human rights. The process of organizing the Beijing tribunal followed a path similar to that of previous hearings convened by the Center for Women's Global Leadership. An international coordinating committee was formed, composed of representatives from networks as well as regional and national sponsoring organizations who identified and developed potential testimonies for the tribunal from their regions and/or areas of work. The final decisions about which testimonies to include and how to frame the issues were made through consultation with this committee. The focus was on the interconnected themes of violence against women in the family and in conflict situations, economic discrimination and exploitation, violations of health and bodily integrity, and political persecution. Testimonies were selected to highlight these themes and the work that tries to address them as well as to reflect the diversity of women's experiences across race, class, sexual orientation, ethnicity, culture, religion, and geopolitical lines (Reilly 1996; Bunch et al. 1996).

The Beijing tribunal was an early formative event at the NGO forum that helped to demonstrate the centrality of human rights to many of the critical areas of concern being debated in the "Platform for Action" at the governmental conference. Previous UN conferences on women had been seen primarily as discussions about "women and development" or "equality," but the Beijing conference expressed the issues more emphatically as questions of human rights. Many people came to understand that the Beijing platform was a referendum on the human rights of women in a whole range of areas. The women's human rights movement that had first become visible in Vienna came of age in Beijing. This shift in consciousness was the result of organizing and lobbying that women's human rights activists had been doing at the local, national, regional, and global level. The function of the Global Campaign for Women's Human Rights was to help give this diverse activity a coherent international expression and visibility. The women's human rights caucus in Beijing worked to incorporate human rights perspectives in many parts of the platform and collaborated with other NGO caucuses to prevent the conservative backlash against women's gains that threatened to use Beijing to undermine the achievements women had made. The international and regional networking that women undertook for Beijing ensured that the "Platform for Action" reasserted the universal and holistic nature of women's human rights.

Since Beijing, the work of the Global Campaign for Women's Human Rights has shifted to the implementation of intergovernmental agreements and human rights treaties. This means both pressuring national governments for domestic-level implementation of the promises they have made at the international and regional levels and keeping the momentum of the international networks going so that governments know that they are being monitored worldwide. Groups from the campaign continue to work together globally to lobby the various human rights mechanisms of the UN to fulfill their commitment to integrate fully gender concerns and awareness into their work. In 1998, the Global Campaign organized to ensure that gender perspectives were part of commemorations of the 50th Anniversary of the Universal Declaration of Human Rights, and it is now working to make certain that the five-year reviews of the various UN World Conferences advance women's human rights.

Diversity, Universality, and Women's Human Rights

The human rights approaches used by women in the campaign have strengthened local mobilization efforts and advanced local objectives, while at the same time linking local agendas to a larger international movement with broad common goals. Women from different regions have been able to use human rights concepts to articulate diverse demands in relation to a broad array of issues. Human rights language creates a space in which different accounts of women's lives and new ways of demanding change can be developed. It provides a set of overarching principles to frame alternative visions of gender justice, without dictating the precise content of those visions. The idea of universal human rights provides a powerful vocabulary for naming gender-based violations and impediments to the exercise of women's full equality and citizenship. Furthermore, the large body of international human rights covenants, agreements, and commitments gives women potential political leverage and concrete points of reference for their organizing and lobbying activities.

Women's human rights networking has also faced criticisms of its efforts to find a common articulation of women's concerns or a common basis for women's organizing. Some argue that to do so is to universalize the category of "woman" and to impose a limited agenda on all women on the basis of the experience of some—usually white, middle class, and living in the global North. As women's movements have grown over the past three decades, grassroots and professional activists and academics have had unprecedented opportunities for dialogue around gender-based oppression. In the course of these important and often contentious debates, women have been pressed to think about the ways in which geography, ethnicity, race, culture, sexuality, class, and tradition shape what it means to be a woman. These issues, combined with the specificities of local and national politics, point to the fact that it is difficult to conceive of women or the women's movement as singular entities.

A major bone of contention has been that patterns of exclusion and invisibility are reinforced by an uncritical assumption that all women share common and easily identifiable experiences and self-understandings. Women of color in the United States, for example, have leveled powerful critiques at the theory and politics of mainstream feminists, arguing that their analyses and visions for change have tended to be formulated around the concerns of economically privileged, heterosexual, white women-citizens. When this happens, inequality and power differentials among women are not adequately taken into account as key factors that shape women's lives. In order to consider how issues such as class, race, culture, or sexuality actually affect women, such factors must be incorporated into the structure of theory and strategy, not simply added on at a later date. Many of these critiques came from the writings and activism of women in the global South. Basu (1995: 4), for example, argues that "women's identities within and across nations are shaped by a complex amalgam of national, racial, religious, ethnic, class, and sexual identities," and that these specificities shape and inform the challenges that women face and the work that women do. If feminism is defined only in terms of Western conceptions, not only is there a danger of inappropriately imposing Western priorities, but there may be a failure to recognize the strength and transformative potential of women's organizing as it exists at local levels. The need to recognize the specificity of local feminisms and women's activism is at the heart of debates about the role of universal claims in women's organizing. The challenge is to reconcile the recognition and strength of the multiplicity of women's experiences with the need to find a common basis for women's international networking and collaboration.

The international movement for women's human rights has consciously sought to respond to these challenges. The global campaign encouraged regional networks in the South to play a leadership role at both the local and international levels. National and local groups participated in defining and implementing international lobbying strategies at UN conferences. The campaign also included many women who worked in mixed sex groups in development or human rights organizations to ensure that women's concerns were viewed from different angles and that they began to form an integral part of these other agendas.

In thinking about how to reconcile differences among women and still find common ways to work politically, Mohanty (1991: 13–14) emphasizes that women can identify opportunities for coherent "Third World feminist" struggles that are based on "common differences." Even though women experience oppression differently, they do so in relation to common systems of power and domination that affect all women in the third world. Similarly, the experience of the women's human rights movement suggests that international networking does not require homogeneity of experience. Rather, the complexity with which different women contend can enrich the movement's understanding of the multiple forces at work, even as it finds common themes in the opposition that women face. For example, economic globalization is experienced in different forms according to context—economic liberalization, structural adjustment, downward pressure on wages, and loss of job security—but women affected by the global economy can join in making common demands. As women have worked to incorporate diverse perspectives into their work, they have also struggled to create alliances across different groups in the face of a conservative, fundamentalist backlash against feminism in many parts of the world. Faced by the need to do justice to the many different ways women experience and act on their concerns *and* the need to make claims in the name of women in order to counter this backlash, what does it mean to say that women's human rights are universal? As Butegwa (1993a) points out, human rights are universal in the sense that all human rights laws, treaties, and procedures theoretically apply equally to all people. In addition, by shifting the focus away from particular experiences to an analysis of the interconnected ways in which power is exercised in the world, an argument can be made that universal human rights provide the only system of accountability that is able to confront the powers that deny women their rights across the globe.

When local women's groups use human rights thinking and practice, especially in the context of international networking, they are actively demonstrating the complementary links that exist between universal ideals and local struggles for justice. The international movement for women's human rights has challenged the idea that we must choose between universality and particularity by developing its ideas and tactics through a process of networking at the local, national, and international levels in all regions of the world. DAWN's experience provides a good illustration of this process.

Women's Regional and International Networks: The Case of DAWN

DAWN is a network of women from the South who are actively engaged in feminist research and analysis of global issues related to economic justice, environmental sustainability, reproductive health and rights, and political restructuring. Launched in the context of the United Nation's Third World Conference on Women held in Nairobi in 1985, DAWN represents Third World women's increasing concerns about the impact of debt, food security, environmental degradation, deteriorating social services, militarism, political conservatism, and religious fundamentalism on the lives of poor women. DAWN's analysis, drawn from the experience of poor women in the South, provided the basis for a platform document for the NGO Forum at Nairobi and underpinned a series of panel discussions on feminist perspectives on development (Sen and Grown 1987). By introducing an analysis that related the daily experiences of women to colonial relations between countries and the macroeconomic policy framework, DAWN gave women a new way of viewing global processes and development issues. DAWN's analysis is characterized by its

- focus on the experience of poor women living in the global South;
- acknowledgement of regional diversity;
- linking of economic, social, cultural, and political factors;
- attempt to link experience at the micro level of women's daily lives to an understanding of the macroeconomic policy framework;
- understanding of the political nature of development;
- use of a feminist framework—rejecting dichotomies, validating women's work and experience, and working in solidarity with women.

This analysis has changed the terms of the debate on women in development (WID) in many arenas. The shift to a more holistic, political analysis of the issues also helped to mobilize women worldwide into a real political constituency.

Following the success of the panels at the Nairobi forum, DAWN's Founders organized a meeting in Rio to launch an ongoing program of research and advocacy.[2] A steering committee, representative of the five regions of the South, was formed and a general coordinator selected (Neuma Aguiar of the University Research Institute for Rio de Janeiro [IUPERJ]). DAWN's first secretariat was established in Rio using IUPERJ as an institutional base, but it was always envisaged that the secretariat would rotate to different regions—to the University of the West Indies in 1990 (with Peggy Antrobus as general coordinator) and to the University of the South Pacific under Claire Slatter six years later. At the general assembly in Rio in 1990, the steering committee was restructured by separating the functions of regional representation (under regional coordinators) and research and analysis (under research coordinators). Research coordinators were selected to facilitate work on environment, reproductive rights and population, and alternative economic frameworks.[3] DAWN's research is developed through regional meetings that enrich the analysis with specific experiences. Participants include activists as well as researchers so that the analysis is informed by political realities and linked to organizing and advocacy at the regional level.

DAWN's experience shows that effective grassroots mobilization requires consistent analysis and strategic thinking. The network's ongoing research program has provided the basis for powerful ideas and strategic thinking and has served as a catalyst for a South-based and South-led global women's movement. In 1996, DAWN's work program was redefined to build on the gains made through the UN conferences while retaining the network's core function of producing cutting-edge feminist analyses of global issues from a Southern perspective. At this meeting in 1996 it was also decided to strengthen engagement at the regional level and give greater attention to regional issues and priorities by linking to, and working in partnership with, existing organizations and institutions. DAWN's mainstreaming activities also included the involvement of network members in the work of progressive networks such as the Society for International Development and Focus on the Global South as well as in NGO initiatives such as the Structural Adjustment Program Review Initiative (SAPRI), which involved a wide range of civil society groups in evaluating World Bank adjustment operations.

From 1997, improved access to e-mail and the Internet brought a new dimension to DAWN's work, strengthening the network by facilitating consultation and collective decisionmaking on a regular basis and building close and supportive relationships through regular communications. The relocation of DAWN's secretariat to Fiji in 1998 was greatly facilitated by the rise of information technology. Basing the secretariat of an active global network in a far-flung, small island state illustrates the potential for new network structures in the age of electronic communications. For DAWN, the policy of rotating the secretariat also ensures that different regions of the South will benefit from its analysis and advocacy work and that DAWN will eventually earn a profile in each of these regions.

Other networks contributed to the global campaign in similar ways. Women in Law and Development in Africa (WiLDAF), for example, took a leadership role in the international women's human rights movement.[4] What is important about the development of WiLDAF and other networks is that the process of formulating mission and priorities, and of raising the necessary support, was broadly participatory. Established in 1990, the planning process originally included women from nine African countries but eventually drew on the ideas, suggestions, and energy of women from more than fifteen as well as from other regional and international networks. The international solidarity network of Women Living Under Muslim Laws (WLUML) defines its mission according to the needs of women living in Muslim communities all over the world.[5] Its structure fosters respect for the diverse "contextual constraints within which women are obliged to live their lives" and for the choices women make (Shaheed 1995: 315). WLUML gains its strength and critical edge by creating links among diverse women living in Muslim contexts, giving women's organizations access both to each other and to information about the sources of law and customary practices. The exchange of information and crosscultural visits and research provide women in the network with an alternative identity through which they develop political analyses and strategies for change. In networks, different groups can use their organizational strengths, commitments, and resources to participate in projects on a flexible basis. Networking allows for coordinated but decentralized and nonhierarchical action around common goals.

Lessons Learned

The chief impact of the global campaign lay in opening spaces for women from different racial and ethnic groups, countries, classes, and occupational backgrounds to meet on a consistent and continuous basis. These meetings enabled women to gain new knowledge and to learn from each other's experience. They facilitated the organization of joint projects and collaborative efforts. They gave birth to issue-based networks at local, regional, and global levels, which in turn provided the research and analysis that served to empower women's advocacy. They helped women to develop self-confidence and leadership skills. They linked activists with researchers and, more importantly, validated and encouraged the pursuit of research among activists, and activism among researchers. They forged and strengthened links between organizing at local and global levels. They facilitated the growth of a global women's movement of the greatest diversity and decentralization, a movement that expanded its agenda, from a narrow definition of "women's issues" to one embracing a range of concern for human rights, and transformed itself into a major constituency for a more humane world.

The Global Campaign for Women's Human Rights has been based on personal and institutional relationships among feminist organizations and regional networks that are comfortable in using loose forms of networking as a primary mode of mobilizing. Its driving force is a shared commitment to action-oriented networking in relation to specific opportunities and events. Participants have varied according to which groups shared a common interest at particular moments in time. Hence, while the campaign cemented working relationships, it has not led to a permanent governance structure or a defined set of members. This has given the campaign great flexibility, but it has also weakened its ability to maintain sustained pressure and pursue commitments on an ongoing basis. One of the keys to the campaign's success has been the unifying value system and legitimacy provided by organizing around human rights for women. Another has been the selection of common issues around which to focus, such as violence against women at the Vienna conference. As the campaign has sought to broaden the agenda of women's human rights issues to more complex problems including the impact of the global economy, it has been more difficult to unite diverse groups around common demands. One of the campaign's other guiding principles has been its commitment to building links among women committed to a common vision of rights but diverse in terms of race, ethnicity, class, religion, sexual orientation, culture, and geography. While the connections have not always reached out as widely as hoped (especially along class lines), the movement has succeeded in creating strong and enduring bonds among diverse groups of women. Networking has also been fostered across professional divisions such as grassroots organizing, service provision, academia, the medical and legal professions, lobbyists, and governmental or UN policymakers. This has been an effective way to learn from diversity in the process of planning actions that incorporate a broad spectrum of strategies.

Networking takes place on many levels, but it is also important to have organizations that are able to serve as nodes of information, conveners, and centers of capacity building and leadership development. The Center for Women's Global Leadership, DAWN, WiLDAF, WLUML, and others all play this role. These nodes not only provide time and space for organizations to make plans but also lay the groundwork for the trust necessary in global work. Face-to-face contact, whether in small meetings, at sessions during world conferences, or while organizing a hearing, proved critical to making the movement strong. In this way, women related to each other through their work but also began to know each other across their differences. Finally, maintaining connections and a fluid sense of exchange between local and global activities have been at the heart of the global campaign. A defining feature is that no one group determines or controls the activities. This allows for local definition of the agenda and of the issues that are important to women in each setting. At the same time, women can use the fact that they are part of an international network to draw on solidarity in enhancing their local organizing. Shaheed (1995: 318) highlights similar themes when she concludes that "positive outcomes are the result of multiple actors working in concert; ... the [WLUML] network sees itself only as an enabling mechanism for rapidly mobilizing support and activating the right connections as needed." Since local and regional organizations have the flexibility to join whichever activities seem appropriate to them, they retain their own autonomy while also cooperating in a larger global endeavor.

The experiences that women have gained in networking around the UN world conferences have provided the basis of trust from which women now work on common and diverse projects in collaboration on a regular basis. In this process, women's networking has developed a model that affirms the universality of human rights while respecting the diversity of particular experiences. This experience may hold the key to success for other movements in their pursuit of global citizen action.

Notes

1. The Global Campaign for Women's Human Rights was coordinated primarily by the Center for Women's Global Leadership in collaboration with many other organizations and networks around the world. For further information about the Center or the Global Campaign, contact the Center for Women's Global Leadership, Rutgers University, 160 Ryders Lane, New Brunswick, NJ 08901; phone (1 732) 932-8782; fax (1 732) 932-1080; email cwgl@igc.apc.org.

2. The founding members were the women who had met in Bangalore. They included Devaki Jain, Gita Sen, and Ela Bhatt (India); Hameeda Hossain (Bangladesh); Noeleen Heyzer (Malaysia); Claire Slatter and Vanessa Griffiths (Fiji); Fatima Mernissi (Morocco); Achola Pala Okeyo (Kenya); Marie Angelique Savane (Senegal); Neuma Aguiar and Carmen Barroso (Brazil); and Peggy Antrobus and Lucille Mair (Caribbean).

3. These themes were modified in 1996 to sustainable livelihoods, reproductive rights and health, and the political economy of globalization.

4. For further information about WiLDAF, contact WiLDAF, P.O. Box 4622, Harare, Zimbabwe; phone (263-4) 752105; fax (263-4) 733670; email wildaf@mango.zw.

5. For further information about WLUML, contact Women Living Under Muslim Laws International Solidarity Network, P.O. Box 28445, London N19 5ZH, UK; phone 44 20 7263 0285.

17

Squatting on the Global Highway: Community Exchanges for Urban Transformation

Sheela Patel, Joel Bolnick, and Diana Mitlin

We learnt the experience of Mahila Milan and we were impressed. But still we did not believe it would work. It started to catch on gradually until, today, people question me when they do not see me every day. I learnt from my neighbour about the savings system. I am shy and can't talk to people easily but I know my neighbour and I decided to give it a try. I did not always want to come to the meetings because I felt uncomfortable but they would come and ask me to join them anyway. They said: you will learn and become less shy over time. At the meetings I was forced to speak by the others. At first I thought they were against me but it worked: Here I am! I live in my own house and I come to India now to share my experiences.

—Xoliswa Tiso, South Africa

Poor people, especially poor women, are skeptical about the solutions presented to them by professional experts, but they are unable to respond in kind. Despite the priority given to participation and empowerment by development agencies, there have been few opportunities for the poor themselves to develop alternatives and present these to their neighbors. In recent years, much has been done to try to ensure the effective participation of poor people, but in most participatory methodologies and programs, the teaching (and, therefore, a critical part of the learning and synthesizing processes) remains in the hands of professionals.

Since 1990, NGOs in Asia and South Africa have supported community-to-community exchanges in order to transform development options, enabling poor people to plan, control, and negotiate their own development strategies. As the process has evolved, international exchanges among the urban poor have spread, offering a practical illustration of both the workings and significance of global civil society. From those exchanges has emerged a people's movement, now linking more than 650,000 members in eleven countries. The links within this movement lie not in formal constitutions or e-mail circulars but in one group of visitors sharing their stories around a fire in someone's shack or mapping a settlement with the local residents. Their activities are not concerned with international lobbying, petitions, treaties, and monitoring the World Bank, although these activities are global in scope. At the heart of this movement is a network of people-to-people exchanges. The squatters in one settlement share their hopes and frustrations, their successes and their problems with others; in so doing, they understand and analyze their situations, gain new insights and strategies, mobilize other residents, and secure the confidence and support they need to move forward.

This movement started in Mumbai in 1987. Groups of pavement dwellers, mainly women, began to develop strategies to address their needs and to share them with their neighbors.[1] Through this sharing, the capacity to teach, disseminate new ideas, explore current events, and analyze settlement and city development options has become embedded in these communities. The women pavement dwellers in India formed a network of women's savings collectives, Mahila Milan, and joined with an existing network of grassroots organizations, the National Slum Dwellers' Federation. The federating process has provided an institution through which their activities could be supported and their exchanges planned and coordinated. As the women of India visited more countries and talked about their approach and their work, the number of savings collectives grew, as did national federations. In 1996, these federations agreed to formalize their international links with the formation of Shack/Slum Dwellers International (SDI). In this chapter we describe the approach of the member organizations of SDI and its significance for people-centered development.

Under Urban Development and Urban Poverty we summarize the urban context in which these organizations have emerged and the scale and nature of the development challenge they face. Under Learning by Doing we then describe the emergence of Mahila Milan and how the need for new models of urban development led to a search for ways of enhancing community learning and, hence, exchanges. In the section titled From Local to Global, we identify and discuss the ways in which this global network can make a difference in the struggles faced by individual settlements and to the capacity of national federations. At the conclusion of the chapter, we consider some of the wider implications of the work of Shack/Slum Dwellers International for people-centered development.

Urban Development and Urban Poverty

Urbanization continues to rise and, by 2025, it is anticipated that most of the people living in the South will be living in towns and cities (United Nations Centre for Human Settlements 1996). At present, an estimated 600 million people living in urban areas are either homeless or living in inadequate, unsafe homes that lack basic services and infrastructure (WHO 1992). As argued by Satterthwaite (1996: 9), between one-third and one-half of urban citizens in the South may have incomes too low to meet basic needs. Existing institutions for urban governance are, for the most part, finding it difficult to address this challenge. Decentralization has placed new roles and responsibilities on local authorities, often without the necessary skills, experience, or resources (McCarney 1996). In the absence of competent authorities, the poor generally find a solution to their needs in the informal sector. Most housing is provided illegally by the poor themselves. Many settlements have been built illegally by squatters and have never received services from government. Residents find water, manage waste, and become the urban planners of squatter areas.

Both governments and development agencies concerned with poverty reduction and urban development programs are increasingly recognizing that residents need to be involved in improvement plans and activities. Governments have been urged to change their approach to the development of informal areas in favor of "enablement strategies." To ensure local ownership, state departments and development agencies have sought both to improve consultation and, in some cases, to offer local residents joint program management (Nelson and Wright 1995). But rarely have these programs and policies resulted in the sustained local improvements and the empowerment of the poor. One of the reasons is that while most low-income settlements have some form of community or grassroots organization, this rarely includes all the citizens in the area, and women and the poorest members are often underrepresented. All too often, such organizations serve the interests of the more dominant individual within the settlement (see, for example, Scheper-Hughes 1992).

Solutions to urban poverty require the involvement and commitment of the urban poor themselves if they are to take place at the scale that is necessary. As important step is an increase in the capacity of grassroots organizations to represent themselves to the powerful professional agencies who control state resources and who set official policies. Equally important is that they both represent and are accountable to the needs of local residents. Understanding how these changes can be achieved is critical to ensuring that the cities of the future address the needs of their poorest citizens. This chapter describes how the approach of one organization has spread to include organizations in eleven countries that now work together in a global movement to support the people's development of low-income settlements.

Learning by Doing

A Strategy for Change

SPARC, originally the Society for the Promotion of Area Resource Centers, is an Indian NGO that started work in 1984 in the E ward in the Byculla area in Mumbai. The ward houses the major Bombay port, vegetable and food markets, and small-scale power looms—all of which have attracted migrants and other day laborers, who work for less than minimum wage and need to live close to their jobs. As a result, the E ward has one of the largest populations of pavement dwellers in the city.

From the beginning, SPARC's focus was the women pavement dwellers who represented the most vulnerable people in the city. Two years after starting work, SPARC entered into a partnership with the National Slum Dwellers' Federation (NSDF), a national organization of leaders of informal settlements around India. The federation was set up in 1974 by community leaders who were disillusioned with welfare oriented interventions of professional agencies and who decided to act independently to secure land tenure and basic amenities. The federation had previously worked with several NGOs but had always found that the NGO sought to control the development process. After observing the manner in which SPARC engaged communities of pavement dwellers in the E ward, the federation began to explore an alliance. The NSDF/SPARC alliance has, from the beginning, combined the strength of both organizations to better address the needs of the poor. SPARC provides the interface with formal development authorities and the federation mobilizes communities at the grassroots; both agencies support the development of new options.

SPARC recognized that women have to play a central role in the survival strategies of the urban poor. Women are the main community managers, creating systems to deal with water and sanitation and delaying the frequent demolition of houses. The informal networks of women that first worked with SPARC began to consolidate around women's groups that promoted savings and loans to their members. Gradually, this network developed into Mahila Milan (Women Together), an organization of women's collectives that manages women's savings and loan groups. Mahila Milan emerged as the third partner of the alliance, together with SPARC and the National Slum Dwellers' Federation.

From the outset, the alliance was conscious of the need to work with government. The tradition of policy advocacy among many Southern NGOs is to consult communities and write up alternative policies that they submit to the city or the state. Often, the policies are good and much needed, but most communities have neither training, the exposure, nor the capacity to take advantage of such processes and, hence, many pro-poor reforms even when introduced remain unused. Thus, there are many ideal policies and programs, but few make any positive impact on the poor and even fewer have a positive impact on a large scale. This may be particularly the case in providing housing and basic services that have traditionally been the responsibility of the state and for which there is little capacity in grassroots organizations and other institutions of civil society.

SPARC and its partners decided to follow another route, that of precedent setting. Precedent setting starts by recognizing that changing policy to practice requires local communities to mobilize for policy changes and then to take these up. The alliance believes that the existing strategies used by the poor are the most effective starting point for improvements, although they may need to be modified. Hence, the alliance supports the refinement of these strategies and then their demonstration to city officials as precedent-setting interventions. Because they emerge from the existing practices of the poor, they make sense to other grassroots organizations, are widely supported, and can easily be implemented on a larger scale. As these "precedents" are put into practice, they show senior policymakers and administrators that it is possible to do things differently. When precedents are accompanied by mass demonstrations of support, this reinforces the conviction that they can go to scale.

How can precedent setting be put in place? Securing changes in policy and practice through precedent setting requires the development of alternatives that are widely supported by grassroots organizations. Once the need for policy change has been demonstrated by precedent, so lobbying of state institutions and local implementation seeks to ensure that the required policy changes are introduced. A good example is found in the impact over time of the housing design and construction done by SPARC. When SPARC and its allies first decided to work on housing issues, the process of direct influence of government seemed enormously difficult. So, rather than react to existing policies, it simply began: the group designed its own houses using low-cost materials. It set up a housing exhibition and used its model to demand changes in the design of other housing built by the government. By 1996, when the Maharashtra government developed a new policy for housing, the strategy of including resettling pavement dwellers was included. Community exchanges for local learning and for mobilization played a critical role in this process.

Community Learning

In SPARC's case, precedent setting is a strategy for influencing policy embedded within a deeper value system. The alliance believes that there can be no social change that benefits low-income communities if the poor do not participate in designing, managing, and realizing the change. Precedents require that community activity. Changes are likely to incorporate existing practices—no one knows how to survive poverty as well as the poor. But they are also likely to involve a refinement of those practices. That requires professional involvement but, most importantly, it requires community reflection, analysis, and learning. To address this need, Mahila Milan and the federation began to use different approaches to engage local savings groups and other residents in grassroots learning. Community-to-community exchanges emerged as the tool to use because such exchanges encouraged reflection and analysis, built confidence among the poor, and mobilized large numbers of people to participate in their own development.

SPARC describes its community exchange program and its significance thus:

> The exchange process builds upon the logic of "doing is knowing." Exchanges lead to good sharing of experience and, therefore, a new set of people learning new skills. ... They draw large numbers of people into a process of change and help to enable the poor to reach out and federate. ... They help to create personalised and strong bonds between communities who share common problems, presenting them with a wide range of options to choose from and negotiate for, and ensuring them they are not alone in their struggles.[2]

Where professionals are the agents of change, the locus of learning is taken away from the community, or is never invested within it. As a result, communities are unable to advance their own strategies and approaches for addressing their own problems. The solutions to urban poverty are driven by the understanding of professionals and, consequently, are often too expensive and inappropriate to the needs of poor people. The ability to create genuine federations and networks of poor urban communities that have a voice in city affairs is denied, along with the empowerment and solidarity that this can build.

When communities share their experiences, learning from one another and jointly implementing the changes that emerge through the exchange process, the problems of disenfranchisement are addressed. Local communities own the refinement of development interventions that are low-cost and appropriate. As they share their experiences, they are drawn together to ensure a political presence within the city and the country.

The organization of exchanges varies between country and according to need, but the process can be summarized as follows: Exchanges are either exploratory or with a specific focus. In exploratory exchanges, one community shares its stories with another in an open-ended manner. The exchange gives an opportunity for the community to look at its needs and how they might better be met. Exchanges with a focus involve communities coming together around a specific activity, such as sharing building skills, resolving internal conflicts and problems in one community, and supporting public events. The visiting community is selected because of what it can bring to the issues currently faced by the host community. In both exploratory and focused exchanges, a group from one community visits another for several days, sharing the lives of the hosts and exploring issues at their own pace. Regional and national leaders play a lead role in identifying which community should visit the other; NGO support organizes transport, reimburses basic costs, and helps to draw out lessons to improve this process.

The Growth of International Exchanges

In 1988, SPARC became one of the founding NGOs of the Asian Coalition for Housing Rights (ACHR), a regional group of professional agencies (particularly NGOs) working with the urban poor to support poverty reduction in urban areas. Through the coalition, SPARC began to share the methodology of exchanges with other NGOs and community-based organizations in Asia. The coalition's early activities included more traditional advocacy and lobbying for policy change, for example, to prevent evictions related to the Olympic Games in Seoul, Korea. Other work has included international support for national policy changes—for instance, supporting member organizations' activities in defense of housing rights. More recently, greater emphasis has been given to learning and to the exchange of ideas and people among member organizations in order to strengthen local capacity. These activities have concentrated on practical learning through visits and exchanges among members (who participate together with the community organizations and local government agencies with whom they are working).

In the early 1990s, SPARC began a regular program of exchanges with communities working with the People's Dialogue on Land and Shelter, a South African NGO. The People's Dialogue was set up in 1991 to support networking among the squatter communities and others living in informal settlements. In 1994, the community-based savings schemes that emerged from the exchanges with India came together to form the South African Homeless People's Federation. This federation in turn initiated an extensive range of exchanges within South Africa and among South Africa and other countries in Africa.

These community-to-community exchanges came together in the

growth of an international movement formalized as the Shack/Slum Dwellers International in 1996. All member organizations share a similar approach to development with three primary characteristics:

- Residents are organized into local community groups based around savings and loans. Savings attracts a high proportion of women members.
- Members of savings groups initiate community driven interventions with community-to-community exchanges being used for reflection and analysis, mobilization, skill development, capacity building, and mutual support.
- Savings groups are consolidated in national federations for squatters and the homeless.

Table 17.1 outlines the growth of this international movement and the following section looks in more detail at the benefits that local communities secure through membership in such an international body.

Table 17.1   The Growth of SDI

1987:	Asian women's gathering in Bombay hosted by SPARC
1988–1990:	Bombay to Bogota exchange (SPARC and FedeVivienda)
1989:	The Asian People's Dialogue in Seoul, sponsored by ACHR, Korea
1991:	SPARC (India), People's Dialogue (South Africa) exchange process started, South African Homeless People's Federation (South Africa) linked to Namibia Housing Action Group (NHAG)
1993:	ACHR: Training and Advisory Program
1993:	SPARC/NSDF/Mahila Milan/ACHR exploration in Cambodia, formation of Squatter Urban Poor Forum in Phnomh Penh (SUPF)
1995:	South African Homeless People's Federation connects to Zimbabwe
1996:	South African Homeless People's Federation links to Kenya initiated; inception of SDI
1997:	Philippines joins the exchange process
1998:	Consolidation of activities in Zimbabwe leading to the formation of the Zimbabwean Homeless People's Federation, links among Namibia, Kenya, and Zimbabwe established

From Local to Global

The main focus of Shack/Slum Dwellers International is to strengthen member activities. Invariably, this has a local focus although there is no conscious decision that this should be the level at which the international federation operates. Rather, the focus emerges from an eagerness to support the ongoing struggles of members to secure land and infrastructure, develop housing, and obtain state finance. As a result, this global process is a movement of solidarity and mutual understanding among the urban poor. It is not a global process that focuses on international policies and practices, but it is global in outreach and efforts to strengthen groups' capacities to deal with what is oppressive and exploitative within their local environment.

International community exchanges are the primary mechanism that draws together the national federations of autonomous savings groups into an international movement. International exchanges cannot replace local and national exchanges, but they can build on active national processes. In a number of countries, exposure visits have taken place without any local federation being in place. In such situations, the international exposure visits seek first to catalyze the creation of a federation and then to support its growth. The older members of the network are now very familiar with such processes.

The participants in international exchanges are generally national or experienced community leaders with something special to offer. The style of learning and teaching is similar to a local exchange, but being international the processes require greater patience as translations are necessary. The full value of the international exchange process may take longer to emerge as community leaders need to understand each other's situations, politics, and culture. But, as indicated below, there are also immediate benefits.

Putting Problems in Perspective

Central to the process of change is the creation of knowledge. Local residents gain new understanding as they tell their stories in a different context. They start to explore some of their own frailties in a nondefensive way as they talk about their experiences, both positive and negative, in order to assist the development of others. International exchanges offer a discontinuity from home situations that suddenly takes community leaders outside of accepted relationships and norms. At the same time, continuity with the development approaches underlying the SDI network orientates participants to a common philosophy. Ultimately, the placement of familiar problems such as relations with local authorities or alternative uses of loan finance in new contexts prompts them to explore alternatives.

Capacity for Change

Planning and management skills play an important part in organizational capacity. Managing exchanges (especially international exchanges) and the events associated with them help to develop local capacity. This process can itself be a catalyst for addressing other problems within the community. As such, it provides practical training in governance. Communities that can organize managing exchanges gain increased confidence and a considerable reputation within the city in which they work. A recent housing exhibition in Kanpur illustrates this process (see Box 17.1).

Placed in the Public Arena

With the status of "international experts," the urban poor themselves become an important attraction. Community leaders often have to deal with guests brought by city officials or NGOs, but they are passive observers during such visits. With an international exchange, community leaders from another country are invited to receptions with senior politicians and to media interviews. Suddenly these individuals find themselves invited to adopt roles from which they have long been excluded. This process makes them reexamine self-expectations and gives them new confidence when they return home.

As the international guests are drawn into local activities, political opportunities arise for the host community. Local residents and government officials interact with an international audience that favors the poor. Controversial issues can be raised and promises recorded. Box 17.2 describes how members of Shack/Slum Dwellers International used this exchange process to support pro-poor savings programs as well as the federation of homeless people in Zimbabwe.

A Sense of Solidarity

Exchanges create a growing solidarity among poor urban communities. It is from this experience that Shack/Slum Dwellers International has grown. Membership provides communities with a feeling of not only ownership over the federation but also involvement in a much larger collective. City-level federations of groups of the urban poor ensure that communities are represented in city decisionmaking and that they have a voice in city affairs. Thus, another benefit of exchanges is to empower poor communities and to work toward more democratic local governance.

Optimizing Investments

International exchanges help to use a national leadership to maximum effect. Through setting and implementing precedents, exchanges have helped to change policy and practice in favor of the urban poor. The growing effectiveness of the international network can be illustrated through land release. It took the Indian federation ten years to obtain their first land

Box 17.1 The Housing Exhibition at Kanpur

The housing exhibition was a chance for the local federation and Mahila Milan groups in the city to present their plans to the city government. They had recently been given land to develop their first 45 houses. Now they could demonstrate both their development process and the homes that they would soon have.

The housing exhibition involved 5,000 local visitors (from other federation groups and government officials), 200 leaders from other cities around India and 45 international guests from seven countries. The meeting lasted for three days and included a "public day" for the local visitors and two days of discussions with those from outside the city. Throughout this period, the local leadership had meetings with city and state officials. The communities from other countries were brought into the dialogue with the state, ensuring that they were introduced gradually and convincingly to new ideas and experiences from Asia and Africa.

In addition to these strategic discussions, the local groups managed the practical aspects of hosting these visitors (food and accommodation) and erected several full-size two-story-house models using timber frames and cloth to give a visual impression of their future plans.

Source: Summarized by the authors from internal SPARC documents, 1998.

---

for housing development; the South African federation spent four years; now, the Zimbabwean federation has secured land after one year of work. Furthermore a recent estimate suggests that U.S.$11.5 million have been secured by the urban poor (primarily from national and local governments), partly as a result of nine international exchanges (mainly those between India and South Africa). In addition to working together to release government monies and share information about donors and development assistance funds, Shack/Slum Dwellers International is now looking at ways to use finances held by one group to assist another.

This discussion has summarized the best of what exchanges have to offer. Of course there are also many different problems associated with exchanges, some more serious that others. One of the more serious problems is that the visiting community might take on the expert role, telling the host community how to proceed, rather than providing support. This can be particularly problematic in a situation that requires innovation because the existing solutions are simply not good enough. There is never a quick answer that can be given by an outsider. Rather the community must strategize together and move forward in ways they negotiate and agree.

However, the exchange process offers at least one positive aspect: The visitors go away. This creates a self-rightening mechanism. What is valuable

Box 17.2 Sharing Experiences in Zimbabwe

Three South African community leaders, Patricia Matelongwe, Rose Maso, and Shalot Adams visited the Dzivarasekwa extension (a low-income resettlement community) for a weekend-long exchange program in August 1998.

Sunday, August 22. Sunday started with the daily collections. The twenty collectors perfected their skills with Shalot. Patricia and Rose and two of the savings group leaders at Dzivarasekwa, Shadreck Tondori and Elizabeth Kananji, went to the broadcasting center for a television interview. In the interview, Patricia outlined the successes of the South African Homeless People's Federation. She explained how they had been first assisted by the Indians and outlined their hope to see their neighbors in Zimbabwe also start savings and credit schemes to solve a multitude of their problems. She emphasised the need for solidarity among the poor people of the world by exchanging ideas that would uplift people's lives.

Shadreck talked about how the group in Dzivarasekwa had started, what they were hoping to achieve, and their call for government to assist them by providing affordable land for them to construct their own houses. Elizabeth talked about the need for women to join housing saving schemes. She told how the saving scheme had changed her life as a woman, how she had created new friendships by joining the saving scheme, and how these bonds were helping her in times of need.

Monday, August 23. Monday morning started with frantic efforts to finish a small-scale house model for the invited delegates who were coming that afternoon. Around two o'clock, the Member of Parliament for Dzivarasekwa, councillors, local government officials, and municipal officials arrived, were shown the life-size house model, and were presented with the results of the remuneration exercise. The saving scheme leadership explained how they were saving and giving out loans and what their hopes were in terms of housing themselves. The delegates seemed impressed with what the groups had achieved in the short time since they had started, and encouraged the groups to continue working and to approach them should they require any assistance. The presence of the South Africans helped the Dzivarasekwa saving scheme organizers in terms of the lessons they learned but it has also resulted in politicians and local authority officials visiting them in their settlement and listening to what they have to say. The continuing solidarity with the South Africans gives hope and inspiration to the Zimbabweans.

Source: Summarized by the authors from internal documents of Dialogue on Shelter in Zimbabwe, 1998.

remains, while what is unnecessary falls aside. Community leaders can refer to new ideas that are helpful to them and leave other ideas unmentioned. In most cases this resolves problems caused by the exchange and yet leaves the host group inspired and supported. It is in addressing problems with exchanges that the importance of the federation, or network, structure emerges. Problems do not matter so much if experiences are embedded within a reflective process. In this way, the federation itself holds knowledge about best practices and can use it to plan future exchanges.

Conclusions

The women of Byculla began by sharing ideas and activities with other groups in Mumbai. There is now an international movement that spans eleven countries and more than 650,000 people. The implications for understanding and addressing poverty reduction are profound.

Community Exchanges and Social Change

The women of Byculla spread their knowledge through visiting other communities, teaching and learning as they went. Immediately they started to invite others to visit them. By working together on a wide range of activities, community members found that they developed essential skills, gained confidence, and could share resources for mutual benefit. International exchanges through a loose network of affiliated groups have added another dimension to their work. In international exchanges, the community leadership reconsiders assumptions and expectations in an atmosphere that is both supportive and challenging. New ideas and directions surface and are rigorously explored through local and national exchanges. The horizontal networking and the subsequent development of links among groups of women enable them all to work more effectively. There are multitudinous and tangible benefits at a local level but, as important, national and international benefits also result.

First, the international network can benefit from the learning and energy that takes place when one country in the network is open to change. More practically, and as we have illustrated in this chapter, the network can help to move resources toward initiatives that succeed due to a particular combination of local circumstances. In this sense, and with obvious analogies to corporate alliances, international networks enable the urban poor to optimize investment strategies. Two recent examples are Cambodia in Asia and Zimbabwe in Africa; in both countries, Shack/Slum Dwellers International has focused support on local savings groups to enable them to capitalize on political opportunities to secure land and other resources from local government.

Second, perhaps associated with globalization and the increased importance of internationally traded goods and services, an increasing unanimity among international development assistance agencies is emerging. Many policies are determined internationally and local actors only hear of these activities when they are imposed on the settlement. Influencing these policies, and following up on the opportunities they represent, requires gathering and analyzing information and arguing for change at an international level. These are all skills that networks learn and teach each other. Furthermore, through international exchanges, the urban poor are developing the capacity to challenge development professionals and consultants who have never been held accountable for their failures.

Third, and related to the ability to use investment knowledge, direct networking of the urban Southern poor breaks down the centralization of power and resources that has traditionally been located in the North. In the past, Northern organizations have often acted as a focal point for change. Not only does the exchange process reposition the locus of power, it also transforms the nature of this power. Exchanges between local communities result in a decentralized strength, rooted in the autonomy of the national and local process. There is no controlling focal point, rather, a set of locally initiated actions meshing together because of two related factors: the mutual value obtained through interaction and the common commitment to a people-driven process of development. Common activities take place when they appear sensible to the participants in the process, not because they are rule bound. As a model of governance, this approach turns on its head many of the hierarchical and directive models that are commonplace today.

Such a process also has implications for the North. On the one hand, there is no role for Northern organizations that seek to act as a filter, dealing out information and resources selectively according to their own agenda. On the other hand, the North itself is a divided society with differential access to income and opportunities; its own stratification is becoming increasingly rigid. As Gaventa (1997: 6) has argued, drawing from exchanges among formal sector workers in the South and the United States, "[We] increasingly found an inter-relationship between issues upon which we worked and those of other countries to the extent that they could not be ignored." The strategies developed through the members of SDI have implications for the urban poor in the North who are increasingly excluded from resources and power. (See also the discussion in Gaventa 1997: 14–15.)

Citizen Action and Social Change

More generally, the movement represented in the thousands of low-income urban residents, primarily women, who make up Shack/Slum Dwellers

International has identified for itself several truths about citizen action at the end of the twentieth century. First, local focus is critical. The policy and programmatic changes that matter to low-income residents cannot be secured at the international level but must be brought down to a local process of change. Mobilization is necessary to secure such policy change, and real mobilization of the poor will only take place if there are immediate benefits to be obtained.

Second, international support in the form of community-to-community exchanges strengthens local knowledge and the local resource base in many ways. This strengthening makes a substantive difference to communities' ability to secure local advancement. Globalization offers benefits to the urban poor through the sharing of knowledge, information, and expertise. International links are required to make the most of these benefits.

Third, the policies and programs of international development assistance agencies do make a difference. Although the national federations believe they have to secure national and local policy changes to advance the cause of the poor, development assistance funds can be important in creating the conditions to obtain and use national funds. The National Slum Dwellers' Federation has maintained its own identity and agenda while leveraging resources from larger organizations.

Fourth, the urban poor require an alternative form of organization to that conventionally found in low-income settlements. Electronic communication and international travel have enabled a movement of autonomous savings groups to define themselves and help their predominately female members to secure housing, land, improved incomes, and better lives for their children. Exchanges are reconstructing civil society in low-income settlements to ensure that it becomes a voice for the poorest and most vulnerable groups. In so doing they are addressing a priority for global development in the twenty-first century.

Notes

1. Pavement dwellings are structures made by using recycled materials, such as wood, bamboo, and plastic, which are often made by leaning these materials against a fence or a wall running along the pavement of a road. These dwellings have led to settlements of those who squat together on a particular street. Unlike other squatters on various private and public lands, these communities have in the past not had any protection of any sort and are considered the most vulnerable and invisible population in the city.

2. Celine d'Cruz, assistant director of SPARC, in conversation with the authors.

18

Do the Facts Matter?
NGOs, Research, and
International Advocacy

Caroline Harper

Much has been made of the ability of NGOs to cross boundaries (both political and geographical), act as interlocutors, and play an increasing role in the international political economy. In part, this is based on a perceived ability for NGOs to enjoy simultaneous access to decisionmakers and grassroots realities, thus linking local and global levels of action and analysis together and influencing policies based on knowledge of their actual effects on the ground (Princen 1994). Joining micro and macro levels in this way is a highly contested arena in which proving or disproving policy impacts lies at the core of the debate. Clearly, policy formulation and implementation are not linear processes. The life of policy is argued by Clay and Schaffer (1984) to be "a chaos of purposes and accidents," in which agency plays an indeterminate role. However, although complex, policy processes are not entirely accidental. There are opportunities for agency, action, and change at every turn (Keely and Scoones 1999). NGOs and other civil society groups pride themselves on being agents of social change, and increasingly social change is mediated through the policy process.[1] A solid understanding of their role in this process is therefore essential. Traditionally, NGOs have been seen as delivering the results of policy decisions, and only more recently as being key players in policy deliberations themselves. Their involvement can be seen in terms of activism, that is, challenging policy prescriptions, networking alternative opinions, and mobilizing the voices of the excluded. All these actions, however, are based on some knowledge of the proposed policy and its potential effects. It is this knowledge and how it is arrived at that are the subjects of this chapter.

If they are to take on an informed role in policy deliberations, NGOs need to develop partnerships and invest time and resources in establishing well-researched and rigorously argued cases for challenging existing policies; they also need to suggest alternatives. Current NGO research experience includes project-based research (feasibility and learning), thematic research (in-depth, explorative, or evaluative pieces), and campaigning or advocacy-led research (often case studies).[2] In reality all three overlap and can be used for many of the same purposes. However, though NGOs have made significant contributions to some areas of development policy through research (Smillie 1995a) (for example in gender, health, and agricultural technology), many remain poorly versed in rigorous research and have not invested significantly in micro-macro links. Such attempts that do exist in this area are highly contested, such as NGO research on the impact of structural adjustment loan (SAL) policies.[3] While NGOs can reveal the consequences of actions on the real lives of people, to be credible such evidence needs to be more than anecdotal. Ideally it should be backed by thorough research, skills still thinly scattered throughout the NGO community (Edwards 1993). Increasingly, NGOs have a role to play in engaging in micro-macro linking in a coherent way. This is enormously challenging, both in tracing policy impacts and creating workable policy alternatives—for example the effects of trade policies on local economies and their concurrent effects on female workers; or multinational sourcing policies, global supply chains, and the employment of children.

There are, of course, NGOs that exist for the purpose of research, and high quality analysis from NGOs is on the increase. However, coming from an activist tradition, NGOs have generally been slow to make the investment necessary to produce well-researched and rigorous policy analysis, seeing such research as costly, a luxury, and impractical.[4] Many NGO advocates have tended to leap from the local to the global, armed only with highly contested anecdotal evidence and frequently bypassing the intermediate stage of research and analysis that lies between grassroots experience and policy change. They have focused on the indisputably important area of building coalitions, strengthening local organizations, winning over the media, targeting key decisionmakers, and linking grassroots activists with politicians. However, NGOs have suffered because of a lack of research capacity in support of both their advocacy work and their project work in the field (Wilkinson 1996).[5]

Clearly, not all policy questions would necessarily benefit from more research, or research specifically by NGOs. The point of this chapter is not to claim that NGO research is more or less important than other kinds of research but to highlight the fact that NGO positions must be substantiated if they are to be properly debated. And that, at root, is an issue of NGO accountability in promoting ideas and values and of ethics in the use of information and partnerships in the policy process. NGOs and other policy actors such as trade unions sometimes appear casual in their treatment of policy related information by failing adequately to use it to substantiate their claims. In addition, the information used may not be merely insufficient, but it also might contain factual errors or, in the worst cases, manipulations aimed at influencing policymakers. To what extent can this result in policy decisions that have negative impacts on the poor?

In highly contested policy processes there are, of course, strong alternative narratives, frequently championed by civil society actors and often in opposition to positions based on "scientific truths." Though many so-called scientific truths are highly contestable, they nevertheless carry considerable authority, particularly in public forums. Elites can also coopt academics and thus the mantle of truth if it suits them. As players in policy processes, NGOs are critical in dislodging dominant positions and building counternarratives. Sound arguments and strong evidence are key to this process. The construction of counternarratives assumes a confrontational approach, exemplified in the high profile NGO campaigns of recent years. However, other, more participatory approaches to policy deliberation (in which research evidence is equally important) may deliver more realistic policy solutions. There is now enough experience to suggest that confrontational and participatory modes of policy work are not mutually exclusive. The challenge lies in combining both approaches to maximum effect, forming partnerships to do so, and recognizing when to take a back seat in the process or take up alternative modes of policy influence. These issues are discussed below.

Advocacy Strategies

Edwards (1993) suggests that there are two types of NGO advocacy: (1) attempts to influence global level processes, structures, and ideologies and (2) attempts to influence specific policies, programs, or projects. Edwards suggests that the latter require technical knowledge based on practical experience and incremental reform based on long-term dialogue, while the former require the mobilization of interest groups. In reality, expertise and mobilization play an equally important role in the best advocacy, though there is still a choice to be made between confrontational and consensual approaches. Keely and Scoones (1999) identify confrontational advocacy as the development of powerful counternarratives that dislodge dominant policy positions. The more consensual or participatory approach, meanwhile, recognizes the "contingency of different knowledge claims and so places more emphasis on developing the institutions that promote communication and address policy issues through participatory processes of augmentation and deliberation" (Keely and Scoones 1999: 31).

The 1990s saw a growing sophistication in policy advocacy, accompanied by greater diversification in forms of NGO engagement. Wapner (1996) identifies three main campaign approaches: global political movements, local politicization, and political internationalism, all of which engage the issue at hand through different forms of mobilization and veer toward the confrontational style of advocacy. The use of international networks in campaigns connected to the Multilateral Agreement on Investment (MAI), landmines, and debt relief have demonstrated Wapner's political internationalism but arguably fell short of grassroots politicization or of inspiring a global political movement, something that can be demonstrated more convincingly by the worldwide environmental campaigns. More focused international campaigns around breast-milk substitutes and child labor have not generated the level of international action inspired by debt relief or landmines but have nevertheless worked at the global level while engaging with specific policies and practices to generate local politicization of segments of the population. Even more focused are campaigns that are situated nationally but supported internationally, such as action against the Kendung Ombo dam in Indonesia and the Mt. Apo thermal plant in the Philippines. Here, local politicization with international support eventually led to major policy changes but questionable impacts on the ground (Cleary 1995, Rumasara 1998; Brown and Fox 1998).

Few of these examples have developed more participatory approaches to advocacy, although local politicization strategies come close to this goal. This weakness is reflected in a failure by global campaigns to make a sustainable difference on the ground, which may reflect a disconnect between the effects of macro-level policy and the influence exerted by those most affected. For instance, evaluations of child labor campaigns in India have found that children can be removed from some industries without attention to their subsequent employment in more abusive forms of work (New Economics Foundation 1998).

Early examples of policymaking processes that lean more toward participatory modes of advocacy include participatory poverty assessments, participatory budget setting and monitoring processes, and possibly (although currently falling short of expectations) the poverty reduction strategy papers (PRSPs) currently being developed by the World Bank and IMF (McGee and Norton 2000). Participatory budget processes present an interesting model whereby research and monitoring of the budget is conducted by NGOs and communities, presenting a tangible means to influence policies and promote transparency. These approaches make use of participatory learning and action (PLA) methodologies that help to build links between policy ownership and the quality of information in the policy process. Generally, only when influence over policy is a reality to those likely to be affected will important information be revealed (Harper 1997). These more participatory modes of policy influence allow for more complex realities, while confrontational approaches frequently exploit public outrage in order to garner political momentum and support. The tension between the two is frequently based on the evidence on which policy claims are made.

Campaigns around conservation and the environment illustrate this dilemma. As Princen and Finger (1994) show, the highly charged debate in 1990 around a worldwide ivory ban was confused by contradictions between the World Wildlife Fund's (WWF) high-profile campaign for elephant protection and its low-profile support for a more complex solution to sustainable wildlife management. This contradiction became public when conservationists aired their disagreements in the British television journal, *BBC Wildlife* (Princen and Finger 1994). A later example of the alleged distortion of facts around the same issue appeared in *New Scientist* magazine, where readers were told of an elephant overpopulation crisis with statistics apparently based on animals that never existed. The article accused environmental groups of perpetuating the myth of a catastrophic decline in elephant numbers across Africa in part because thirty organizations were identified as depending on that myth for their financial survival (*New Scientist* 1999). In the mid-1990s, the debate in the UK concerning the disposal of the Brent Spa oil rig raised public consciousness of marine pollution but also stimulated a public debate about the validity of the scientific evidence presented by corporations and their NGO critics.

Notwithstanding the complexity of the actual evidence in these cases, the point to note is that pressure groups were accused of drawing conclusions that went far beyond the available evidence, and of using research as a commodity to fit their cause.[6] In doing so they risked credibility, not just with policymakers but also with the public. As a result, concerns about NGO evidence and campaigning strategies are increasingly being raised in international forums. For example, Clare Short (the UK minister for international development) claims that "single issue campaigning can lead to a kind of irresponsibility—organisations say ridiculous things to raise their profile and money."[7] In the worst cases NGOs are seen by scientists and researchers as cherry picking from the evidence, with the alleged result that "the reputation of genuine conservationists ... has been sullied by groups who use science as a commodity to fit their cause" (*New Scientist* 1999). In advocacy activities NGOs can also be accused of using bullying and shaming tactics to persuade analysts and decisionmakers to promote their particular cause, rather than addressing the evidence or the issues themselves.[8]

Accessing and Using Research-Based Evidence

Confrontational and participatory advocacy strategies both use research-based evidence. Each employs contested judgments, but confrontational approaches tend to deploy those judgments in the context of high-profile public spaces such as the media and at international forums. In these policy spaces, NGOs are sometimes accused of oversimplification, ignoring research, manipulating information, displaying inconsistency, and neglecting the ethics of information. Why would NGOs deliberately or inadvertently be guilty of these charges? In some cases, NGOs simply do not have an in-depth, nuanced, or sophisticated understanding of the issues, nor do they have the resources to gain such understanding.[9] Alternatively, they may want to promote a particular agenda and manipulate information for ideological ends. NGOs may also believe that complex messages have to be simplified in order to build constituencies for support: Sensational messages generate greater momentum in the campaign. Because the quest for profile is also driven by fund-raising imperatives, campaign themes may be determined by current international debates, passing fashions, or those issues that will sell to the public—not by practice-based evidence.

Confrontational advocacy strategies require NGOs to come up with clear-cut answers to complex questions. Although many do have considerable knowledge and experience, this approach may fail to recognize the validity of different knowledge claims. Negotiating these claims is easier through participatory policy processes, since devising participatory solutions requires that all the actors have solid grassroots connections and the ability to facilitate a genuine process of action-learning—learning by reflecting on action. NGOs that rely purely on confrontational approaches may have difficulty in making these connections. Compounding the problem is the reluctance of NGOs to engage with the scale of investment and long time frames required for research. Inconsistency in confrontational campaigns can distort the policy process, waste resources, undermine NGO credibility, and result in negative impacts on the ground. A rigid focus can obscure or marginalize other factors that may be more significant. Low-quality analysis reflects badly on other members of the campaign and may distance NGOs from the "serious" players in development policy formulation.

The Case of Child Workers

Advocacy motivated by outrage and that motivated by complexity are not necessarily mutually exclusive modes. However, tensions between the two do have to be carefully managed, and both need to use research-based evidence with care. The world-wide campaign against child labor conducted since the early 1990s tends toward confrontation, characterized by the promotion of alternative narratives and the promulgation of simple solutions. Parts of the campaign have begun to use participatory approaches through attempts to involve children themselves in the debate and by involving Southern NGOs in both debates and policy implementation. In arriving at solutions, the campaign has had to move toward consensus building, but there remains a large gap between policy advocates and the children affected by policy, both nationally and internationally. The child labor campaign shows how advocating simple solutions can have drastic effects on poor people.

The Harkin Bill provides a good example. Proposed in 1993 in the United States as a ban on all textiles produced with child labor, the bill immediately provoked large-scale redundancies among young female workers in Bangladesh. Far from removing the problem of child labor, it forced young girls into much more abusive forms of work such as street trading, domestic work, and prostitution (Boyden, Ling, and Myers 1988; Sobhan and Hussein 1995). Although couched in terms of human rights, the bill was widely suspected of being driven by protectionist concerns in the United States, since textile prices would rise once Bangladeshi employers contracted more expensive adults into the labor force (in reality, the huge difference in wage rates would have made any impact on U.S. producers very small). Trade unions in the North have primarily taken an abolitionist stance regarding child labor and tend to advocate education as a solution. Ideally, quality education would be available to all children, but the reality of poverty means that, even if better schooling were available, children would continue to work until they could enter education with some sense of security. Northern trade unions, however, encouraged their members to believe that "[all] child labor is evil. ... It cannot be excused" (Kearney 1998), attacking in the process NGOs who advocate for alternative solutions.

Clearly the issues here are complex. Northern protectionism, adult wage rates, endemic poverty that forces children into work, and assumptions that child work is implicitly bad, confuse both advocates and policymakers. However, though complex, considerable research has already been conducted on child labor that casts doubt on the assumptions of the abolitionists:

- that education poses a solution;
- that it is possible to replace child workers with adult workers from the same family and that child work displaces adult labor;
- that childhood should be a time free from work and that work is not beneficial to children in the long term;
- that *all* child work is a problem that justifies international intervention (as opposed to extremely hazardous and exploitative forms of labor);[10]
- that, by enforcing minimum-age laws, the term *childhood* applies to

the same period of time across all cultures (Save the Children Fund 1998).

As researchers, parents, and child workers themselves have testified, none of these assumptions is true. Abolitionists tend to look at work in isolation from other crucial aspects of children's lives, particularly relationships to kin and the environment that surrounds them. As a result, "child laborers" become a specific social construct rather than an extremely heterogeneous group.[11] The policies that arise from such misplaced assumptions (such as minimum-age laws) lack any justification in empirical evidence and are rarely evaluated. Enforcement is impossible, not least because the analysts ignore the fact that children frequently make the decision to work on their own.

In 1996, the United States–based International Labor Rights Fund (ILRF) began its Foul Ball campaign to "call attention to the plight of thousands of children working full time to stitch soccer balls in the Sialkot region of Pakistan."[12] The ILRF confused the type and conditions of loans given to families in Sialkot and their conditions of labor with extreme forms of "debt bondage," from which families cannot extricate themselves. NGOs in the United States led by the so-called soccer moms picked up the campaign and, with the ILRF, played a significant role in pushing for a ban on child labor in Sialkot. In doing so, they widened still further the gap between research findings and policy demands. While undoubtedly well-intentioned, the soccer moms campaigned on the basis of poorly analyzed potential impacts and without consulting those who would be affected. Many observers, particularly Pakistani organizations, feel that the campaign detracted attention from even more serious abuses of children in extremely hazardous work, such as those engaged in the nearby surgical instruments industry.[13] It is not surprising that children in Sialkot are still stitching footballs from the security of their homes, since this provides reasonably paid piecework that can be performed at any time, and between other activities.

Simple messages are easier to communicate and can be used more effectively to raise an NGO's profile with potential donors. At a time when aid agencies were trying to unite against the detrimental effects of bans against products made by child workers, some campaigning groups in the North, including Christian Aid, broadcast simple messages to ban child labor (BBC Radio Four "A.M." program, May 12, 1997). This message reached a wider public audience and generated major coverage in the media, but it also undermined public education by other organizations such as Save the Children Fund and Anti-Slavery International, which aimed to deliver a more complex picture. NGOs tread a delicate path in their pursuit of high profile international campaign targets. Most claim that their policy work is rooted in practice, but the campaign themes are often determined by issues that will sell to the public or are of current but passing importance to international agencies.

There are, of course, genuine differences in the worldviews of different NGOs. Some see globalization as something to be halted in favor of grass-roots self-reliance; some opt for constructive engagement; and others see it as "a progressive social revolution in the making" (Edwards et al. 1999). Each approach has advantages and disadvantages, but every worldview implies a different set of policy recommendations that need substantiation. NGOs are world leaders in criticizing policies and advocating general visions, but they are less adept at saying how change might be promoted at any level of detail. Some advocates of the view that child labor should be universally banned have a vision of a world wherein children do not work. Such a vision may inspire, but does it advance the cause on the ground? Kearney (1998) provides a case in point from the Northern trade union movement:

> There are many apologists for child labor today. ... We need to nail the argument that only some child labor is intolerable. ... Is 20 hours a day working in factories intolerable? ... Is domestic work for 6–7-year-olds working 18–20 hours a day tolerable? ... In reality no child labor is tolerable. There is another dangerous body of opinion around at the moment. This suggests that children should be allowed to work but that schooling should be provided in the evenings. ... Would these apologists for child labor themselves be fit to begin a school day after 10-12 hours of hard manual labor? There is no room for compromise.[14]

By deliberately conflating tolerable and intolerable work and accusing fellow activists of being apologists, this misleading but powerful agenda presents itself as fact. But the wrong message can build momentum for the wrong actions, and that momentum can be difficult to reverse. The campaign on child labor since 1995 has tried both to put the issue onto the public and policy agendas and to urge a more subtle understanding of the issues involved. As a result of NGO research on the ground, Northern trade unions increasingly recognize that in some circumstances a child is better off in work than out of it. The new International Labour Organization (ILO) convention on the worst forms of child labor (ILO 1999, number 182) acknowledges that when children are removed from work, means must be put in place to assist their transition to education.

Conclusions

It is increasingly clear that "engaging with others over the long term in a process of mutual learning becomes more important than claiming that NGOs have the answers and merely wish to convert others to their point of view" (Edwards et al. 1999). This is a challenge to NGOs that cling to an outdated mode of policy advocacy based on simple answers and driven by institutional imperatives such as fundraising and profile. By contrast, sustainable development requires all development actors to engage in genuinely collaborative relationships, to "forge transnational alliances that more fully represent poor people's interests, and move from development as delivery to development as leverage, evolving new and better relationships with a wide range of institutions" (Edwards et al. 1999). These institutions include those with the research capacity that NGOs lack but must acquire if they are to unravel the huge complexity of the issues they confront. Simple outrage will not bring us to satisfactory policy conclusions, but elaborate arguments may lack the power to motivate political will for change. Therefore, the future of NGO advocacy is likely to rest on a combination of passion and expertise, requiring those who work with outrage and those who work with complexity to join forces in new alliances. Such alliances should be more effective in translating the gains of international legislation into actual improvements in the lives of the poor.

Questions about accountability in NGO campaigns will continue to grow in importance, particularly if NGOs succeed in altering the direction of official policy. Seen by many to be self-appointed advocates, NGOs will have to identify more clearly who they represent, and by what standards they act in their role as advocates for change.[15] A central part of this debate will revolve around the ethics of information use. NGOs will have to increase their own involvement in research, build research capacity among their partners in the South, and develop more collaborative relationships with academics. In a world of highly contested and contestable evidence, NGOs must ensure that their messages carry weight and authority. Although donor agencies have incorporated collaboration as a condition of funding development research, this remains an area fraught with difficulty and constrained by academic incentives in favor of original empirical research and publication, making dissemination, empowerment, policy influence, and policy processes of secondary importance. In a context in which there are no simple answers to sustainable development dilemmas, participatory and consensual modes of policy advocacy will need to take a more central place in NGO campaigns.

The campaign against child labor shows that NGOs (and perhaps more so, trade unions) have sometimes failed to engage with research-based evidence responsibly, thereby distorting the policy process and risking a range of negative effects on the poor themselves. This is especially true for confrontational approaches to policy influence, where organizations may be anxious to steal the headlines, keep an issue on the political agenda, or promote a particular philosophy. Though bringing an issue to popular attention is valuable, participatory modes of policy advocacy provide an essential balance in generating solutions that reflect an understanding of the causes of the problem and engage stakeholders in implementing viable, sustainable solutions. The more subtle understanding of child work now espoused by senior politicians and decisionmakers is a good illustration of this shift.[16]

Different policy spaces require alternative modes of policy advocacy. Confrontational approaches can develop validity and strength by linking their counternarratives to stronger bodies of evidence. Participatory approaches that recognize and reconcile different claims can benefit from the public and political gains of high-profile campaigning. New research methodologies are vital to both approaches, and NGOs must therefore develop their ability to gain, understand, and use research-based evidence to greater effect. For some critics the "age of innocence is over. ... More reflection and less action is sometimes in order; ... NGO resources can and should legitimately be spent on analysis" (Gordenker and Weiss 1995). By forming alliances with Southern researchers in academic institutions or NGOs, and by using Northern expertise wisely, NGOs can influence the flow of resources and ideas across the globe. In doing this more systematically, they will be taken more seriously by key policy actors. NGOs must learn to marry different forms of policy advocacy together, balancing outrage with complexity and refining the art of moving continuously between the two. Contact with grassroots realities and mediation between different claims through participatory processes are skills that NGOs already bring to the table. These skills now need to be extended upward into more sophisticated modes of advocacy at the national and international levels.

Notes

The views expressed in this paper are those of the author and not necessarily those of Save the Children Fund–UK. Thanks to Rachel Marcus for comments on an earlier draft.

1. In the main I am drawing lessons from Northern NGO experience.

2. I do not use the term *advocacy* to denote a specific activity, but something inherent in all the activities of an NGO striving for change. Campaigns however, can denote a specific time-bound activity to enhance advocacy strategies.

3. The feasibility of some questions are very debatable, for example NGOs have spent many years attempting to prove the impact of SA programs, which has proved an almost impossible research question to address and is a highly contested policy space.

4. NGOs for financial or other reasons also tend to be reactive and fail to plan for the time necessary to produce authoritative work; however, when long-term work is undertaken it lends the organization considerable credibility. The Save the Children fund for example gained credibility in the areas of revolving drug funds, child work, and health financing from serious investment or collaboration in research.

5. A Catholic Institute for International Relations (CIIR) study on the effectiveness of NGO campaigning on trade issues found the widespread view among NGO participants and outsiders that the campaign was under-resourced in terms of research and lobbying capacity (Wilkinson 1996).

6. Researchers also somewhat selectively use evidence to prove particular ideas and while they do acknowledge other evidence before drawing conclusions they cannot actually gather *all* available evidence. However, as academics they are assumed to have been more rigorous than campaigning NGOs.

7. Clare Short, secretary of state for international development at a commonwealth Business Council conference on trade negotiations.

8. For example when legitimate concerns about debt relief practicalities were raised at an international forum, a member of the NGO Jubilee 2000 responded with scorn regarding the political orientation and commitment of the questioner, rather than addressing the question itself.

9. Simon Maxwell, director of ODI, maintains that unlike in 1990 NGOs now simply cannot afford academic advice. As academics have moved into the consultancy market and in the UK increasingly rely on self-funded staff, so advisory rates, particularly on important economic issues, have grown beyond the reach of most NGOs.

10. The debate has now moved to this tighter focus after several years of deliberation.

11. Comments by Bill Myers at the Save the Children Fund roundtable on child work research.

12. See the ILRF website, available at http://laborrights.org.

13. Rachel Marcus, based on discussions with Pakistani and international organizations, personal communication with the author.

14. Neil Kearney, International Textile, Garment, and Leather Workers Federation (ITGLEF) (submitted speech to a conference funded by the UK Department for International Development in Manchester, July 1998).

15. See "Citizens' Groups: The Nongovernmental Order," *The Economist* (December 11, 1999).

16. Leading up to the 1999 WTO negotiation, senior politicians such as Clare Short, minister for international development in the UK, persuasively argued the case against boycotts and bans linked to child work.

19

What Makes
International Campaigns Effective?
Lessons from India and Ghana

Jennifer Chapman

NGO campaigns seek to bring about positive changes in policies and in people's lives, but their impact is rarely straightforward. Campaigns often have unclear origins and may evolve in new directions over time, transmuting to focus on other issues, leading into new campaigns on related problems, and altering their demands to grow, narrow, or widen at different times. The effectiveness of NGO influence is rarely dependent on a single event or campaign. Instead, the cumulative effect of campaigning tends to create critical moments that then have a major impact on policy and practice. Campaigns may focus at the international level, the national level, or the grassroots level—or in a combination of all three, with different actors as targets in each. Work at different levels may be carried out by different organizations working independently, and gains at one level may work against progress at others. In other campaigns, or at other times, work at different levels comes together to produce an effect greater than the sum of its parts.

NGO campaigns are not necessarily linked to one particular organization; a range of active groups may flow in and out of campaigns over time. Some organizations resonate with the spirit of the times and take off and grow in their involvement, only to decline or fall away later on, perhaps producing a multiplicity of new actors with different approaches and ideas. Institutions that remain the same in name can change their nature or their approach, especially when they lose key individuals who have left to start new institutions, possibly working on related issues. At some times a few key individuals can make all the difference, while at others the activism of many is called for. Individual motivation is a key driving force, but these motives are varied and sometimes confused. Some campaigners make an issue their life's work, while others will stay for a short period before moving on to another issue that appears more pressing. Campaigning organizations provide jobs and security for some, but they also rely on voluntary effort, and this can prove to be dangerous work. Many who are paid for their involvement could receive greater monetary rewards elsewhere, but they gain in other ways, finding excitement in a movement that attacks the status quo. NGOs often provide opportunity for travel, increased personal status, and, possibly, a chance to make a real difference.

Another common characteristic of campaigns is that they are based on oral histories made up of multiple and often conflicting perspectives. An effective campaign is based on the making and telling of stories and the extent to which different parties accept their validity. In some senses these stories are myths: This is not to doubt their historical veracity, but powerful narratives can exclude complexities that detract from their appeal, and to challenge them invites suspicion of alternative political agendas (Stoll 1998). Such suspicion is not without grounds, and some challengers do try to undermine the stories of others in a campaign, providing alternatives that then compete for support. Such storytelling can take many forms, including the simplification of complex problems into an easily communicable form, not necessarily based on hard evidence. Heroes or heroines are created, whose exploits become mythologized and who become part of the motivating force that draws in new supporters. Common narratives are also an element in enhancing the legitimacy of a campaign. These stories are not always created directly by the organizations involved; indeed the media has a large and powerful role to play. But successful campaigning organizations will attempt to manipulate and use the media themselves. In return, opponents will try to dissect the narratives of a campaign in order to undermine its legitimacy.

Thus, campaigns are both fluid and difficult to assess. They cannot be understood as a linear or logical sequence of separate events. Neither can they be grasped in their entirety at any point in time. In order to shed more light on these complex dynamics, the New Economics Foundation (NEF) undertook a study of NGO campaigns in two areas, summarized in Boxes 19.1 and 19.2: the campaign against breast-milk substitutes in Ghana, and against child labor in the Indian carpet industry.

Key Challenges

Working Simultaneously at Different Levels

To bring about changes in practice as well as policy, it is rarely sufficient to concentrate on one key target such as local industry. Instead, work has to be conducted at the international, national, regional, and grassroots levels and

Box 19.1 The Promotion of Breast-Feeding in Ghana

The international campaign to promote breast-feeding in Ghana is a long established effort with significant involvement by Northern NGOs campaigning against large Northern corporations, especially Nestle, under the umbrella of the Infant Baby Food Action Network (IBFAN) and the World Alliance on Breastfeeding Action (WABA).[1] Coordinated work on the issue of breast-feeding in Ghana began in 1987 after a Ghanaian doctor noticed the negative results of a donation of free samples of infant formula to clinics. He formed the Ghanaian Infant Nutrition Action Network (GINAN) and pressed the government to take action. Work on controlling the marketing of breast-milk substitutes progressed fairly quickly at first, with a committee functioning within a year and a Ghanaian code on their use drafted by 1989, though it is still waiting to enter into law because of bureaucratic delays. Concurrently with this work, GINAN has been monitoring the marketing of breast-milk substitutes in Ghana using the international code as a benchmark.[2]

In addition to lobbying against substitutes, the campaign also actively promoted breast-feeding. Health workers required training and support, and Ghana became involved in the "Baby Friendly Hospital Initiative" started by UNICEF and the celebration of World Breastfeeding Week. More recently, support has been provided to nursing mothers, with the training of grassroots "breast-feeding advisers" and the formation of local support groups.

The campaign shows clearly that GINAN had a catalytic effect in getting things moving in Ghana. It was necessary for Ghanaian organizations to start to work on the issue before things began to happen, in spite of a long running international campaign on the same subject. At the same time, collaboration between GINAN and international NGOs was vital for success. Being a member of IBFAN and WABA has helped legitimize the work of GINAN as well as providing channels for sharing and disseminating information and resources. The work in Ghana has also benefited greatly from experience and knowledge gained in similar campaigns in other countries.

targeted at a variety of groups (UN bodies, government officials, market traders, health workers, parents, villagers, and others). This in turn may lead to a broadening of the campaign, for example, from child labor to education or from the marketing of breast-milk substitutes to infant health promotion. Working at these different levels is an immense challenge, but it is not necessary to do everything at the same time. In both case studies, the work started in a small number of arenas and expanded as the campaign progressed. The challenge is to select the arenas that will be most effective in moving the campaign forward at different times and to link up with the appropriate organizations. Table 19.1 illustrates these conclusions for the two case studies.

**Box 19.2 The Campaign Against
Child Labor in the Carpet Industry in India**

This campaign was strongly influenced from the outset by Southern NGOs and was targeted at local industry, although Northern NGOs, consumers, and importers played critical roles because the carpet industry is a major exporter.[3] Within India, the campaign had its roots in earlier work on bonded labor; this developed into a focus on bonded children and then specifically on children bonded to carpet manufacturers. This narrow focus was instrumental in attracting international media attention.

The campaign used many different strategies. It started with raids to free bonded children, which still continue. Around 1990 a consumer campaign, promoted by the South Asian Coalition on Child Servitude (SACCS) and German NGOs, was initiated in Germany, one of two main destinations for Indian carpets. The campaign sought to educate consumers about the plight of children exploited in the production of hand-knotted carpets. At the same time, the Harkin Bill was pending in the United States, which threatened to legislate against the importation of goods made with child labor. These pressures prompted talk of a labeling system. Initially this was discussed between the government-supported Carpet Export Promotion Council (CEPC), NGOs, and industry. However the government and industry representatives (from the larger companies) eventually dropped out. Nevertheless, the talks continued and led in 1994 to the formation of the Rugmark labeling scheme.

NGOs have not had a significant impact on introducing new laws or policies in the carpet industry, but they have had a major influence on the implementation and interpretation of laws and policies already in existence. They worked with the judiciary and government officials to enforce existing laws, threatened export markets sufficiently to bring about some changes within the industry without implementing a boycott, established the Rugmark label as a constructive outcome from the consumer campaign, and had a significant impact at the grassroots and on the emergence of local civil society organizations. There is some evidence of a reduction in child labor in the specific industries and areas targeted, although whether there has been a reduction in child labor overall is widely debated. These results have been achieved by NGOs and activists within India, although they received resources and support in the international dimension of their work from Northern NGOs. The campaign has also had an impact in moving forward the debate on child labor as a whole. It has fed into work on children in the carpet industry in other countries and work on child labor in other industries in India such as firecrackers and footballs. It has also contributed to the Indian campaign for universal primary education.

Table 19.1   What Is Most Helpful at Different Levels of a Campaign?

Levels	Arenas	What Is Particularly Helpful
International	international NGOs, multilateral organizations, national governments, consumers, voters, industry	• the existence of international codes and legislation • an active international campaign • the existence of international conventions • consumer activism • independent monitoring
National/ Regional	national government, regional government, judiciary, public opinion, national NGOs, industry	• progressive legislation to uphold rights • legal pressure points (e.g., supreme court) • history of social activism and NGO activity • high levels of public awareness • labeling systems • independent monitoring
Grassroots	communities, grassroots NGOs, families, individuals	• active civil society organizations • high levels of public awareness • active individuals

Collaborating Across Diverse Organizations: Pyramids, Wheels, and Webs

It is clear that no one organization can campaign effectively at every level, since each requires different attitudes, strategies, and skills. To achieve the right mix of contributions, different types of organizations need to work together. In particular, campaigns rarely work exclusively with outsider strategies (wherein NGOs campaign against their targets) or insider strategies, wherein they work closely with government agencies or industry to bring about change. Outsider or insider strategies may be more effective in moving the campaign forward when targeting different groups at different times. Collaboration is therefore vital. However, this can also lead to conflict when NGOs use different campaign styles. In this case, collaboration can undermine the progress of the campaign as a whole.

The New Economics Foundation study identified three structures for organizing constructive collaboration: the pyramid, the wheel, and the web. Pyramids have a coordinating secretariat who disseminates information through the campaign; wheels have one or more focal points for information exchange, but information also flows directly among the members; in the web, no focal points exist, so information flows to and from all the members in roughly equal quantities. Each structure has both advantages and disadvantages, summarized in Table 19.2.

Collaboration among campaign members may be constrained by different philosophies, strategies, and tactics; by competition for credit, profile, publicity, resources, legitimacy, and credibility; or by power relations and value conflicts. Close collaboration is therefore usually confined to organizations that are similar in type and that work at adjacent levels. Northern NGOs do collaborate with Southern NGOs, but they tend to be middle-class organizations based in cities. Many NGOs are unable to see that different approaches may be essential to move a campaign forward at different levels. They may also ignore the fact that government and the legal system are important actors in getting results, for example in developing a more effective legislative framework to provide an essential lever for campaigners; ensuring that the law is enforced, though in practice it is often campaigning NGOs that pressure the government and judiciary to implement the law using direct action (like in the raids to free bonded child laborers in the Indian case study); carrying out large-scale programs for which NGOs cannot raise the necessary resources; changing attitudes and practice in government-run institutions; ensuring a level playing field for companies; and providing a sense of permanency. Laws do not collapse in

Table 19.2 Structures for Collaboration

Structure	Advantages	Disadvantages
Pyramid	• dynamic • quick to act • can speak with authority for many member organizations • can mobilize a lot of people • helps to get access to top-level of policy	• members may feel loss of identity • strengthening civil society at grassroots may not be given adequate attention • danger of speaking for people rather than helping them to speak for themselves
Wheel	• more independence at the grassroots • good for information exchange and sorting • centers of specialization in large networks can aid in information sorting	• can be harder to show a united front or common identity • process of change is slow • campaign may miss opportunities for sudden changes in practice
Web	• good for information exchange	• slow to take action • may have to change into a wheel or pyramid before effective campaigning action can be taken

the way that codes of conduct for industry often do when they are subject to self-enforcement alone. Eliciting government cooperation requires at least some contact with, and support from, insiders as well as recognition that many government personnel and employees among corporations are actively seeking change. NGOs are only one set of players among many.

Developing and Maintaining Credibility

All the actors in a campaign spend time and energy establishing and maintaining their own legitimacy and contesting that of their opponents. This is often essential for their survival, in terms of campaigning successfully and raising adequate resources. At the same time, the pressure on organizations to show results can lead them to downplay the role of others. The desire of NGOs to establish their own legitimacy can create tensions when collaborating with other NGOs, especially if they are potential competitors for funds. There are different ways in which legitimacy is claimed by NGOs, and most draw on more than one at the same time. These choices have implications for the nature of NGO campaigning, summarized in Table 19.3.

Motivating Campaigners and Keeping Them Involved

Individual champions play a key role in campaigning and are crucial to success at both the national and the grassroots levels. In the case studies, they were people with a flair for motivating others who combined a social conscience with a strategic vision of how to push the issue forward. In both Ghana and India, they were particularly important in getting the issue onto the national policy agenda and in ensuring real change at the grassroots. During the later stages of a campaign, however, such individuals are insufficient to meet wider goals. Even where campaigning NGOs represent an extension of their leaders, wide change in practice requires the mobilization of a constituency around the issue. In the case study in India, the campaign mobilized ordinary citizens into marches and was able to link this to a national platform for action. Given the long time frames required for achieving social change, a key issue facing most campaigns is how to continue to mobilize people over the necessary length of time. Giving participants an active role, recognizing their contributions, celebrating their successes along the way, and developing practical tools that promote concrete changes are all important in this respect.

Finding the Right Blend of Tactics

In order to affect change, campaigns must find events or stories that engage public attention. This is often easier when disaster strikes or when the

Table 19.3   Possible Consequences of Different Bases for NGO Legitimacy

Approach to Claiming Legitimacy	Possible Consequences
Practice to policy—seeking to influence policy by pointing to practical experience on the ground	• complex message, difficult communication tool • less open to dispute • works well for grassroots NGOs • can be challenged if NGOs claim to speak for people they have not genuinely consulted
Values—NGOs promote a particular value that is widely recognized within society or enshrined in international law	• extremely powerful when combined with pictures, stories, and myths and when related to universal values • powerful when values are enshrined in international conventions, etc. • can lead to accusations of selecting values in order to attract Northern funds, especially in professional rather than voluntary organizations • can be challenged for talking rather than doing • can be accused of speaking for beneficiaries rather than enabling them to express their own views
Knowledge and research—acting as an expert on a particular issue	• works well when there is consensus on topic or you have credible allies • particularly useful and relevant for more technically based policy issues • can be open to challenge by views based on alternative research • open to question of who sponsors research or organization
Grassroots and other civil society organizations—legitimacy via adhering to and strengthening democratic principles and practice	• works well at grassroots • necessary for civil society aims • long-term engagement required • may mean campaigning opportunities missed • weak impact at higher policy levels
Alliances and networks—legitimacy gained from other members of network who secure legitimacy from one of above	• quickly spreads work to a wide audience • gives strength of numbers • disputes over who owns work • successful alliances often require significant management input

campaign can use extreme examples that can be easily communicated; clear targets and identifiable villains help. However, moving the campaign from awareness and discussion to practical action needs further impetus, such as the threat of a consumer campaign or the use of legal action against abuses.

Different levers tend to be useful at different levels, as summarized in Table 19.4.

There can be some tension between the use of these different levers. For example, a narrow focus was instrumental in getting people involved in the two case studies, but at the grassroots a narrow focus is harder to justify and maintain, since problems and potential solutions are far more complex. The most effective campaigns manage these tensions by allowing different foci to coexist and change over time. For example, the focus of the campaign on child labor in the Indian carpet industry shifted considerably over the years, yet fundamentally it remained the same campaign with mainly the same actors (see Figure 19.1). At times the focus narrowed to achieve a clear campaign message, while at other times it widened to reflect the real complexity of the issues at hand.

Figure 19.1 shows how two organizations involved in the child labor campaign in India changed their focus over time. The South Asian Coalition on Child Servitude (SACCS) has moved from a focus on child labor, through a specific campaign on the carpet industry, to a recognition of the wider problems affecting children. By contrast, the Centre for Rural Education and Development Action (CREDA) began with (and has since returned to) a broad focus on children's education, having also participated in the carpet industry campaign. The campaign took off when these different NGOs, along with others from the international arena, converged on the carpet industry from their different perspectives. A narrow focus like this can yield results, but it can also distract from the wider problem and target responses too narrowly. For example, schools reserved for ex-carpet weavers, who are primarily boys, entrenched existing gender biases in education. Grassroots voices may also be bypassed in the campaign in the desire for quick results. But if grassroots participants feel no sense of

Table 19.4   Levers that Help to Move Campaigns Forward

Attracting Attention	Taking Action
• effective communication tools (e.g., visible suffering) • judicious use of the media • critical events • obvious villains • a narrow focus (e.g., on carpet children or breast-milk substitutes) • social entrepreneurs with strategic vision	• consumer action (or the threat of it) in the North • use of the law • social entrepreneurs with strategic vision • international attention, a framework for global action, and lessons of experience from elsewhere • involvement of government • mass movements • shareholder action

Figure 19.1 The Shifting Focus of the Child Labor Campaign

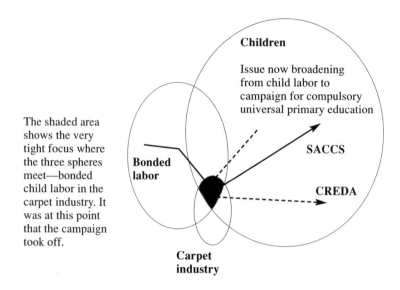

ownership over the solutions recommended, they are less likely to cooperate. For example, parents of child laborers might move their children into other jobs when employment opportunities in the carpet factories are curtailed by the campaign. Table 19.5 summarizes these difficult dilemmas.

The limitations of the focused approach become particularly apparent when one examines the factors that influence decisions taken by individuals at the grassroots—for example, how children allocate their time or how mothers choose to feed their infants. As Table 19.6 shows, factors susceptible to international pressure form only a very small part of the picture but are, understandably, the ones that receive most attention by international NGOs.

Table 19.5 Advantages and Disadvantages of a Focused Approach

Advantages	Disadvantages
• moves national and international campaigns forward quickly • works well as a communications tool • makes people at a distance from the problem feel that they can do something to help • helps to identify a clear target	• can oversimplify and distract from wider problems and deeper causes • can target responses too narrowly • can make grassroots involvement more difficult • can undermine civil society in nascent democracies

Table 19.6 Factors That Influence How Mothers Feed Their Infants in Ghana

| | Mothers' behavior is most susceptible to influence by: | | | | | | | | | | |
Factor	International NGOs	National NGOs	Local NGOs	Community Groups	Health Workers	Ministry of Health	Law	Baby-Food Industry	Employers	Multilateral Agencies	Media
Marketing	X	X				X	X	X		X	X
Mothers' knowledge	X	X	X	X	X	X					X
Other commitments, e.g., work		X	X	X			X		X		X
Community support and attitude			X	X	X						X
Norms in health system	X	X			X	X	X	X		X	

By contrast, many of the factors that influence a child's or mother's behavior are only susceptible to pressure at the community level. The question for NGOs is when and where to use each of the many levers available to them in a campaign like this. When should gains at the national or international levels take precedence over what is required at the grassroots, and vice versa? What should the balance be between a focused approach that might affect short-term impact and a holistic approach that aims to achieve long-term change? Most difficult of all, who should make these decisions?

Developing and Implementing Effective Tools for Change

Campaigning alone is rarely enough to achieve changes in policy and practice: Other tools are essential. Traditionally, legislation or formal conventions were seen as the natural goal of NGO campaigns, but more recently, codes of conduct, labeling schemes, and social auditing have grown in popularity. These tools are seen to be more appropriate where national legislation and international conventions do not exist, remain too weak to have any effect, or face problems in implementation through the legal system and by government.

The selection of campaign tools can become another arena for conflict among members, that is, opponents may try to use similar tools for their own ends. For example, the Rugmark scheme against child labor tried to involve large exporters but failed to sustain their support once international pressure subsided. The subsequent success of establishing the Rugmark label with smaller exporters led to the introduction of a rival labeling system from industry. The challenge is to develop tools that move the campaign forward and achieve real change, rather than just creating a new arena for contestation or allowing opponents to set the agenda.

Ensuring Real Change at the Grassroots?

Much can be achieved in terms of policy change and awareness without grassroots involvement. However, such involvement is essential to ensure real, responsive change on the ground and to ensure consistency between the campaign's goals and achievements. In India for example, child laborers would not have been moved out of the carpet industry and into less exploitative forms of work without careful efforts at the grassroots. In Ghana, if the campaign had not spent time on grassroots involvement, mothers would be likely to continue feeding inappropriate foods such as water to their infants even if breast-milk substitutes were entirely unavailable. The links between policy and project work have always been key to the legitimacy of NGO campaigns. International development NGOs first took up advocacy work in the 1970s that drew on their practical experience on the ground (working from "practice to policy"). Resources began to be moved from development projects into advocacy work, although recently this trend has been modified to strengthen links among macrolevel policy proposals and concrete microlevel experiences (Edwards and Hulme 1992). The research on which this chapter was based went further, confirming not only the essential links between advocacy and project work but showing also that in order to realize the goals of a campaign, long-term work at the grassroots is needed even after policy change has been achieved. The global landmines campaign analyzed by Matthew J.O. Scott in Chapter 9 provides a good example of this dilemma.

The role of the grassroots in NGO campaigns is complex. In some campaigns, grassroots constituencies are treated largely as recipients of messages handed down from above. Mothers in Ghana are told the correct way to feed their infants despite the constraints they face in doing so. Villagers in India are encouraged to remove their children from the labor market and put them into full-time education despite the need of families for income. Weak information from the grassroots can lead to inappropriate policy responses, as in the case of the Harkin Bill, which attempted to impose blanket restrictions on imports to the United States that used any form of child labor without regard to local circumstances. In Chapter 18, Caroline Harper argues that the result in Bangladesh was to force children into even more abusive forms of labor, including prostitution.

Campaigns are linked together both vertically—from the grassroots to policy activists—and horizontally, across organizations at each level. However, maintaining enough space and support for grassroots constituencies is often difficult when agendas change quickly and require urgent action. High levels of trust, close personal contacts, and nonhierarchical campaign structures are all important here, but organizations can establish none of these things quickly. However, even where grassroots constituencies are not directly involved in setting campaign goals, the campaign can stimulate new forms of grassroots activism. In the carpet weaving zone of India, activists have formed over 200 village-level Child Labor Vigilance Committees, and in Ghana, volunteer mothers run grassroots support groups to encourage exclusive breast-feeding (Chapman 1999, 2000). These local institutions may hold the key to ensuring real change in campaigns.

Campaign Assessment

Most campaigning NGOs use a variety of indicators to assess their work. Such indicators may involve statistical survey data (for example, breast-feeding rates in Ghana), simpler quantitative measures (such as the number of activists or newspaper reports on the campaign), significant events (such as a landmark judgment), or more qualitative measures (for instance, changes in political will or the extent of demands made by communities). Most of these indicators are specific to each campaign, even to different NGOs within them, since different organizations in the same campaign may adopt very different strategies. Therefore, they may not help to analyze the overall lessons or successes of a campaign. In any case, the fluidity, complexity, and dynamism of campaigns call for the use of flexible indicators. For example, some have proclaimed the international campaign over breast-milk substitutes a failure in terms of its lack of success in getting national governments to enact the international code on marketing (Bernard 1999). But this conclusion ignores the campaign's successes in other areas, such as the promotion of breast-feeding and the encouragement of civil society and grassroots activism, dimensions of the campaign that were not envisaged at its start.

Indicators may also vary according to the levels or arenas in which the campaign operates, and different indicators may have different meanings for each of the participants. The motivating narratives of the campaign may lead organizations to be selective in the indicators they use. For example, in a country with high rates of child labor, the number of children taken out of work and placed in school is an obvious yardstick of success, especially when the drama of rescue raids is part of the story. Yet this indicator alone is insufficient if other child workers take their place in the factory.

Conclusions

It is clear from the case studies that collaboration among Northern and Southern NGOs is instrumental in moving campaigns forward. That said, the role Northern NGOs can play in bringing about real change in Southern countries is limited. Northern NGOs have often provided critical support by giving their Southern counterparts an international platform for their concerns, providing access to international experience, encouraging consumer action in Northern markets, and supplying the necessary funding. In general however, they have not been able to sustain social movements or grassroots bases for their campaigns—factors that severely limit long-term impact.

In controversial campaigns such as child labor in the carpet industry, respecting national sensitivities is especially important. For example, international backers had to withdraw from a prominent role in setting up the Rugmark label when it came under fire for external leadership. Local ownership is essential. Achieving short-term policy change is rarely an effective endpoint in a campaign, since government agencies or corporations can renege or ignore policies after they have been adopted. Both case studies show how important it is to ensure that new policies and laws are actually implemented. In Ghana the international code on breast-milk substitutes needs constant monitoring, with violations continuously exposed, to ensure that its provisions are made real. The Indian example shows how NGOs can push the judiciary to enforce existing laws and, where these are insufficient, set up their own initiatives such as the Rugmark label with built-in provisions for verification.

However, on issues such as infant feeding and child labor, changes in policy, even if implemented, are not sufficient to change attitudes, knowledge, and behavior. Policy change must be complemented by alternatives at the grassroots so that affected people can make their own informed choices about their interests. This often requires that local people carry out activism in parallel with activism at the national and international levels.

Northern NGOs have often concentrated on work at the international level with policy elites. While this work is necessary, it is insufficient if it is not reinforced by work at the national and grassroots levels. A key challenge for the future will be building new forms of global alliance that facilitate collaboration among levels while giving greater support and voice to the intended beneficiaries of a campaign and those working most closely with them.

Notes

The author would like to acknowledge the help and input of Subodh Boddisitwa and Shamshad Khan in India, Charles Sagoe-Moses in Ghana, Thomas Fisher at NEF, and Tina Wallace at Oxford Brookes University throughout the research project that formed the background to this chapter. The research was carried out during 1997–1998 for the New Economics Foundation and funded by the UK Department for International Development (DFID) through ESCOR. DFID supports policies, programs, and projects to promote international development. DFID provided funds for this study as part of that objective, but the views and opinions expressed are those of the author alone.

1. The research in Ghana was carried out in collaboration with GINAN.

2. The International Code of Marketing of Breast-Milk Substitutes was adopted by the World Health Assembly (WHA) in 1981.

3. The research in India was carried out in collaboration with the Centre for Rural Education and Development Action (CREDA) and the South Asian Coalition on Child Servitude (SACCS).

20

Global Citizen Action: Lessons and Challenges

John Gaventa

The Significance of Global Citizen Action

Across the globe, citizen action is widely recognized as part of the discourse and practice of democratic politics and social change—at least at the local level (Barker 1999). Through community organizations, social movements, issue campaigns, and policy advocacy, citizens have found ways to have their voices heard and to influence the decisions and practices of larger institutions that affect their lives. A number of writers have documented this rise in civic action empirically, even referring to a "global associational revolution that may prove to be as significant to the latter 20th century as the rise of the nation-state was to the latter 19th century" (Salamon 1994). Theorists of democracy also have given renewed recognition to the role and importance of civil society in governance itself: For many, democratic governance includes the role of citizen action outside of, and in relation to, the formal political sphere, not participation by citizens in government alone (Minogue 1997, Rhodes 1996).

The essays in this volume take us beyond citizen action at the local level into relatively new territory—that of "global citizen action." The broadening of citizen action into the global sphere recognizes a new contemporary reality in which power relations at local and global levels are increasingly intertwined and in which "governance involves more than the state, community involves more than the nation, and citizenship involves more than national entitlements and obligations" (Scholte 1999: 22). By bringing together a series of in-depth case studies from both practitioners and academics, this volume gives us fresh and detailed empirical insights about the meaning and possibilities of citizen action at the global level as well as about what the notion of global citizen itself implies. It adds to an important and growing literature that is concerned with activism beyond national borders (Keck and Sikkink 1998), global social movements (Cohen and Rai 2000; Wilson and Whitmore 2000), global civil society (Clark et al. 1998; Smith 1998), and global governance (Deacon et al. 1997, Edwards 1999, Scholte 1999).

Since the 1970s many activists have heard and been guided by the adage "think globally, act locally." These essays would suggest the reverse: *Think locally* about the impacts of global institutions and global forces. *Act globally* on them (Chapter 2). The first part of this equation—the local effects of global institutions and forces—has received a great deal of attention in the burgeoning literature on globalization. Public understanding is growing of the ways in which our daily lives and choices are affected by the practices of transnationals, world trade and financial flows, the global media, and the policies of multilateral institutions. But what does it mean to act globally? The essays in this volume provide several suggestions. In one sense, global action is *action on or against global institutions*, whose policies and programs have significant impact at the local, national, and regional levels. In recent years, such citizen action has been dramatically illustrated in a series of large public protests, such as those at the G8 meetings in Birmingham in May 1998, where 60,000 people joined hands against world debt; in Hydrabad, India, in 1998 where 200,000 largely peasant farmers protested the policies of the WTO; in Seattle in November 1999, where workers, environmentalists, and others protested over trade and "global capitalism"; and in the similar protests at the World Bank and IMF meetings in April 2000. The essays in this volume document other examples of long-term, transnational engagement by NGOs and other civil society groups—such as churches, trade unions, and community groups—to affect the policies of these global institutions, be they the World Bank, the International Monetary Fund, United Nations agencies, international development banks, or the World Trade Organization. These struggles and campaigns have sought not only to organize around specific issues and policies but also to make these suprastate institutions more accountable, democratic, and transparent (Chapter 7).

In another sense, the essays in this volume suggest that global action occurs when citizens link across borders in *campaigns on issues of mutual concern*. While *global* in the sense of covering the entire planet would be too grandiose a term for many of these examples, they illustrate the importance of solidarity and support across national borders. Sometimes, such campaigns focus on collective action on a specific issue—such as the practices of a multinational. Where globalization makes it harder for nation-states to regulate large multinationals for fear of capital flight or relocation of industries, transnational civil society organizing helps to fill the void by providing checks and balances against the behavior of otherwise unaccountable suprastate organizations (Chapter 14). In other cases such as the Slum/Shack Dwellers movement (Chapter 17) or the spread of participatory methods and approaches (Chapter 13), transnational solidarity takes the form of horizontal sharing, learning, and support through which global linkages can help to empower local voices.

In yet a third sense, citizens act globally in order *to realize or promote a set of rights offered to them by global treaties or agreements.* In numerous historical and contemporary examples, global forms of action have contributed to greater awareness and understanding of rights, which have in turn led to new international agreements or conventions. This volume offers such examples as the Jubilee 2000 campaign to articulate the right to freedom from debt (Chapter 10), the global movements which led to the UN Declaration for the Elimination of Violence Against Women (Chapter 16), and the campaigns for conventions to regulate landmines (Chapters 3 and 9). These campaigns continue a long and pivotal history of citizen action on human rights, such as the antislavery movements and the international movement for women's suffrage (Keck and Sikkink 1998). Global citizen action is also critical to the enforcement and implementation of *existing* international treaties and convenants. As Lent and Trivedy show for Mozambique and Guatemala in reference to the United Nations Convention on the Rights of the Child, it is only through citizen action at the local level, reenforced by global networks that the promise of such international agreements can be realized. Further, we have seen that global declarations of human rights offer important spaces and levers around which other mobilization efforts can occur. As Bunch et al. point out in Chapter 16, "human rights language creates a space in which different accounts of women's lives, and new ways of demanding change can be developed. ... The idea of universal human rights provides a powerful vocabulary for naming gender-based violations and impediments to the exercise of woman's full equality and citizenship."

The appeal to universal human rights takes us, however, to another concern about the concept of global citizen action. What do we mean by "citizenship" at the global level? The debate is a complex one, which raises thorny issues of universalism and particularity, global governance and national sovereignty. To some, citizenship is a bundle of rights and entitlements gained in relationship to a nation-state. The absence of a clear government at the global level makes the concept of a global citizen a non sequitur. To others, however, universal rights are already established in documents like the Universal Declaration of Human Rights and other international legal instruments. In a recent strategy paper, British Secretary of State for International Development Clare Short argues that human rights are essential to the achievement of international targets to reduce poverty because "they provide a means of empowering people to make effective decisions about their own lives" (Department for International Development 2000). Moreover, she argues, such rights must be extended on a global scale to include those of participation, inclusion, and obligation (that is, assurance that obligations to protect and promote rights are fulfilled). An understanding of citizenship as participation puts less emphasis on rights as entitlements, to be bestowed by a nation-state or another form of government, and more emphasis on citizenship as something that is realized through responsible action (Lister 1998; Cornwall and Gaventa 1999).

From this perspective, global citizenship is the exercise of the right to participate in decisionmaking in social, economic, cultural, and political life, within and across the local, national, and global arenas. This is true especially at the global level: Where the institutions and authority of global governance are not so clear, the rights of citizenship are made real not only through legal instruments but through the process of citizen action, or human agency, itself. Rights to participation in global decisionmaking also carry with them a set of responsibilities, which, in the absence of external rules and standards, must be self-developed and self-imposed—a challenge that many global civic actors have yet to fulfill (as the contributors to this volume discuss).

Even if we accept this conception of global citizenship, another important set of empirical questions remain to be answered: Can global citizen action really make a difference? Under what conditions? Much is known about the possibilities and limits of citizen action at the local and national levels. How can citizens go further to influence powerful actors in distant places?

One line of argument might be that effective global citizen action is desirable but impossible—global decisions are shaped by structures and forces beyond the reach of action by ordinary people. But the essays in this volume suggest another story. As civil society actors have linked together around the world, their influence on the global stage has been impressive. We have seen the utility and impact of citizen organizing on numerous issues including landmines, housing, sustainable tourism, dams, children's rights and labor, violence against women, fair trade, and infant health. Global citizen action has contributed to large-scale cancelation of third world debt (Chapter 10), to the "democratization of foreign policy (Chapter 9), and to the challenging of power relationships at multiple levels. To some degree, global citizen action has helped to change—or at least restrain—the practices of large institutions ranging from the World Bank, IMF, and WTO to multinational corporations; and it has clearly affected international treaties and conventions including those relating to nuclear weapons, human rights, and the environment. Beyond specific policy changes, global citizen action has made a number of other contributions to global governance, including encouraging civic education, magnifying citizen voice to policymakers, stimulating public debates, increasing transparency and accountability, legitimizing and democratizing global institutions, building social cohesion, and promoting ecological integrity (Chapter 7).

While the essays in this volume strengthen our understanding of both the concept and contributions of global citizen action, numerous questions have also been raised about the practice of global citizenship. In Chapter 3, Florini argues that the question is not whether global civil society has power but whether this is a force for "good or bad." In addition to listing the contributions made by global civil society, Scholte also cites, in Chapter 7, a number of its weaknesses, including its poor grounding, lack of or selective dialogue, unrepresentativeness, and weak internal democracy. In his Introduction to the volume, Michael Edwards summarizes the critical tensions raised by the rise of civil society on the global stage, including questions of

- Legitimacy, accountability, and representation: "how to structure global citizen voice in ways that combat rather than accentuate existing social, economic, and political inequalities";
- Building from the bottom up: "how to connect ordinary citizens to global regimes"; and
- Moving from campaign slogans to constituencies for change—how to advocate responsibly from a genuine social base.

Thus, although citizen action has certainly expanded from the local to the global level, there are many challenges, and much to be learned, about how the rights and responsibilities of global citizenship are effectively and ethically carried through. As Florini warns, "If transnational civil society networks are to flourish as significant contributors to the management and resolution of global problems, they will have to do better."

Lessons for Good Practice

Fortunately, the essays in this book also provide many lessons for improving the practice of global citizen action as well as some pointers to the broader challenges that remain to be addressed in the future. While these lessons are numerous, five principles stand out, each of which carries specific implications for good and effective practice.

Global citizen action implies—and must embrace—a diversity of approaches and outcomes. The diversity of the cases in this volume clearly point to the principle that there is no single blueprint, no universal path, through which global citizen action can occur. At one level, this lesson has to do with choices about strategies and tactics. As Brown and Fox point out in their analysis of campaigns to influence the World Bank, "Different goals require different kinds of coalitions." The goals and strategies that are possible will vary from context to context, based on differences in values, organizational forms and capacities, leadership, and political space. A campaign that assumes that one size fits all, that one solution or approach is best in all cases, may mean domination by more powerful actors who design the size and shape of the campaign.

Recognizing diversity does not mean ignoring commonality. Rather, affirming diversity while working for common or universal goals has proven critical to a form of global citizen action that is more inclusive than the one-size-fits-all approach. In their case study of international work for the rights of women, Bunch et al. observe that campaigns that universalize the category of woman may suppress attention to power and inequality among women and "impose a limited agenda on all women on the basis of experience of some—usually white, middle class, and living in the north." Building on Mohanty's (1991) concept of common differences, they describe the importance of understanding how women in different parts of the world and in differing circumstances may experience oppression differently, even though they do so "in relation to common systems of power and domination."

An intellectual understanding that global citizen action needs to affirm difference within a framework of commonality has significant organizational implications (Edwards 1999). The international movement for women's human rights balanced the tension between commonality and particularity through a form of networking at the local, national, and international levels that allowed "for decentralized, co-ordinated and non-hierarchical action around common goals" (Chapter 16). In the process, it "developed a model that affirms the universality of human rights while respecting the diversity of particular experiences. This experience may hold the key to success for other movements in their pursuit of global citizen action" (Chapter 16). Other studies point to the importance of constantly grounding concerns about global issues in local understanding and experience (Chapters 12 and 17) and to the importance of regional coalitions that can link local realities to global institutions and issues (Chapters 5 and 6).

Incorporating diversity and particularity in global work also has practical implications for dealing with conflict. Those organizations and campaigns that have stayed together, and have had the most impact, have learned how to accommodate differences without overruling them, and to accept the importance of ongoing negotiation and collaboration as a prerequisite for effective action. On the other hand, when differences among actors are too great, "collaboration can undermine the progress of the campaign as a whole" (Chapter 19). In her study of campaigns against child labor in the Indian carpet industry and against breast-milk substitutes in Ghana, Chapman found three organizational structures for constructive collaboration—the pyramid, the web, and the wheel. Each has advantages and disadvantages, again depending on the goals and contexts of the global effort concerned.

Global citizen action implies action at multiple levels—local, national, and international— which must be linked through effective vertical alliances. The most effective and sustainable forms of global citizen action are linked to constituency building and action at the local, national, and regional levels. It is equally important that such actions be "vertically aligned" so that each level re-enforces the other. One of the clearest examples of "vertical alignment" is the case of the Uganda Debt Network (Chapter 10). Here, participation in a global campaign (Jubilee 2000) led to a favorable decision on debt relief for Uganda. At the same time, advocacy by civil society at the national level contributed to greater budget transparency and to greater government responsiveness to the needs of poor people, including the establishment of the Poverty Action Fund. Through projects such as the Ugandan Participatory Poverty Assessment Process (involving Oxfam, other NGOs, and the Ministry of Finance), attention was paid to national budgeting processes that would help to ensure that debt relief funds were used to meet the needs of poor people (McGee and Norton 2000). At the same time, active education and mobilization work at the local level helped to strengthen the awareness and voice the priorities of poor people throughout the process. In this case, no level would have been fully successful without action at each of the others.

Alignment of action at multiple levels—particularly action that is synergistic and mutually reinforcing—does not happen without the creation of "vertical alliances" that allow the different levels to communicate about—if not to coordinate—their work. Building vertical alliances often requires people to learn to work together across boundaries of geography, culture, and power. Brown and Fox observe that power and communication gaps within civil society need "bridges or organizational chains" to connect organizationally distant partners. Such partnerships require the development of relationships of mutual trust and influence that are usually built through face-to-face encounters, often in informal spaces such as "over the pool table" (Chapter 3). Other case studies point to the importance of finding allies in high office and sometimes in unlikely places (Chapters 9 and 15) and of being willing to build networks that cut across power relations at every level (Chapter 16).

Building strong vertical alliances also has implications for redefining the links between Northern and Southern organizations. A number of case studies address the challenge of how to create and sustain more equitable, democratic, and accountable relationships among NGOs based in the North, which often campaign and speak "on behalf" of the South, and those in the South, which must organize to affect the centers of power and decisionmaking in the North. Chiriboga's case study of ALOP, a network of Latin American NGOs, points to the importance of regional associations as a "bridge" between South and North. The chapter on Jubilee 2000 also reflects on the North-South imbalances that have characterized the campaign in terms of access to resources, information, and global decisionmaking. It points to the national (as well as global) campaigning and to South-South sharing of experiences as steps that can be taken to remedy these problems (Chapter 10).

Vertical links are also strengthened through "horizontal" networks and partnerships, which themselves are strongly linked to local realities. While some essays in this volume have focused on the process of building vertical links between ordinary people and global decisionmakers, others focus on the strength that comes from horizontal sharing and network building. Slum dwellers were able to build an international movement through community exchanges that started slowly and gradually spread across eleven countries (Chapter 17). South-South sharing and training contributed to the global spread of participatory approaches in research and development planning (Chapter 13). In the case of the landmines campaign, the emergence of a "network of networks" was critical to success (Chapter 9).

In developing and promoting these horizontal links, almost every case study refers to the valuable role of rapid communications—especially the Internet—in supporting information sharing and coordinated action. This is consistent with other studies that have analyzed the role of globalized forms of communication for social movements, such as the use of the Internet by the Mexican Zapatistas in their human rights campaign (Schulz 1998). However, as Brown and Fox found in their study of four cases of World Bank influence, the Internet is insufficient: Face-to-face communication is critical for developing mutual trust. In the case of crossborder organizing on free trade for example, a series of direct dialogues allowed activists in the United States, Mexico, and Canada to agree on common principles and clarify differences, forging a strong foundation for success (Chapter 11). Other chapters show how successive UN world conferences provided critical arenas in which dialogue occurred and where personal relations of trust were formed, facilitating subsequent collaboration.

In addition to face-to-face contacts at global conferences and events, community-based, people-to-people exchanges are also important in building global networks. Both the case of the Slum/Shack Dwellers International (Chapter 17) and of the spread of participatory research experiences (Chapter 13) point to the importance of direct exchanges for accelerating the process of learning, and for providing significant events wherein local people can express and share their knowledge and expertise. In both cases, the rapid spread of knowledge and practices at the local level also affected policies by setting precedents and creating models that then attracted attention and influenced the practices of larger institutions. In the case of the Slum/Shack Dwellers International movement, horizontal exchanges also contributed to changing the locus of power between Southern and Northern NGOs by circumventing the filtering of resources and information that often occurs when networks are coordinated through the North. In other cases, direct people-to-people exchanges have contributed to new forms of North-South interaction based on mutual learning and solidarity (Gaventa 1999).

Global citizen action is strengthened by participatory forms of research, increasingly sophisticated policy analysis, and continuous organizational learning. To be credible, effective, and accountable, global citizen action must pay attention to its own knowledge and learning strategies. Knowledge strategies can be important tools for linking micro and macro realities, for policy advocacy on complex issues, and for building continuous organizational responsiveness and flexibility.

One of the key issues facing the legitimacy of international NGOs is that of voice. How do they link their own voices as advocates with the knowledge and voices of local people on whose behalf they sometimes claim to speak? Whose realities are represented (Chambers 1997; Holland 1998)? One important strategy that is emerging to answer this question is the use of participatory research methods to ensure a stronger link between the views and realities of local people and those being articulated by global policy actors, be they NGOs or international organizations. In Mozambique for example, the Agenda for Action for Children took the view that children had a right to be heard on issues that affect them and sought to include children in the rights assessment and visioning process. In Uganda, the use of participatory poverty assessments helped to link poor people's voices to national and international debates. More recently, a large scale Consultations with the Poor exercise in twenty-three countries (in which a number of international NGOs were involved) has used participatory research to influence both national debates on poverty and the *World Development Report 2000* (Narayan et al. 2000).

While participatory research methods help to maintain the legitimacy of global civil society actors by linking their policy positions to the voices of others, NGOs often use expert-based advocacy strategies as well. In so doing, credibility is gained by employing high standards of rigor, analysis, and ethics-in-reporting—which may require the development of greater research capacity for many NGOs. New styles of participatory advocacy that blend the best of both approaches may also help to reconcile trade-offs among speed, accuracy, and participation (Chapter 18). Similarly, as the case of the NAFTA trade campaign suggests, credibility is strengthened by being able to propose policy alternatives proactively, not simply protesting against existing arrangements (Chapter 11).

While more inclusive and increasingly sophisticated research approaches are required by civil society actors to maintain legitimacy on international issues, they also must be able to create internal learning strategies that allow them to be responsive to differing voices and constituencies and constantly to improve their own practices (Chapter 5). Grounding learning in the concrete realities and experiences of poor people creates a capacity for global movements to self-correct and to sustain themselves when the international advocates or "experts" have left the scene (Chapter 17). NGOs must also be able to strengthen their participatory processes for monitoring and assessing their own effectiveness (Chapter 19) and to use the results of such exercises for organizational learning (Gaventa and Blauert 2000).

Global citizen action requires constant attention to internal forms of governance that are participatory, transparent, and accountable. The essays in this volume point to numerous examples wherein the legitimacy, credibility, and effectiveness of global citizen action is affected not so much by the quality of *external* strategies and linkages as by attention to the ethics and consistency of *internal* behaviors and practices. In an era of globalization, when messages and symbols are created and transmitted almost instantaneously, corporations and other global actors have learned that one or two examples of socially irresponsible practice can do enormous damage to their credibility on other issues and in other places. As a result, they are committing greater resources to monitor and improve the quality and ethics of their work. International civil society actors must be willing to do the same.

The cases presented in this book provide a number of examples of attempts by international civil society actors to alter their internal governance strategies to become more participatory and accountable to their constituencies. Elsewhere, Edwards (2000) has argued that civil society must continue to promote innovations in three crucial areas:

- The principle of "a voice not a vote," structured to give every interest in civil society a fair and equal hearing and building from the bottom up so that global campaigns are built on strong local foundations. One way to do this would be through a set of compacts among governments, businesses, and NGO networks that lay out the roles and responsibilities of each set of actors around particular issues or institutions.

- A seat at the global negotiating table in return for transparency and accountability on a set of minimum standards for NGO integrity and performance, monitored largely through self-regulation. Codes of conduct may be the best way to enforce a sense of self-discipline in global citizen action, perhaps with an international ombudsman to arbitrate in particularly difficult disputes.
- A "level playing field" for NGO involvement, with special backing for voices that are currently left out of the global debate. That means additional support for capacity building, economic literacy, and financial autonomy among NGOs and other civil society groups in developing countries, and more opportunities to guarantee their direct participation in the international arena.

Other chapters suggest the value of rotating and decentralized leadership, as in the case of DAWN (Chapter 16); using the Internet to promote transparency about internal decisionmaking, as in the Commission on Sustainable Development (Chapter 15); and building regional networks and associations as in the NGO Working Group on the World Bank (Chapters 5 and 6).

Challenges for the Future

Despite its successes, global citizen action is still in the early stages of its evolution, and numerous challenges lie ahead. A first set of challenges arise partly from civil society's success: The increasing legitimacy and opportunities for civil society participation in global debates and in global institutions also pose risks of cooptation. Global civil society actors may find themselves spending more time and resources on servicing the participation agendas of global agencies rather than furthering the demands of grassroots constituencies. Given their new-found acceptance as global players, international NGOs may find themselves lulled into an overestimation of their own importance. Chapter 8, by Tussie and Tuozzo, reminds us that while the World Bank and other international financial institutions may have increased their rhetorical acceptance of participation, its actual practice is confined to certain limited areas of lending—leading the authors to question whether the commitment to participation represents "a window of opportunity" or mere "window dressing." Newell also cites the use by corporations of symbolic action, in which they may adopt a socially or environmentally responsible position in one highly visible aspect of their operations while ignoring its application to other, perhaps even more significant areas. In the landmines campaign, Scott concludes that, though NGOs successfully organized to sit at the negotiating table, "they felt as if decisions were still being made at another table in another room" (Chapter 9).

To ensure that new opportunities for civil society participation in global decisionmaking are genuinely widened, a second set of challenges must be addressed. These involve strengthening the capacities of civil society to participate fully, inclusively, and effectively at the global level. In many parts of the world, the opportunities and demands for citizen action now outmatch the capacity of civil society to deliver. In the absence of strong, accountable organizations and the experience and skills to engage effectively, the openings for greater civil society participation risk being filled with unaccountable and ill-equipped actors. Increasingly, the rush to participation mandated from above—as seen, for example, in new World Bank policies such as the Poverty Reduction Strategy Paper that requires national participatory poverty planning as a condition for debt relief—risks contributing to poor quality practices that simply relegitimize the status quo or dilute the possibilities for more authentic bottom-up participation in the future. Greater attention must be paid to minimum standards of quality in civil society participation, both for civil society's own internal practices, and the ways in which civil society consultation and participation is used in larger policy processes (McGee 2000).

However, the responsibility to extend and ensure the breadth, depth, and quality of global citizen action does not rest with civil society alone. A third set of challenges has to do with institutional change. National experiences in scaling up participation over the last decade show that the greatest obstacles may rest, not with the capacity of those who are seeking to participate, but in the ability of large institutions to adopt and embrace participatory approaches to change (for example, Blackburn with Holland 1998; Blackburn, Chambers, and Gaventa 2000). For global policy institutions to embrace participatory approaches fully will mean radical organizational transformation, whether in international NGOs, multilateral or bilateral agencies, donors, or corporations. Only when large-scale institutions alter their internal incentives and rewards, decisionmaking structures, and knowledge systems will decisionmaking at the global level become truly inclusive and participatory.

Finally, the most fundamental challenge for global citizen action hearkens back to the need to address the theory and practice of global citizenship. What level of civil society participation and power are possible and desirable in the global arena? Where do the rights and responsibilities of global citizenship intersect with other rights and responsibilities in the household, in local and national governments, and in the marketplace? How can citizen voice in global debates be structured in ways that promote a genuine sense of equality and democracy in global civil society itself?

These questions are demanding, and their answers are as yet unclear. However, a century ago we could not have imagined the extent to which citizens across the world have since succeeded in their struggles for more complete and inclusive democracies in their localities and national polities. In the twenty-first century, the globalization of power demands a new form of global citizen action that extends the theory and practice of democracy still further. The chapters in this volume provide valuable insights into the emergence of a new arena of global citizenship and the continuing struggles of citizens across the globe for their rights of participation, inclusion, and accountability.

Acronyms

AAWORD	Association of African Women for Research and Development
ACHR	Asian Coalition for Housing Rights
AERC	African Economic Research Consortium
AGM	annual general meeting
ALOP	Latin American Association of Popular Organizations
APEC	Asia-Pacific Economic Cooperation
ASEAN	Association of Southeast Asian Nations
ASICL	African Society for International and Comparative Law
BCAS	Bangladesh Centre for Advanced Studies
BIC	Bank Information Center
BO	bridging organization
CAS	country assistance strategy
CASA	Citizen Evaluation of Structural Adjustment
CCIC	Canadian Council for International Cooperation
CCW	Convention on Certain Conventional Weapons
CELS	Centro de Estudios Legales y Sociales
CEN	Canadian Environmental Network
CERES	Coalition for Environmentally Responsible Economies
CIPRODENI	Coordinador Institutiónal Pro Derechos de la Niñez
CoC	Center of Concern
CRC	Convention on the Rights of the Child
CTBT	Comprehensive Test Ban Treaty
CONAIE	Federation of Indigenous Peoples
CNS	Conselho Nacional dos Seringueiros
CSO	civil society organizations
CWC	Conventional Weapons Convention
DAWN	Development Alternatives with Women for a New Era
DFID	UK Department for International Development

DND	Department of National Defence (Canada)
ECOSOC	Economic and Social Council
ED	executive director
EDF	Environmental Defense Fund
ELCI	Environment Liaison Centre International
ENGOs	environmental NGOs
ESAF	Enhanced Structural Adjustment Facility
FLACSO	Facultad Latinoamericana de Ciencias Sociales
FSC	Forestry Stewardship Council
GDP	gross domestic product
GOP	Government of the Philippines
GRO	grassroots organization
GTZ	German Technical Assistance
HIPC	Highly Indebted Poor Countries Initiative
IAMA	Instituto de Antropologia e Meio Ambiente
ICBL	International Campaign to Ban Land Mines
ICC	International Chamber of Commerce
ICFTU	International Confederation of Free Trade Unions
ICPD	International Conference on Population and Development
ICVA	International Council of Voluntary Agencies
IDA	International Development Agency
IDA-10	International Development Agency-10
IDB	Inter-American Development Bank
IDR	Institute for Development Research
IDS	Institute of Development Studies at the University of Sussex
IEA	Instituto de Estudos Amazónicos
IEDECA	Instituto de Ecologia y Desarrollo de las Comunidades Andinas
IFC	international facilitating committee
IFI	international financial institutions
IIDH	Instituto Interamericano de Derechos Humanos
IIE	Institute for International Economics
IIF	Institute of International Finance
ILO	International Labour Organization
IMF	International Monetary Fund
INGI	International NGO Group on Indonesia
INGO	international nongovernmental organizations
IEDECA	Instituto de Ecologia y Desarrollo de las Comunidades Andinas
IFCB	International Forum on Southern NGO Capacity Building
ILSA	Instituto Latinoamericano de Servicios Legales Alternativos

INGOF	International Non Governmental Organizations Forum
IP	indigenous peoples
ISC	international steering committee
ISO	international standards organization
LRP	lead regional partner
MCPA	Mine Clearance Planning Agency
MDB	multilateral development bank
MERCOSUR	Common Market of the Southern Cone
NGO	nongovernmental organization
NGOWG	NGO Working Group on the World Bank
NHAG	Namibia Housing Action Group
NPT	Nonproliferation Treaty
NRA	National Rifle Association
NRM	National Resistance Movement
NSDF	National Slum Dwellers' Federation
ODI	Overseas Development Institute
PAF	Poverty Action Fund
PDF	Philippine Development Forum
PIN	public information notice
PLA	participatory learning and action
PPNN	Programme for Promoting Nuclear Nonproliferation
PRA	participatory rural appraisal
PRODEN	Commission Pro Convención de Derechos de la Niñez
PRSP	Poverty Reduction Strategy Program
REDE	Rede Brasilera Frente a la Banca Multilateral
RRA	rapid rural appraisal
SAPRI	Structural Adjustment Participatory Review Initiative
SDI	Shack/Slum Dwellers International
SIDA	Swedish International Development Authority
SIFs	social investment funds
SPARC	Society for the Promotion of Area Resource Centers
SUPF	Squatter Urban Poor Forum (Phnomh Penh)
TNCs	transnational corporations
UDN	Uganda Debt Network
UNCED	UN Conference on Environment and Development
UNCHS	UN Commission on Human Settlements
UNCSD	United Nations Commission on Sustainable Development
UNCTAD	United Nations Conference on Trade and Development
UNCTC	United Nations Committee on Transnational Corporations
UNDP	United Nations Development Programme
UNED-UK	United Nations Environment and Development UK
UNGASS	United Nations General Assembly Special Session
UNICEF	United Nations Children's Fund

UNNGLS	UN Non-Governmental Liaison Service
WBCSD	World Business Council on Sustainable Development
WBNGOC	World Bank NGO Committee
WCD	World Commission on Dams
WHO	World Health Organization
WID	women in development
WiLDAF	Women in Law and Development in Africa
WLUML	Women Living Under Muslim Laws
WSSD	Summit for Social Development
WWF	World Wildlife Fund
WTO	World Trade Organization

References

Acuña, C. H., and M. F. Tuozzo (2000) "Civil Society Participation in World Bank and IDB Programs: The Case of Argentina," *Global Governance* 6(4): 433–456.

Administrative Staff College of India (1996) *Eliminating Child Labour Through Community Mobilisation, Child Labour Action, and Support Project.* New Delhi: ILO.

Ahumada, C. (1999) *The Colombian Case,* Working Paper No. 7. Buenos Aires: FLACSO/Argentina.

Allain, A. (1991) *IBFAN on the Cutting Edge.* IBFAN: London.

Anheier, H., and L. Salamon (1994*) The Emerging Sector: The Nonprofit Sector in Comparative Perspective—An Overview.* Baltimore: Johns Hopkins University Press, Institute for Policy Studies.

Anheier, H., and L. Salamon (eds.) (1998) *The Nonprofit Sector in the Developing World: A Comparative Analysis.* Baltimore: Johns Hopkins University Press.

Annan, K. (1998) "The Quiet Revolution." *Global Governance* (4): 123–138.

Archibugi, D., and D. Held (1995) *Cosmopolitan Democracy.* Cambridge: Polity Press.

Arzobispado de Guatemala, Oficina de Derechos Humanos (1998) *Nunca Más (Never Again), Report on the Recuperation of the Historical Memory (REMHI).* Guatemala: ODHAG.

Asahi, S. (1997) "NGOs, Governments Work Together to Achieve Peace." *Asahi News Service:* October 20, 1997.

Axworthy, L. (1998a) "Towards a New Multilateralism," in M. Cameron et al. (eds.) *To Walk Without Fear: The Global Movement to Ban Landmines.* Toronto: Oxford University Press.

Axworthy, L. (1998b) "Lessons from the Ottawa Process," *Canadian Foreign Policy* 5(3): 1–2.

Bankwatch (1999) *Activities and Workplans.* <http://www.bankwatch.org/ngowbwg/NGOWGinfo/Activities%20and%20Workplans.htm>. December 22, 1999.

Barker, J. (1999) *Street-Level Democracy: Political Settings at the Margins of Global Power.* West Hartford: Kumarian Press.

Basu, A. (1995) *The Challenge of Local Feminisms: Women's Movements in Global Perspectives.* Boulder, CO: Westview Press.

Beier, J. M., and A. Denholm Crosby (1998) "Harnessing Change for Continuity:

293

The Play of Political and Economic Forces Behind the Ottawa Process."
Canadian Foreign Policy 5(3): 85–104.

Bernard, A. (1999) "Globalisation and Civil Society: The Babymilk Campaign."
Paper presented at NGOs in a Global Future: Marrying Local Delivery to
Worldwide Leverage, January 1999, Birmingham, UK.

Bigg, T., and F. Dodds (1997) "NGOs and the UN System Since the Earth Summit:
The NGO Steering Committee for the Commission on Sustainable
Development," in *Implementing Agenda 21: NGO Experiences from Around
the World.* Geneva: UN-NGLS.

Black, M. (1992) *A Cause for Our Times: Oxfam, the First 50 Years.* Oxford: Oxfam.

Blackburn, J., with J. Holland (1998) *Who Changes? Institutionalizing
Participation in Development.* London: Intermediate Technology Publications.

Blackburn, J., R. Chambers, and J. Gaventa (2000) "Mainstreaming Participation in
Development." Working Paper Series, No. 10. Washington, D.C.: World Bank.

Boli, J., and G. M. Thomas (eds.) (1999) *Constructing World Culture: International
Nongovernmental Organizations Since 1875.* Stanford: Stanford University
Press.

Boswell, R. (1997) "Mines Treaty Boosts Spirits at 'Lost Causes.'" *The Ottawa
Citizen,* December 5.

Boyden, J., B. Ling, and W. Myers (1998) *What Works for Working Children.*
Stockholm: Radda Barnen and UNICEF.

Brandt Commission (1980) *North-South: A Programme for Survival.* UK: Pan.

Bronfenbrenner, K. (1996) "Final Report: The Effects of Plant Closing or Threat of
Plant Closing on the Rights of Workers to Organize." Cornell University,
School of Industrial and Labor Relations.

Brown, L. D., and J. A. Fox (eds.) (1998) *The Struggle for Accountability: The
World Bank, NGOs, and Grassroots Movements.* Cambridge: MIT Press.

Buchanan, P. (1999) *A Republic, Not an Empire.* Washington, D.C.: Regnery
Publishing.

Bunch, C., and C. Reilly (1994) *Demanding Accountability: The Global Campaign
and Vienna Tribunal for Women's Human Rights.* New Brunswick, NJ: Center
for Women's Global Leadership and New York: UN Development Fund for
Women (UNIFEM).

Bunch, C., M. Dutt, and S. Fried (1996) "Beijing '95: A Global Referendum on the
Human Rights of Women." *Canadian Women's Studies* 16(3).

Butegwa, F. (1993a) "Limitations of the Human Rights Framework for the
Protection of Women," in *Claiming Our Place: Working the Human Rights
System to Women's Advantage.* Washington, D.C.: Institute for Women, Law,
and Development.

Butegwa, F. (1993b) *The World Conference on Human Rights: The WiLDAF
Experience.* Harare: Women in Law and Development in Africa.

Cameron, J., and R. MacKenzie (1995) *State Sovereignty, NGOs, and Multilateral
Institutions.* Council for Foreign Relations. Washington, D.C. (mimeo.).

Cameron, M. (1998) "Democratization of Foreign Policy: The Ottawa Process as a
Model," *Canadian Foreign Policy* 5(3): 147–163.

Cameron, M. A., R. J. Lawson, and B. W. Tomlin (eds.) (1998) *To Walk Without
Fear: The Global Movement to Ban Landmines.* Toronto: Oxford University
Press.

Campodónico, H. (1999) "The Peruvian Case," Working Paper No. 6. Buenos Aires:
FLACSO/Argentina.

Casaburi, G., and D. Tussie (1997) "Governance and the MDBs New Lending
Strategies," Working Paper No. 1. Buenos Aires: FLACSO/Argentina.

Caulkin, S. (1997) "Amnesty and WWF Take a Crack at Shell." *The Observer,* May 11.

Center of Concern (1999) "Democratizing Reform of the Bretton Woods Institutions: Networking Priorities Among NGO Activists and Scholars." Washington, D.C.: Center of Concern.

Chambers, R. (1997) *Whose Reality Counts.* London: Intermediate Technology Publications.

Chapman, J. (1999) "The Response of Civil Society in Ghana to the Globalization of the Marketing of Breastmilk Substitutes." Paper presented at the International Roundtable on Responses to Globalization: Rethinking Equity and Health, July 12–14, jointly organized by the Society for International Development, World Health Organization, and the Rockefeller Foundation. Geneva: World Health Organization.

Chapman, J. (2000) "The Importance of People on the Ground in International Campaigns," in D. Lewis and T. Wallace (eds.) *After the "New Policy Agenda?" Non-governmental Organisations and the Search for Development Alternatives.* West Hartford: Kumarian Press.

Charnovitz, S. (1997) "Two Centuries of Participation: NGOs and International Governance." *Michigan Journal of International Law* 18(2): 183–286.

Chatterjee, P., and M. Finger (1994) *The Earth Brokers: Power, Politics, and World Development.* London: Routledge.

Chetley, A. (1986) *The Politics of Baby Foods: Successful Challenges to an International Marketing Strategy.* London: Frances Pinter.

Chu, K.-Y., and S. Gupta (1998) *Social Safety Nets: Issues and Experience.* Washington, D.C.: International Monetary Fund.

CIVICUS (1994) *Citizens: Strengthening Global Civil Society.* Washington, D.C.: CIVICUS.

CIVICUS (1997) *The New Civic Atlas: Profiles of Civil Society in 60 Countries.* Washington, D.C.: CIVICUS.

Clark, A.-M. (1995) "Non-Governmental Organizations and Their Influence on International Society. *Journal of International Affairs* 48(2): 507–525.

Clark, A.-M., E. J. Friedman, and K. Hochstetler (1998) "The Sovereign Limits of Global Civil Society: A Comparison of NGO Participation in UN World Conferences on the Environment, Human Rights, and Women." *World Politics* 51(1): 1.

Clark, J. (1991) *Democratizing Development: The Role of Voluntary Agencies.* London: Earthscan and West Hartford: Kumarian Press.

Clay, E., and B. Schaffer (eds.) (1984) *Room for Manoeuvre: An Exploration of Public Policy in Agriculture and Rural Development.* London: Heinemann.

Cleary, S. (1995) "In Whose Interest? NGO Advocacy Campaigns and the Poorest." *International Relations* 12(5) 9–36.

Cohen, R., and S. Rai (eds.) (2000) *Global Social Movements: Towards a Cosmopolitan Politics.* London: Athlone Press.

Comisión para el Esclarecimiento Histórico (1998) *Guatemala: Memoria del Silencio: Conclusions and Recommedations of the Historical Truth Commission.* Guatemala: United Nations.

CODE-NGO (Committee of Development NGOs) (1997) "Code of Conduct for Development NGOs—Whitelist Project." CODE-NGO Strategy Paper: 1998–2000, Manila, Philippines.

Cornwall, A., and J. Gaventa (2000) "Repositioning Participation in Social Policy." Background paper prepared for the IDS conference The Future of Social Policy, October 28–29, Brighton (mimeo.).

Correa, S., with R. Reichmann (1994) *Population and Reproductive Rights: Feminist Perspectives from the South.* St. Michael, Barbados: DAWN, and London: Zed.

Covey, J. (1994) *Accountability and Effectiveness of NGO Policy Alliances.* Boston: Institute for Development Research.

Covey, J. (1995) "Accountability and Effectiveness in NGO Policy Alliances," in M. Edwards and D. Hulme (eds.) *Beyond the Magic Bullet: NGO Performance and Accountability in the Post Cold-War World.* London: Earthscan and West Hartford: Kumarian Press.

Covey, J. (1998) "Critical Cooperation? Influencing the World Bank," in J. Fox and L. D. Brown, *Accountability Within Transnational Coalitions: The Struggle for Accountability.* Cambridge: MIT Press.

Cox, R. W. (1999) "Civil Society at the Turn of the Millennium: Prospects for an Alternative World Order." *Review of International Studies* 25: 3–28.

CQ Researcher (1997) "Banning Land Mines." *CQ Researcher* 7(30): 700.

Congressional Quarterly Almanac (1994) "Foreign Aid Bill Clears Easily." *Congressional Quarter Almanac* 50: 505–512.

CRIES-INVESP (1997) "1 er Foro de la Sociedad Civil del Gran Caribe. Colombia: CRIES-INVESP. 53.

Culpeper, R. (1997) *Titans or Behemoths? The Multilateral Development Banks.* Boulder, CO: Lynne Rienner.

Deacon, B., M. Hulse, and P. Stubbs (1997) *Global Social Policy: International Organizations and the Future of Welfare.* London: Sage.

De la Rosa, J. (1999) "Five Years and Beyond," in J. Foster et al. (eds.) *Whose World Is It Anyway?* Ottawa: United Nations Association of Canada.

Department for International Development (1998a) "Challenging Child Labour." Report of a DFID workshop. London: DFID.

Department for International Development (1998b) "Strengthening DFID's Support for Civil Society." London: DFID.

Department for International Development (2000) "Strategies for Achieving the International Development Targets: Human Rights for Poor People." London: DFID.

De Senillosa, I. (1998) "A New Age of Social Movements: A Fifth Generation of Non-Governmental Development Organizations in the Making?" *Development in Practice* 8(1): 40–53.

Dubash, N.K., and M. Oppenheimer (1992) "Modifying the Mandate of Existing Institutions: NGOs," in I. Mintzer (ed.) *Confronting Climate Change: Risks, Implications, and Responses.* Cambridge: CUP.

Dutt, M. (ed.) (1995) *The Cairo Hearing on Reproductive Health and Human Rights.* New Brunswick: Center for Women's Global Leadership.

Dutt, M., S. Fried, and D. Holcomb (eds.) (1995) *The Copenhagen Hearing on Economic Justice and Women's Human Rights.* New Brunswick: Center for Women's Global Leadership.

Earth Summit '92 (1992) "Agenda 21," Chapter 38, *Institutional Structure*, Section 3. London: The Regency Press.

"Ecuador Opening National SAPRI Forum" (1999) http://www.igc.apc.org/dgap/saprin/ecforum.html. December 1, 1999.

Edwards, M. (1993) "Does the Doormat Influence the Boot? Critical Thoughts on UK NGOs and International Advocacy." *Development in Practice* 3(3).

Edwards, M. (1999) *Future Positive: International Cooperation in the 21st Century.* London: Earthscan and Sterling, Virginia: Stylus.

Edwards, M. (2000) *NGO Rights and Responsibilities: A New Deal for Global Governance.* London: Foreign Policy Center.

Edwards, M., and D. Hulme (eds.) (1992) *Making a Difference: NGOs and Development in a Changing World.* London: Earthscan.

Edwards, M., and D. Hulme (eds.) (1995) *NGO Performance and Accountability: Beyond the Magic Bullet.* London: Earthscan and West Hartford: Kumarian Press.

Edwards, M., D. Hulme, and T. Wallace (1999) "NGOs in a Global Future: Marrying Local Delivery to Worldwide Leverage." *Public Administration and Development* 19: 117–136.

Ethical Consumer Magazine (1998) Special issue on ethical consumerism. January: 1.

Fernández, M., and N. Adelson (2000) "The Participation of Civil Society in World Bank and IDB Programs: The Case of Mexico. Special issue of *Global Governance* 6(4).

Finger, M. (1995) "The UNCED Process," in T. Princen and M. Finger (eds.) *Environmental NGOs in World Politics.* London: Routledge.

FIRE (Feminist International Radio Endeavor, Radio for Peace International) (1992) Satellite FIRE meeting "La Nuestra," San Jose, Costa Rica.

Fisher, J. (1998) *Nongovernments: NGOs and the Political Development of the Third World.* West Hartford: Kumarian Press.

Florini, A. M. (2000) "Lessons Learned," in A. M. Florini (ed.) *The Third Force: The Rise of Transnational Civil Society.* Tokyo and Washington, D.C.: The Japan Center for International Exchange and the Carnegie Endowment for International Peace.

Fourth World Conference on Women (1995) *Beijing Declaration and Platform for Action.* UN Doc. A/CONF.177/20. New York: United Nations.

Fowler, A. (1997) S*triking a Balance: A Guide to Enhancing the Effectiveness of NGOs in International Development.* London: Earthscan.

Fox, J., and L. David Brown (1998) *Accountability Within Transnational Coalitions: The Struggle for Accountability.* Cambridge: MIT Press.

Frandsen, J. (1997) "International Campaign to Ban Land Mines Receives Nobel Peace Prize." *Gannett News Service,* December 9.

Franklin, A., and B. Franklin (1996) "Growing Pains: The Developing Child Rights Movement in the UK," in J. Pilcher and J. Wragg (eds.) *Thatcher's Children? Politics, Childhood, and Society in the 1980s and 1990s.* Brighton: Falmer Press.

Frynas, J. G. (1999) "Legal Change in Africa: Evidence from Oil-Related Litigation in Nigeria." *Journal of African Law* 43: 121–150.

Gaventa, J. (1998) "Crossing the Great Divide: Building Links Between NGOs and Community Based Organisations in North and South," in D. Lewis (ed.) *International Perspectives on the Third Sector.* London: Earthscan.

Gaventa, J. (1999) "Citizen Knowledge, Citizen Competence, and Democracy Building" in S. Elkin (ed.) *Democracy and Citizen Competence.* Philadelphia: Penn State Press.

Gaventa, J., and J. Blauert (1999) "Learning *to* Change by Learning *from* Change: Going to Scale with Participatory Monitoring and Evaluation, in M. Estrella et al. (eds.) *Learning from Change: Issues and Experiences in Participatory Monitoring and Evaluation.* London: IT Publications.

Gibbs, C., C. Fumo, and T. Kuby (1998) "Non Governmental Organizations in Bank Supported Projects." Operations Evaluation Department, World Bank, Washington, D.C.

Giddens, A. (1998) *The Third Way: The Renewal of Social Democracy.* Cambridge: Polity Press.

Global Governance (2000) "Civil Society and Multilateral Development Banks." Special Issue, 6(4).

Gordenker, L., and T. G. Weiss (1995) "NGO Participation in the International Policy Process." *Third World Quarterly* 6(3).

Gorelick, S. (1997) "Big Mac Attacks: Lessons from the Burger Wars." *The Ecologist* 27(5): 173–175.

GPC (1997) Lima: Proyecto Grupo Propuesta Ciudadana (mimeo.).

Guhar, R., and J. Martinez-Alier (1997) "The Merchandising of Biodiversity," in R. Guhar and J. Martinez-Alier (eds.) *Varieties of Environmentalism: Essays in North and South.* London: Earthscan.

Harper, C (1997) "The Power in Participatory Practice: Strengthening Participation in Donor Assisted Projects and Policy." Presentation for OECF and World Bank Symposium on Aid Effectiveness, Japan (mimeo.).

Havel, V. (1998) Speech to Parliament, December 9, 1997. Translated and printed in *New York Review of Books* XLV(4).

Helie-Lucas, M. (1993) "Women Living Under Muslim Laws," in J. Kerr (ed.) *Ours by Right: Women's Rights as Human Rights.* Ottawa: North-South Institute.

Higgott, R., and Bieler, A. (eds.) (1999) *Non-State Actors and Authority in the Global System.* London: Routledge.

Holland, J. (1998) *Whose Voice? Participatory Research and Policy Change.* London: Intermediate Technology Publications.

Holloway, R. (1997) *How Civil Is Civil Society?* Washington, D.C.: PACT (mimeo.).

Howell, M. (1999) *The NGO Steering Committee and Multi-Stakeholder Participation at the UN Commission on Sustainable Development.* Montreal: Montreal International Forum.

Hulme, D., and M. Edwards (eds.) (1997) *NGOs, States, and Donors: Too Close for Comfort?* New York: St. Martin's Press.

Humphreys, D. (1997) "Environmental Accountability and Transnational Corporations." Paper presented at the International Academic Conference on Environmental Justice: Global Ethics for the 21st Century," October 1–3, University of Melbourne, Victoria, Australia.

IDB (InterAmerican Development Bank) (1993) "Gestion Para un Desarrollo Eficaz." Task Force on Portfolio Management. IDB, Washington, D.C.

IDR (1997) *Advocacy Sourcebook: Frameworks for Planning, Action, and Reflection.* Boston: Institute for Development Research.

IDS (1996) "The Power of Participation: PRA and Policy." Policy Briefing 7. Brighton: Institute of Development Studies.

IGC (1999) "Ecuador Opening National SAPRI Forum." http://www.igc.apc.org/dgap/saprin/ecforum.html. December 1, 1999.

ILO (1999) "C182 Worst Forms of Child Labor Convention 1999" ("Convention Concerning Prohibition and Immediate Action for the Elimination of the Worst Forms of Child Labor"), adopted June 17, 1999, at Geneva ILO Session 87.

IMF (1995) "Social Dimensions of the IMF's Policy Dialogue." International Monetary Fund Pamphlet Series No. 47. Washington, D.C.: International Monetary Fund.

IMF (1997) *Annual Report 1997.* Washington, D.C.: International Monetary Fund.

IMF (1998) "Report of the Group of Independent Persons Appointed to Conduct an

Evaluation of Certain Aspects of the Enhanced Structural Adjustment Facility." Washington, D.C.: International Monetary Fund.

IMF Study Group (1998) "IMF Study Group Report: Transparency and Evaluation." Washington, D.C.: International Monetary Fund (mimeo.).

Inspection Panel of the World Bank (1998) *World Bank's Inspection Panel: The First Four Years (1994–1998)*. Washington, D.C.: World Bank.

International Center for Not-for-Profit Law (for the World Bank) (1997) *Good Practices for Laws Relating to NGOs: Draft Handbook*. NGO Unit, World Bank, Washington, D.C.: World Bank.

International Confederation of Free Trade Union. Web site. <http://www.icftu.org/>.

International Conference on Population and Development (1994) *Program of Action of the United Nations*. Doc. A/CONF.171/13. New York: UN.

James, E. (1989) *The Nonprofit Sector in International Perspective: Studies in Comparative Culture and Policy*. New York: Oxford University Press.

Johnson, R. (2000) "Advocates and Activists: Conflicting Approaches on Non-Proliferation and the Test Ban Treaty," in A. M. Florini (ed.) *The Third Force: The Rise of Transnational Civil Society,* Tokyo and Washington D.C.: The Japan Center for International Exchange and the Carnegie Endowment for International Peace.

Jordan, L., and P. van Tuijl (1997) "Political Responsibility in NGO Advocacy: Exploring Emerging Shapes of Global Democracy." BIC-NOVIB (mimeo.). Washington, D.C.

Jubilee 2000. Web site. <www.oneworld.org/jubilee2000/> or (in the United States) <www.j2000usa.org/j2000>.

Juyal B. N. (1993) *Child Labour in the Carpet Industry in Mirzapur-Bhadoi*. New Delhi: International Labour Organisation.

Kaul, I., et al. (eds.) (1999) *Global Public Goods: International Cooperation in the 21st Century*. Oxford: Oxford University Press.

Kearney, N. (1998) in Department for International Development (1998) *Challenging Child Labour: Report of a DFID Workshop*. London: DFID.

Keck, M., and K. Sikkink (1998) *Activists Beyond Borders: Trans-National Advocacy Networks in International Politics*. London: Cornell University Press.

Keely, J., and I. Scoones (1999) "Understanding Environmental Policy processes: A Review." Institute for Development Studies working paper. Brighton: IDS, University of Sussex.

Kendig, K. (1999) *Civil Society, Global Governance, and the United Nations*. Tokyo: United Nations University.

Khagram, S. (2000) "Towards Democratic Governance for Sustainable Development: Transnational Civil Society Organizing Around Big Dams," in A. M. Florini (ed.) *The Third Force: The Rise of Transnational Civil Society*. Tokyo and Washington, D.C.: The Japan Center for International Exchange and the Carnegie Endowment for International Peace.

Kneale, J. (1998) "Diplomatic Language: Enhancing International Communication into the 21st Century." *Bout de papier* 15(1): 12–13.

Korten, D. C. (1990) *Getting to the 21st Century: Voluntary Action and the Global Agenda*. West Hartford: Kumarian Press.

Kuenyehia, A. (1995) "Organizing at the Regional Level: The Case of WiLDAF," in M. Schuler (ed.) *From Basic Needs to Basic Rights: Women's Claim to Human Rights*. Washington D.C.: Women, Law, and Development International.

LaRue, F., H. Taylor, and C. Salazar-Volkmann (1998) "¿Se pueden negar los

Derechos Humanos de los niños?" Case study. UNICEF, European Union, Radda Barnen, CALDH and GTZ, Guatemala City.

Leroy, J.-P., and M.-C. Couto Soares (1998) *Bancos Multilaterales e Desenvolvimento Participativo no Brasil: Dilemas e Desafios.* Rio de Janeiro: FASE/IBASE.

"Lessons from the Ottawa Process" (1998) *Canadian Foreign Policy* 5(3): 1–2.

Lewis, W. (1997) "Shell to Face Shareholder Vote on Ethics." *Financial Times* (April 12).

Lister, R. (1998) "Citizen in Action: Citizenship and Community Development in a Southern Ireland Context." *Community Development Journal* 33(3): 226–235.

Lockwood, M., and P. Madden (1997*) Closer Together, Further Apart: A Discussion Paper on Globalization.* London: Christian Aid.

Martinez-Alier, J. (1997) "The Merchandising of Biodiversity," in *Varieties of Environmentalism: Essays from North and South.* London: Earthscan. 109–127.

Mathews, J. T. (1997) "Power Shift." *Foreign Affairs* 76(1): 50–66.

McCarney, P. L. (ed.) (1996) *The Changing Nature of Local Government in Developing Countries.* Toronto: Centre for Urban and Community Studies, University of Toronto, and Federation of Canadian Municipalities International Office.

McCarthy, K. D. (1992) *The Nonprofit Sector in the Global Community: Voices from Many Nations.* San Francisco: Jossey-Bass Publishers.

McCully, P. (1993) "NGO Participation and Evaluation," in P. McCully and M. McCoy (eds.) *The Road from Rio.* Utrecht: ANPED, WISE, and International Books.

McGee, R., and A. Norton. (2000) "Participation in Poverty Reduction Strategies: A Synthesis of Experience with Participatory Approaches to Policy Design, Implementation, and Monitoring." Institute of Development Studies working paper. Brighton: IDS.

Mekata, M. (2000) "Building Partnerships Toward a Common Goal: The Experiences of the International Campaign to Ban Landmines," in A. M. Florini (ed.) *The Third Force: The Rise of Transnational Civil Society.* Tokyo and Washington, D.C.: The Japan Center for International Exchange and the Carnegie Endowment for International Peace.

Miller, V. (1994) *Policy Influence by Development NGOs: A Vehicle for Strengthening Civil Society.* Boston: Institute for Development Research.

Minogue M. (1994) "The Principles and Practice of Good Governance." British Council Briefing, *Law and Governance,* Issue 4. Manchester: British Council.

Mode Research Pvt. Ltd. (1996) "An Evaluation of the Action Programme Implemented by CREDA as a part of ILO's IPEC." Submitted to ILO, New Delhi. New Delhi: Mode Research Pvt. Ltd,.

Mohanty, C. (1991) "Cartographies of Struggle: Third World Women and the Politics of Feminism," in C. Mohanty, A. Russon, and L. Torres (eds.) *Third World Women and the Politics of Feminism.* Bloomington, Indiana: Indiana University Press.

Morales, A., and M. I. Cranshaw (1997) *Regionalismo Emergente, Redes de la Sociedad Civil e Integracion Centroamericana.* San Jose: FLACSO-IBIS.

Muchlinski, P. (1999) "A Brief History of Business Negotation," in S. Picciotto and R. Mayne (eds.) *Regulating International Business: Beyond Liberalization.* Basingstoke: Macmillan.

Mucke, P. (1997) "Non Governmental Organizations," in F. Dodds et al. (eds.) *The Way Forward Beyond Agenda 21*. London: Earthscan.

Murphy, D., and J. Bendell (1997) *In the Company of Partners*. Bristol: Policy Press.

Murphy, D., and J. Bendell (2000) "Planting the Seeds of Change: Business-NGO Relations and Tropical Desforestation," in J. Bendell (ed.) *Terms of Endearment: Business, NGOs, and Sustainable Development*. Sheffield: Greenleaf Publishing.

Narayan, D., R. Chambers, M. Shah, and P. Petesch (2000) *Voices of the Poor: Crying Out for Change*. Washington, D.C.: World Bank.

National Charities Information Bureau (1996) *Statement of Purpose and Standards of National Philanthropy*. New York: NCIB.

Nelson, N., and S. Wright (1995) "Participation and Power," in N. Nelson and S. Wright (eds.) *Power and Participatory Development: Theory and Practice*. London: Intermediate Technology Publications. 1–18.

Nelson, P. (1995) *The World Bank and NGOs: The Limits of Apolitical Development*. London: Macmillan.

Nelson, P. (1996) "Internationalising Economic and Environmental Policy: Transnational NGO Networks and the World Bank's Expanding Influence." *Millennium* 25(3).

Nelson, P. (1997a) "Los Nuevos Mandatos de Transparencia, Fiscalización y Participación de los BMDs," in D. Tussie (ed.) *El BID, el Banco Mundial y la Sociedad Civil: Nuevas Formas de Financiamiento Internacional*. Buenos Aires: FLACSO/Argentina and Oficinas de Publicación del CBC.

Nelson, P. (1997b) *Who Runs the World? A Partial Evaluation of a Two Year Christian Aid Campaign*. London: CAID.

Nelson, P. (1999) *"Democratizing Reform of the Bretton Woods Institutions: Networking Priorities Among NGO Activists and Scholars*. Washington, D.C.: Center of Concern.

Nelson, P. (2000) "Whose Civil Society? Whose Governance? The World Bank and the IDB." Special issue of *Global Governance* 6(4).

New Economics Foundation (1997) *Towards Understanding NGO Work on Policy*. London: NEF.

New Economics Foundation (1998) "Effective NGO Campaigning." Summary paper (draft). London: New Economics Foundation.

Newell, P. (2000) "Environmental NGOs and Globalization: The Governance of TNCs," in R. Cohen and S. Rai (eds.) *Global Social Movements*. London: Athlone Press. 117–134.

New Scientist (1999) "Reed Business Information," *New Scientist* (January).

Newsweek (1999) "It's Not a Pretty Picture." (March 8), Stoker McGuire et al.

NGO Steering Committee to the UN Commission on Sustainable Development (1998) *Guidelines*. New York: NGO Steering Committee to the UN Commission on Sustainable Development (also available at http://www. csdngo.org/csdngo).

Nyamugasira, S. (1998) "NGOs and Advocacy: How Well Are the Poor Represented?" *Development in Practice* 8(3): 297–308.

O'Brien, R. et al. (1998) *Challenging Global Governance: Social Movements and Multilateral Economic Institutions*. Cambridge: Cambridge University Press.

O'Brien, R. et al. (2000) *Contesting Global Governance: Multilateral Economic*

Institutions and Global Social Movements. Cambridge: Cambridge University Press.

OECF/WB (1997) Symposium on aid effectiveness. September 18. Tokyo, Japan.

Osunsade, F. L., and P. Gleason (1992) *IMF Assistance to Sub-Saharan Africa*. Washington, D.C.: International Monetary Fund.

Outreach (1999) *Outreach* 4(15). <http://www.csdngo.org/csdngo>.

Pace, R. W., and V. Maria (1997) *Reviewing the Spirit of Rio: A Survey of the Successes and Failures of the Commission on Sustainable Development*. New York: International NGO Task Group on Legal and Institutional Matters.

Padbury, P. (1997) *International Co-operation Among NGO Networks: Experiments, Reflections, and a Survey on Next Steps*. UN Document A/Conf.165/INF/8. Ottawa: Alternative Futures Institute.

Palmer, G. (1993) *The Politics of Breastfeeding*. London: Pandora.

Participatory Research in Asia (1997) *Study of Social Policy Mapping of NGOs in South Asia*. New Delhi: PRIA.

Pearce, J. (1997) "Between Co-option and Irrelevance? Latin American NGOs in the 1990s," in D. Hulme and M. Edwards (eds.) *NGOs, States, and Donors: Too Close for Comfort?* London: Macmillan.

Pearce, J. (1998) "Building Civil Society from the Outside: The Problematic Democratisation of Central America," *Global Society* 12(2): 563–580.

Picciotto, S., and R. Mayne (1999) *Regulating International Business: Beyond Liberalization*. Basingstoke: Macmillan.

Princen, T., and M. Finger (eds.) (1994) *Environmental NGOs in World Politics: Linking the Local and the Global*. London: Routledge.

Reilly, N. (ed.) (1996) *Without Reservation: The Beijing Tribunal on Accountability for Women's Human Rights*. New Brunswick: Center for Women's Global Leadership.

Reinicke, W. (1998) *Global Public Policy: Governing Without Government*. Washington, D.C.: Brookings Institution.

Resolution on the Special Rapporteur (1994) "Resolution Integrating the Rights of Women into the Human Rights Mechanisms of the United Nations." UN Doc. E/CN.4/1994/L.8/Rev.1 New York: United Nations.

Reygadas, R. (1998) *Abriendo Veredas*. México City: Convergencia de Organismos Civiles para la Democracia.

Rhodes, R. (1996) "The New Governance: Governing Without Government." *Political Studies* 44: 652–667.

Robinson, S., and L. Biersteker (1997) "First Call: The South African Children's Budget." IDASA Publications. Cape Town.

Rodman, K. (1997) "Think Globally, Sanction Locally: Non-state Actors, Multinational Corporations, and Human Rights." Paper presented at the Warwick University conference Non-state Actors and Authority in the Global System, October 31–November 1.

Rodman, K. (1998) "Think Globally, Punish Locally: Non-State Actors, MNCs, and Human Rights Sanctions." *Ethics and International Affairs* 12: 19–43.

Rodrigues, M. (2000) "Searching for Common Ground: Transnational Advocacy Network and Environmentally Sustainable Development in Amazonia." University of California–Santa Cruz (http://www.ucsc.edu/cgirs/conferences/humanrights/rodrigues.pdf).

Roe, E. (1995) Critical Theory, Sustainable Development, and Populism." *Telos* 103: 149–162.

Rosenau, J., and E. Cziempel (eds.) (1992) *Governance Without Government:*

Order and Change in World Politics. Cambridge: Cambridge University Press.

Royo, A. (1998) "The Philippines: Against the Peoples' Wishes—the Mount Apo Story," in L. D. Brown and J. A. Fox (eds.) *The Struggle for Accountability: The World Bank, NGOs, and Crossroots Movements.* Cambridge: MIT Press.

Rumasara, A. (1998) "The Struggle of the People of Kedung Ombo," in L. D. Brown and J. A. Fox (eds.) *The Struggle for Accountability: The World Bank, NGOs, and Grassroots Movements.* Cambridge: MIT Press.

Runyan, C. (1999) "Action on the Front Lines." *World Watch* (November/December).

Sachs, W. (1997) "Ecology, Justice, and the End of Development." *Development* 24(2).

Salamon, L. (1994) "The Rise of the Nonprofit Sector: A Global Associational Revolution," *Foreign Affairs* 73(4).

Salamon, L., and H. Anheier (1998) *The Emerging Sector Revisited: A Summary.* Baltimore: Institute of Policy Studies and Johns Hopkins University Press.

Satterthwaite, D. (1996) "Urban Poverty: Reconsidering Its Scale and Nature." IIED Paper Series on Poverty Reduction in Urban Areas. London: IIED.

Save the Children Fund (1998) *Child Labour Research, Future Directions.* London: SCF-UK.

Scheper-Hughes, N. (1992) *Death Without Weeping: The Violence of Everyday Life in Brazil.* Berkeley: University of California Press.

Schmidheiny, S. (1992) *Changing Course: A Global Business Perspective on Development and the Environment.* Cambridge: MIT Press.

Scholte, J. A. (1997) "The Globalization of World Politics," in J. Baylis and S. Smith (eds.) *The Globalization of World Politics: An Introduction to International Relations.* Oxford: Oxford University Press. 13–30.

Scholte, J. A. (1999) "Global Civil Society: Changing the World?" Centre for Study of Globalisation and Regionalisation Working Paper No. 31/99. University of Warwick, Warwick, UK.

Scholte, J. A. (2000a) "Global Civil Society," in N. Woods (ed.) *The Political Economy of Globalization.* Basingstoke: Macmillan. 173–201.

Scholte, J. A. (2000b) *Globalization: A Critical Introduction.* Basingstoke: Macmillan.

Scholte, J. A. (2000c) "In the Foothills": Relations Between the IMF and Civil Society," in R. A. Higgott et al. (eds.) *Non-State Actors and Authority in the Global System.* London: Routledge. 256–273.

Schulz, M. S. (1998) "Collective Action Across Borders: Opportunity Structures, Network Capacities, and Communicative Praxis in the Age of Advanced Globalization." *Sociological Perspectives* 41: 587–616.

Sen, G., and C. Grown (1987) *Development, Crises, and Alternative Visions: Third World Women's Perspectives.* New York: Monthly Review Press.

Shaheed, F. (1995) "Linking Dreams: The Network of Women Living Under Muslim Laws," in M. Schuler (ed.) *From Basic Needs to Basic Rights: Women's Claim to Human Rights.* Washington, D.C.: Women, Law, and Development International.

Simmons, P. J. (1998) "Learning to Live with NGOs." *Foreign Policy* 112: 82–96.

Sinnar, S. (1995/1996) "Mixed Blessing: The Growing Influence of NGOs." *Harvard International Review* 18(1): 54–57.

Smillie, I. (1995a) *The Alms Bazaar.* London: IT Publications.

Smillie, I. (1995b) "Painting Canadian Roses Red," in M. Edwards and D. Hulme (eds.) *NGO Performance and Accountability: Beyond the Magic Bullet.* London: Earthscan.

Smith, J., et al. (eds.) (1997) *Transnational Social Movements and Global Politics: Solidarity Beyond the State.* Syracuse: Syracuse University Press.

Smith, N. C. (1990) *Morality and the Market: Consumer Pressure for Corporate Accountability.* London: Routledge.

Sobhan, B., and H. Hossain (1995) *Child Labour: A Bangladeshi Perspective.* Dhaka: Ain-O-Shalish Kendro.

Soros, G. (1998) *The Crisis of Global Capitalism: Open Society Endangered.* London: Little, Brown.

Spiro, P. J. (1995) "New Global Communities: Nongovernmental Organizations in International Decision-Making Institutions. *The Washington Quarterly* 18(1): 45–56.

Stevis, D., and V. J. Assetto (2001) *The International Political Economy of the Environment: Critical Perspectives.* Boulder: Lynne Rienner.

Stoll, D. (1998) "Life Story as Mythopoesis," *Anthropology Newsletter* 9(11).

SustainAbility (1996) "Strange Attractor: The Business-ENGO Partnership Strategic Review of BP's Relationships with Environmental NGOs; Summary of Findings: Trends." *SustainAbility* (July).

Tandon, R. (1989) *NGO-Government Relations: A Source of Life or the Kiss of Death?* New Delhi: Society for Participatory Research in Asia (PRIA).

Tandon, R. (1995) *Networks as Mechanisms of Communications and Influence.* New Delhi: Society for Participatory Research in Asia (PRIA).

Tarrow, S., and M. Acostavalle (1999) "Transnational Politics: A Bibliographic Guide to Recent Research on Transnational Movements and Advocacy Groups." Working Paper, Contentious Politics Series, Lajarsfeld Center. New York: Columbia University.

Thukral, E. G. (1997) *Combating Child Labour Through Elementary Education and Social Mobilisation.* New York: UNDP.

Tomlin, Brian. (1998) "On a Fast Track to a Ban: The Canadian Policy Process," in M. A. Cameron et al. (eds.) *To Walk Without Fear: The Global Movement to Ban Landmines.* Toronto: Oxford University Press.

Toye, J. (1999) "Nationalising the Anti-Poverty Agenda." *IDS Bulletin* 30(2).

Transform (1998) The Harare Declaration. London: Transform.

Tussie, D. (ed.) (1997) *El BID y el Banco Mundial: Nuevas Formas de Financiamiento Internacional.* Buenos Aires: Publicaciones FLACSO/Argentina y Centro Publicaciones del Ciclo Basico Común.

Tussie, D., with M. F. Tuozzo (1997) "Argentina's Big Bang Reform: The Interplay of Domestic Actors and Multilateral Development Banks." Working Paper No. 2. Buenos Aires: FLACSO/Argentina.

Udall, L. (1998) "The World Bank and Public Accountability: Has Anything Changed," in L. D. Brown and J. A. Fox (eds.) *The Struggle for Accountability: The World Bank, NGOs, and Grassroots Movements.* Cambridge: MIT Press.

Union of International Associations (1999) "International Organizations by Type (Table 1)." *Yearbook of International Organizations.* <http://www.uia.org/uiastats/stybv196.htm>.

United Nations Centre for Human Settlements (Habitat) (1996) "Global Report on Human Settlements." Oxford: Oxford University Press for the United Nations Centre for Human Settlements.

University of Maryland (2000) "Americans on Globalization: A Study of U.S. Public Attitudes." University of Maryland, Program on International Policy Attitudes, College Park, Md.

Valderrama, M. (1998) *Los Acelerados Cambios de las ONGs Latinoamericanas y el Fortalecimiento Institucional*. Buenos Aires: ALOP-FICONG.

Verdesoto, C. L. (1996) *Temas para una Sociedad en Crisis*, Foro de la Ciudadanía. Quito: Fundación Esquel.

Vianna, A. (1998) The Strategy of Multilateral Banks in Brazil: Critical Analysis of Unpublished Documents. Red Brazil, Brasilia, DF.

Vianna, A. (2000) "Civil Society Participation in World Bank and IDB Programs: The Case of Brazil." Special issue of *Global Governance* 6(4).

Vidal, J. (1996) *McLibel: Burger Culture on Trial*. Basingstoke: Macmillan.

Vidal, J. (1997) "Industry Terrified at the Outbreak of Ethics." *The Guardian*, Ecosoundings, April 23.

Vogel, D. (1978) *Lobbying the Corporation: Citizen Challenges to Business Authority*. New York: Basic Books.

Wapner, P. (1995) *Environmental Activism and World Civic Politics*. New York: SUNY.

Waterman, P. (1998) *Globalization, Social Movements, and the New Internationalism*. London: Mansell.

Weiss, T., and L. Gordenker (1996) *NGOs, the UN, and Global Governance*. Boulder: Lynne Rienner.

WHO (1992) "Our Planet, Our Health." Report of the WHO Commission on Health and Environment. Geneva: World Health Organization.

Wilkinson, M. D. (1996) "Lobbying for Fair Trade: Northern NGDOs, the European Community, and the GATT Uruguay Round." *Third World Quarterly* 17(2).

Williams, J., and S. Goose (1998) "The International Campaign to Ban Landmines" in M. A. Cameron et al. (eds.) *To Walk Without Fear: The Global Movement to Ban Landmines*. Toronto: Oxford University Press.

Willetts, P. (1996) *The Conscience of the World: The Influence of NGOs in the UN System*. London: Hurst and Co.

Wilson, M. G., and E. Whitmore (2000) *Seeds of Fire: Social Development in the Era of Globalism*. Toronto: Fernwood Books and the Canadian Consortium for International Social Development.

Wolf, M. (1999) "Uncivil Society." *Financial Times*, September 1.

"Women, Law, and Development in Africa" (1990) *Origins and Issues* 10.

Wood, A. (1997) *The IMF's Final Frontier? Assessing "Second Generation" Reforms*. London: Bretton Woods Project.

Wood, A., and C. Welch (1998) *Policing the Policemen: The Case for an Independent Evaluation Mechanism for the IMF*. London/Washington, D.C.: Bretton Woods Project/Friends of the Earth-U.S.

Woods, N. (1999) "Good Governance in International Organizations." *Global Governance* 5: 39–61.

World Bank (1991) Operational Directive on Poverty Alleviation. 4.15 (revised 1993) p. 11. Washington, D.C.: World Bank.

World Bank (1993) *Getting Results: The World Bank's Agenda for Improving Development Effectiveness*. Washington, D.C.: World Bank.

World Bank (1998a) *The Bank's Relationship with NGOs*. Washington, D.C.: World Bank.

World Bank (1998b) "Involving Non Governmental Organizations in Bank Supported Activities." GP 14.70 (March). Washington, D.C.: World Bank.

World Conference on Human Rights (1993) *The Vienna Declaration and Programme of Action*. UN Doc. A/CONF.157/23. New York: United Nations.

World Summit on Social Development (1995) "Copenhagen Declaration of Social Development and Programme of Action." UN Doc. A/CONF.166/9, April 19. New York: United Nations.

Wuthnow, R. (1994) *Sharing the Journey: Support Groups and America's New Quest for Community*. New York: Free Press.

The Contributors

Peggy Antrobus, a native of Grenada, has served as adviser on women's affairs to the government of Jamaica and set up the Women and Development Unit at the University of the West Indies. From 1991 to 1996, she served as general coordinator of the network of third world women promoting Development Alternatives with Women for a New Era (DAWN), and she continues as a member of DAWN's steering committee.

Joel Bolnick is cofounder and director since 1990 of People's Dialogue. He is coordinator of the Shack/Slum Dwellers International Support Group Board and a member of the Asian Coalition for Housing Rights.

L. David Brown is director of International Programs at the Hauser Center for Nonprofit Organizations and visiting professor of public policy at the Kennedy School of Government at Harvard University. He is chairman of the Institute for Development Research and is on leave from being professor of organizational behavior at Boston University. He is coauthor of *The Struggle for Accountability: NGOs, Social Movements, and the World Bank* (with Jonathan Fox); he has been a Fulbright lecturer in India; and he served as a Peace Corps community organizer in Ethiopia.

Charlotte Bunch is the founder and executive director of the Center for Women's Global Leadership at Rutgers University. Founder of Washington, D.C., Women's Liberation and of *Quest: A Feminist Quarterly*, her most recent books are *Passionate Politics: Feminist Theory in Action* and *Demanding Accountability: The Global Campaign and Vienna Tribunal for Women's Human Rights.* Inducted into the National Women's Hall of Fame in 1996 and recipient of the Eleanor Roosevelt Human Rights Award in 1999, Bunch serves on the board of the Ms. Foundation for Women.

Tony Burdon is a policy advisor for Oxfam-GB, working on finance and social policy. He has worked in development for fifteen years, mostly in Africa but also in the Middle East and Central America. He was Oxfam-GB's country representative for Uganda between 1993 and 1997. Burdon serves on the boards of Eurodad and Jubilee 2000 UK.

John Cavanagh is the director and **Sarah Anderson** is a fellow at the Institute for Policy Studies in Washington, D.C. They are coauthors of *Field Guide to the Global Economy* (New Press, 2000). **Karen Hansen-Kuhn** is Latin American Program Director at the Development Group for Alternative Policies (DGAP).

Jennifer Chapman has been working on international development issues for fifteen years. Her career has spanned work with government, NGOs, academia, the private sector, and industry. Most recently she has carried out research on advocacy and campaigning by Southern NGOs with the New Economics Foundation in London.

Manuel Chiriboga V. is an Ecuadorian citizen with degrees in sociology and development studies. He has taught at the Facultad Latinoamericana de Ciencias Sociales, FLACSO, and at the Pontificia Universidad Católica del Ecuador. Currently he is the executive secretary of ALOP, a Latin American NGO network, and was chair of the NGO Working Group on the World Bank and cochair of the World Bank NGO Committee. He is also a steering committee member of the Coalition Against Hunger and Rural Poverty and the International Forum on Capacity Building.

John D. Clark is currently working at the World Bank in Washington, D.C. For six years he was the head of the NGO Unit and has recently moved to a position in the East Asia Region. Before joining the Bank he held various posts with Oxfam-GB and is the author of a number of books including *Democratizing Development* (1991).

Carole J.L. Collins was national coordinator for Jubilee 2000 USA during 1998–1999. A coauthor of *From Debt to Development: Alternatives to the International Debt Crisis* (1986), she has worked and written on debt and development issues, especially in Africa, for over two decades. She served as the Quaker International Affairs Representative for southern Africa (based in Zimbabwe) from 1986–1990.

Felix Dodds is executive director of the United Nations Environment and Development Forum and cochair of the CSD NGO Steering Committee. He has been active in all the UN Commission on Sustainable Development meetings and coordinated lobbying teams for the Habitat II and the Earth Summit II Conferences. His previous books include *Earth Summit 2002: A New Deal* (2000) and *The Way Forward: Beyond Agenda 21* (1997).

Michael Edwards is director, Governance and Civil Society, for the Ford Foundation in New York. Prior to joining the foundation he was the senior civil society specialist at the World Bank in Washington, D.C. Michael spent fifteen years as a manager in international relief and development NGOs, including periods with Oxfam-GB and Save the Children-UK. His most recent book is *Future Positive: International Cooperation in the 21st Century.*

Ann M. Florini is senior associate at the Carnegie Endowment for International Peace, where she directs the Projects on Transparency and Transnational Civil Society. She received her Ph.D. in political science from UCLA and an MA in public affairs from Princeton University. She is coauthor of *Secrets for Sale: How Commercial Satellite Imagery Will Change the World* and editor of *The Third Force: The Rise of Transnational Civil Society* (2000).

Jonathan Fox is chair of Latin American and Latino studies and associate professor of social sciences at the University of California, Santa Cruz. His next book is *Cross-Border Dialogues: Mexico-US Social Movement Networking.* His current research focuses on accountability and participation in multilateral development bank-funded projects in Latin America, and he works closely on these issues with Mexican social organizations and public interest groups.

Samantha Frost was a consultant to the Center for Women's Global Leadership for several years and received her Ph.D. in political science from Rutgers University. She is currently research assistant professor of communications and assistant professor of women's studies at the Univeristy of Illinois, Urbana-Champaign.

Zie Gariyo has a social studies degree from Makerere University in Uganda and has worked on development issues for over a decade. After a stint as a researcher at the independent Center for Basic Research, he headed the Uganda NGO Forum before becoming head of the Uganda Debt Network in 1996.

John Gaventa is a fellow at the Institute of Development Studies, University of Sussex, where he coordinates a program on citizen participation and participatory methods. Prior to moving to IDS, he worked for a number of years on issues of citizen action in the United States, both as a sociologist at the University of Tennessee and at the Highlander Research and Education Center. He has published widely on issues of power and participation.

Caroline Harper is currently head of Research and Development at SCF-UK in London. Previously she worked for bilateral and multilateral development agencies as a social development specialist and development anthropologist in East and Southeast Asia. She has a particular interest in the social impacts of economic policies, social change and social policy, and poverty and the processes of policy formulation.

Tom Lent is a consultant on organizational development in Latin America for Save the Children-Norway, based in Guatemala, where he has worked on and off for fifteen years. Previously he worked for Save the Children-U.S. as international director of training, Save the Children-Norway, based in Zimbabwe, as international training coordinator, and Peace Corps volunteer in Afghanistan. He has a BA and an MA in international relations, School of International Service, American University.

Diana Mitlin is an economist with the Human Settlements Programme of the International Institute for Environment and Development (IIED) and is currently working with the South African NGO People's Dialogue on Land and Shelter in Cape Town. She is also on the editorial board of the journal *Environment and Urbanization.*

Paul Nelson is assistant professor in the Graduate School of Public and International Affairs, University of Pittsburgh, where he teaches and conducts research on NGOs, development policy, and international organizations. Before joining the university in 1998 he worked as policy analyst for several U.S.-based development NGOs and continues to work as a consultant on international NGO advocacy. He is the author of *The World Bank and NGOs: The Limits of Apolitical Development* (1995).

Peter Newell is a research fellow at the Institute of Development Studies, Sussex University. His key research interests lie in corporate social and environmental responsibility and international environmental politics. He has books forthcoming on the global politics of climate change and EU environmental policy and is currently researching the politics of crop biotechnology regulation in developing countries.

Sheela Patel is the founding director of SPARC, Society for the Promotion of Area Resource Centers, an NGO in Bombay that works in an alliance with NSDF (National Slum Dwellers' Federation) and Mahila Milan, two organizations that together work in thirty-two cities and towns in India on issues of equity and social justice for the urban poor in cities.

Niamh Reilly worked for six years as senior program associate for the Center for Women's Global Leadership. She has a Ph.D. in political science from Rutgers University and is the coauthor of *Demanding Accountability: The Global Campaign* and *Vienna Tribunal for Women's Human Rights* and the editor of *Without Reservation: The Beijing Tribunal on Accountability for Women's Human Rights.* She lives in Ireland and is currently the executive director of WHRNET—a women's human rights electronic communications technology.

Jan Aart Scholte is reader in international studies at the University of Warwick (UK). His publications include *International Relations of Social Change* (Open University Press, 1993*), Contesting Global Governance* (coauthor, 2000), and *Globalization: A Critical Introduction* (2000). He has also codirected a project on civil society and global finance whose work will be published in 2001.

Matthew J.O. Scott served on the steering committee of Mines Action Canada from 1996–1999 and as the NGO representative on the Canadian delegation to the Sydney Regional Landmines Conference in July 1999. He has evaluated landmine programs in Angola and Cambodia with World Vision, a global Christian humanitarian NGO. He currently serves as World Vision's representative to the United Nations in New York.

Kamal Singh is a South African community and rural development activist, where he was involved with a variety of antiapartheid processes, through youth, community, and worker organizations. Between 1996 and 2000, he was part of the Participation Group at the Institute of Development Studies. During this time he was responsible for networking and South-South interactions with participation-related networks across the globe. He currently lives in Senegal, West Africa.

Roy Trivedy works for the Department for International Development (DFID) in the Africa Policy and Economics Department, based in London. He was program director for Save the Children-UK in Mozambique from April 1997 to April 2000 and also worked for Save the Children in India and with Oxfam-GB in Malawi. From 1990–1993 he was the international officer for the British Labour Party.

María Fernanda Tuozzo is a Ph.D candidate at the University of

Warwick. She holds an MSc in Latin American politics from the Institute of Latin American Studies at the University of London. She has previously been a researcher at FLACSO/Argentina (Latin American School of Social Sciences) in the Research Program on International Economic Institutions and in 1997 was awarded a research grant from the National Council for Technical and Scientific Research (CONICET) in Argentina.

Diana Tussie holds a Ph.D in international relations and economics from the London School of Economics. In 1996 she was selected as distinguished Fulbright scholar in international relations and became a member of the executive board of the International Studies Association. At present she is a senior research fellow in the International Relations Department at FLACSO/Argentina and CONICET.

Index

About the Book

As late as 1990, there was little talk of civil society in the corridors of power. But now, the walls reverberate with the sound of global citizen action—and difficult questions about the phenomenon abound. This book presents the cutting edge of contemporary thinking about nonstate participation in the international system.

Against the background of the changing global context, the authors present case studies of the most significant social movements and NGO networks influencing the course of world politics today. Their timely analysis encompasses the conflicting interests and agendas associated with civil society, shedding much-needed light on the forces that will help to determine the future of global governance.

Michael Edwards is director of Governance and Civil Society at the Ford Foundation. Among his most recent publications is *Future Positive: International Cooperation in the 21st Century*. **John Gaventa** is a fellow at the Institute of Development Studies, University of Sussex, where he coordinates a global program on citizen participation. He is perhaps best known for his book *Power and Powerlessness in an Appalachian Valley*, winner of numerous awards.